P9-DUY-470

THE EARLY CHILDHOOD
CURRICULUM

THE EARLY CHILDHOOD CURRICULUM

Suzanne L. Krogh
Kristine L. Slentz
Western Washington University

LEA

LAWRENCE ERLBAUM ASSOCIATES, PUBLISHERS

2001   Mahwah, New Jersey   London

Copyright © 2001 by Lawrence Erlbaum Associates, Inc.
All rights reserved. No part of this book may be reproduced in
any form, by photostat, microform, retrieval system, or any other
means, without the prior written permission of the publisher.

Lawrence Erlbaum Associates, Inc., Publishers
10 Industrial Avenue
Mahwah, New Jersey 07430

Cover design by Kathryn Houghtaling Lacey

Library of Congress Cataloging-in-Publication Data

Krogh, Suzanne.
    The early childhood curriculum / by Suzanne L. Krogh and Kristine L. Slentz.
        p.   cm.
    Includes bibliographical references and index.
    ISBN 0-8058-2883-4 (pbk. : alk. paper)
    1. Early childhood education—United States—Curricula.   2. Curriculum
planning—United States.   I. Slentz, Kristine.   II. Title.

    LB1139.4 .K73 2001
    372.19—dc21   00-034714
                                                                        CIP

Books published by Lawrence Erlbaum Associates are printed on acid-free paper,
and their bindings are chosen for strength and durability.

Printed in the United States of America
10 9 8 7 6 5 4 3 2 1

To our families, friends, and colleagues who supported
and motivated us, and tolerated our occasional
preoccupation—you know who you are

CONTENTS

3   MATHEMATICS: HOW MUCH, HOW MANY, WHAT SIZE, WHAT SHAPE   76

4   SCIENCE: CURIOSITY ABOUT THEIR WORLD   110

To Our Readers and Their Instructors: An Introduction to the Series

The book you are now beginning is one of a series of four interrelated texts. Taken together, they provide an introduction to the broad field of early childhood education. Usually, such introductions are provided to students in one large survey textbook. Over the years, however, our knowledge of early development as it relates to education has increased enormously at the same time that legislative and cultural issues have grown in number. Add to that the fact that more and more early childhood centers and classrooms include youngsters who would once have been segregated in self-contained special education classes and it becomes evident that now all teachers of young children need to understand development and education across a broad spectrum of abilities. We thus are faced with a problem: Introductory textbooks must either get much longer and heavier, or simply skate across the surface of their topics.

Meanwhile, college and university instructors must decide how to fit this expanded knowledge and information into their courses. The answers they arrive at are many and various, making the traditional all-purpose textbook a source of frustration for many.

This series of textbooks has been designed to alleviate the frustration by offering four modules divided by general subject areas:

- an overview of history and the current field of early education;
- typical and atypical growth and development, infancy through the third grade;
- models and methods of teaching and guiding behavior; and
- curriculum, with a focus on preschool and the primary grades.

By creating this modular scheme, we have been able to treat each topic in more depth and incorporate discussions of abilities and needs across all levels, including developmental delays and giftedness. Instructors are invited to mix and match the texts as appropriate to their own interests and needs.

The titles of the four books in the series are:

Volume I: Early Childhood Education: Yesterday, Today, and Tomorrow
Volume II: Early Childhood Development and Its Variations
Volume III: Teaching Young Children
Volume IV: The Early Childhood Curriculum

We hope you find this new approach to early childhood courses a useful and refreshing one. We welcome your feedback and ideas.

—Suzanne Krogh
  Elementary Education
  Western Washington University
  Suzanne.Krogh@wwu.edu

—Kristine Slentz
  Special Education
  Western Washington University
  Kristine.Slentz@wwu.edu

PREFACE

The word *curriculum* refers to the collection of courses designated by a school or university. For the most part, the identity and content of the courses are determined by what is found useful to a particular society. Once, the study of Latin was considered a basic for the creation of educated gentlemen; today, it is difficult to find a class in it. Instead, college students—both male and female—opt for courses in languages that will provide practical knowledge for their upcoming careers.

School and university curricula are traditionally divided into rigidly defined segments known as *subjects*, with elementary school subjects being more general and basic (math, social studies) and high school or university subjects being more specialized and narrow (calculus, anthropology).

For early childhood education, the traditional definition of curriculum and division into subjects presents something of a challenge when we also consider the need to teach in ways that are developmentally appropriate. Infants, toddlers, preschoolers, and even primary grade children don't look at learning as divided into adult-defined categories. All of life is their school, and designating some of it as math or science or art can be an intrusion on their more integrated approach to learning. (We might do well to consider if the same could often be true at the adult level as well!) Yet, adults who have become teachers are accustomed to using subject areas as a convenient way to categorize and make sense of the content of learning. These two conflicting variables—the needs and interests of children versus those of adults—create a dilemma for the early childhood practitioner. Should curriculum description and design be approached from the more holistic child-view or from the structured adult definition?

For the purposes of this text, we answer: both. Traditional subjects—reading, language arts, math, science, social studies, art, music, movement—offer an organizing framework or a series of checkpoints for the adult curriculum planner. That is, subject areas can be considered and then combined into a more meaningful whole; or, the more meaningful interests can be considered first, then later categorized into subjects. Teachers who work with infants, toddlers, and younger children can generally plan curriculum with little regard for formal subjects. Teachers in the primary grades, and even kindergarten, have a greater responsibility for dealing with them. While they can frequently integrate subjects, awareness of, and concern for, each one is an important part of curriculum planning.

The structure of this textbook considers the differing needs of teachers at the varying age levels. Chapter 1 provides an overview of curriculum design, with statements from professional organizations on what is appropriate for young children, including those with special needs. In addition, there are some practical suggestions for creating activities, lessons, and schedules. A theme that runs throughout is that of curriculum integration, as that is the way young children most naturally learn.

This theme is continued in the succeeding chapters, although they are divided into the traditional curricular subjects, one or more subjects per chapter. As appropriate, there are position statements and benchmarks for learning as provided by national subject-matter organizations. These are important for teachers to know so that they have standards and goals in mind as they plan their children's learning. At the same time, each chapter also provides suggestions for integrating its subject matter with other subjects and with children's more natural learning.

The balance between naturally integrated learning and subject-oriented curriculum is a theme throughout this entire text. The chances are good that this same balance is one that you will need to achieve in your professional career as well.

THE EARLY CHILDHOOD
CURRICULUM

CHAPTER

1

PLANNING AND CREATING
THE CURRICULUM

*Curriculum is happening all around the home, the school, the playground,
and wherever young children gather. Perceptive teachers can help enrich and
enhance what is happening.*

Barbara J. Taylor

▼ *Chapter Objectives*

After reading this chapter, you should be able to:

- ▼ Identify the positions of the NAEYC and DEC regarding appropriate curriculum for young children.
- ▼ Define the differences and benefits of an emergent and a traditional curriculum.
- ▼ Define an integrated curriculum, and explain how one works as well as its pros and cons.
- ▼ Explain the similarities and differences in curricular approaches for different ages and abilities of children.

As you think about and apply chapter content on your own, you should be able to:

- ▼ Create plans for activities and lessons.
- ▼ Observe the ways in which curriculum emerges from children and is designed by adults.
- ▼ Integrate assessment techniques into curricula you develop.
- ▼ Consider a range of learning needs when developing curricula.

T he terms *instruction* and *methodology* refer to the ways in which we teach children; *curriculum* is the content that is taught. This chapter and those following are devoted to the content of children's learning, although at times the instructional implications also are discussed.

In the United States, there is no national curriculum to tell every teacher what should be taught and in what order, although discussions about creating just such a unified approach occasionally occur during policy discussions about school improvement. Since the late 1980s, a national curriculum that includes early childhood has been instituted in Great Britain. Its critics "note the irony in a capitalist, free-market-loving government's enacting such a curriculum" (Unks, 1995, p. 422), and it may be this disconnect that ultimately keeps the United States from creating similar nationwide requirements at any grade level.

At this time, curriculum in the public schools is typically decided by local school districts or, at least in part, by individual schools. Nonpublic schools, particularly preschools and child-care centers, must decide for themselves what is important content for their young learners. For the early years, more than with any other age group, the *what* of children's learning is the responsibility of the teacher, working either alone or in cooperation with others in the school or center. Thus, if you find yourself working with prekindergarten youngsters, you will need extensive knowledge about developmentally appropriate curriculum. One could also argue that the same is true for teachers of older children. Although state and district education agencies generally have much to say about what should be learned between kindergarten and the third grade, an aware teacher is in a better position to make decisions about what to emphasize, what can be visited just briefly, ways in which some curricula can be integrated, and how best to prepare children for the inevitable standardized tests.

CURRENTLY RECOGNIZED CURRICULAR CONCEPTS

In your course work and in centers and schools, you will come in contact with a variety of terms that pertain to curriculum decisions for early learning. Some of these represent concepts currently accepted by early childhood specialists, and some are decried as inappropriate, even though they are perhaps popular. Major curricular terms in American early education today include the following. If you have read other books in this series, some of the curricular concepts will be familiar to you.

Integrated Curriculum

When academic subjects are brought together to make a more meaningful learning experience, we say that the curriculum has been integrated. For high school and college courses, this may mean joining two classes in a team-teaching endeavor. In the early childhood years, during which formal courses are not the norm, integration frequently takes place as part of an emergent curriculum or theme-based learning, both of which are described in the sections that follow. A slightly different approach is to "begin with the discipline frameworks and identify the connections, the ways that curriculum can be integrated and made more meaningful for learners. Integrated curriculum is the answer to achieving coverage of the curriculum while also promoting meaningfulness" (Bredecamp, 1997, p. xvi).

Emergent Curriculum

This term was first coined by Elizabeth (Betty) Jones (1970) in a publication from the National Association for the Education of Young Children (NAEYC) and has since entered the vocabulary of all early educators who value learning that comes from and is determined by the daily lives of young children and their caregivers and teachers. Arguing against formulaic curricula and commercial packages that seem to promise magical results, Jones and John Nimmo (1994) said that "there is no magic except the magic we create for ourselves." It is children who "are the wizards, inviting us to join them in their magic making" (p. 3). Yet, Jones (1999) pointed out that emergent curriculum "is scary for some teachers. For those who haven't yet learned how to plan well, it may be too much to undertake." She added, however, that "for those with some practice in observing and reflecting on child behavior, it's a well-timed challenge in taking children's interests seriously and becoming co-players with them" (p. 16).

There are currently two well-known models of emergent curriculum. The first model is from the United States and is called the *project approach* in which teachers and primary grade children negotiate, plan, and participate in an in-depth study of their choice (Katz & Chard, 1989). Such studies might last for a few weeks or even months. The second model can be found in the city preschools of Reggio Emilia, Italy (Edwards, Gandini, & Forman, 1993). Here too, the children and teachers negotiate their choices, planning, and learning. Because the children are generally too young to communicate their learning and research findings through the written word, they are encouraged to explore and share their ideas through the arts.

Theme-Based Learning or Thematic Curriculum

A theme or central idea is selected by the teacher, and related learning activities then are designed and taught. Proponents of theme teaching argue that this approach helps children make meaning of their learning experiences as they "form connections among individual bits of information. These connections contribute to children's concept development and are the most important reason for advocating a theme-oriented approach to teaching" (Kostelnik, Soderman, & Whiren, 1999, p. 507).

As in project learning or the Reggio Emilia schools, themes permit children to focus deeply on a single topic over a period of time. In addition, themes that are developed in response to children's interests keep them excited about learning. Thematic teaching has its dangers in that teachers may create activities whose connection to the theme is contrived, "cutesy," or devoted to fun and games, a situation that can lead to shallow or misguided learning. Kostelnik and colleagues (1999) gave as an example the popular theme "letter of the week." Perhaps the teacher has chosen the letter G this week and is confident that the children are getting the connection as they use green paint at the easel, snack on grapes, and growl like lions. However:

> In reality, the children may be focusing on the subject of their paintings rather than on the color, they may be thinking of grapes as fruit rather than a *g* word, and they may be more aware of the loudness or mock ferocity of their growling than the consonant sound they are making. Since *g* is not a concept and does not directly relate to children's real-life experiences, these are poor attempts at theme teaching. (p. 511)

Effective themes, according to Kostelnik and colleagues (1999) are those that relate to children's life experiences, represent a concept, are supported by a body of factual content, and lend themselves to possible development as projects (see the previous section entitled *Emergent Curriculum*).

Subject-Based, Discipline-Based, or Traditional Curriculum

Basing the curriculum on academic disciplines or subjects such as reading, language arts, math, science, social studies, art, music, and physical education leads to learning experiences that are created and controlled mainly by adults. This does not mean that they cannot be enjoyable and interesting to children. It, however, does place most decision-making power in the hands of the educators, with little room for input from those who do the actual learning. This approach is probably appropriate in a society with top-down power, but it is less helpful in a society that strives to raise citizens for democracy. At the early childhood level, one way to lead children toward democracy is to give them choices in their learning.

Additionally, dividing the curriculum by subject areas can be confusing to young children who are just becoming acquainted with the world and everything in it. When they explore a pond for the first time, they don't see it in terms of a science lesson but in relation to all its sensory delights. (Take a moment here to consider the possibilities of teaching something about the pond using every one of the subject areas listed in the preceding paragraph.)

Teachers of children in the primary grades of necessity, will need to concern themselves with teaching individual subjects. Helping children learn to read is, for most, the critical core of the curriculum. The content of children's reading is frequently divided according to predetermined textbooks in specified academic areas. To the extent that it is necessary to assist children in understanding this content according to the prescribed curriculum, teachers must comply. Wherever and whenever possible, it is recommended that children be provided choices and cross-curricular meaning through the other approaches we describe here.

Philosophically Prescribed Curriculum

Throughout the history of early education, there have been a number of philosophers, educators, and theorists who have observed young children, then prescribed curriculum they deemed most appropriate. Generally, these approaches have been an improvement on the early education of their time, have lasted until the next improvements emerged, and then have faded from sight, perhaps leaving behind a remnant or two.

One example of such a curriculum is that developed by Friedrich Froebel, the 19th-century German who created and named the *kindergarten* (German for children's garden). Children between the ages of 3 and 6 spent their days working in identically laid out gardens, participating in specially composed singing games, and interacting with materials designed to teach a series of specific skills. Although we no longer see kindergartens that look just like Froebel's, his influence lingers on in such activities as weaving with colored construction paper, sewing with yarn on cardboard, and in whole-class circle games.

A second example, still in existence, is the curriculum developed by Maria Montessori, an Italian doctor who was inspired, in part, by Froebel's materials. Observing and working with the same age children, she focused on creating curricula that permitted youngsters to advance in their learning to the greatest extent possible. Her learning materials were nearly as prescribed and rigid as Froebel's, but Montessori also was dedicated to creating citizens for democracy and thus built a variety of choices into the curricula and the teaching methods. Montessori schools still can be observed in many countries, including the United States, but her influence is felt in other learning sites as well. Cardboard cutout letters for creating simple words and phrases, mushroom-shaped tone bells, and metal templates for making geometric designs are examples of materials that have made their way to non-Montessori schools.

Pushed-Down and Watered-Down Curricula

These approaches to early childhood curriculum are two sides of the same coin. They seem to appear when parents, school systems, legislators, and other adults who hope to raise the educational performance of young children insist on a curriculum that is inappropriate for them. Typically, any or all of these adult groups decide that the children aren't learning enough for their age and then go about "fixing" the problem.

It is entirely possible that the children in question could be learning more, but adults who have no background in child development and education tend to believe that the appropriate response is to push down to the earlier age group the curriculum of older children. Then, when it becomes apparent that the youngsters are having difficulties coping, the new curriculum is watered down to a (usually mind-numbing) basic level. If the children still have trouble coping, the blame is then placed on them or their teachers or both, rather than on the inappropriate curriculum that has come to fill their days.

One of the authors observed just such a situation in a state in which she previously lived. In this case, the adults providing the push were members of the state legislature, and the pushed-down curriculum was designated for grades K–3. She recalls walking down a school hallway one day when a first-grade teacher, apparently having just reached her breaking point, leaned out of her classroom and yelled, "We know better than to teach like this!" then disappeared into her classroom again. Over a period of 10 years, teachers, principals, and university educators managed to overturn the legislative mandates, and with a new state superintendent of schools, a new, developmentally appropriate curriculum was developed. By that time, unfortunately, many thousands of children had received curriculum that was inappropriate to their age.

About watering down the curriculum, a number of researchers and writers have noted that:

> Such intellectually impoverished curriculum underestimates the true competence of children, which has been demonstrated to be much higher than is often assumed. Watered-down, oversimplified curriculum leaves many children unchallenged, bored, uninterested, or unmotivated. In such situations, children's experiences are marked by a great many missed opportunities for learning. (Bredecamp & Copple, 1997, p. 20)

The pushed-down curriculum, on the other hand, creates other problems:

> When next-grade expectations of mastery of basic skills are routinely pushed down to the previous grade and whole-group and teacher-led instruction is the dominant teaching strategy, children who cannot sit still and attend to teacher lectures or who are bored and unchallenged or frustrated by doing workbook pages for long periods of time are mislabeled as immature, disruptive, or unready for school. (Bredecamp & Copple, 1997, p. 20)

Individualized Educational Plans

Preschool and primary children who are eligible for special education services have a portion of their curriculum identified by their Individualized Educational Plans (IEPs). The IEP contains goals and objectives developed to address the individual learning needs of each eligible child. The IEP usually addresses more specific curriculum objectives in the same content areas as the regular classroom curriculum. IEP goals and objectives for preschool children usually are written in specific developmental areas such as motor, cognitive, language, and social domains. School-age children are more likely to have goals and objectives for specific subject areas. The most common goals and objectives on IEPs are in the areas of cognition and communication for preschoolers and in reading for primary school students.

The Individualized Family Service Plan (IFSP) is used for infants and toddlers who qualify for early intervention services and includes developmental goals for children as well as family-centered goals. School districts that serve infants and toddlers in special education programs generally address only the developmental goals for children on IFSPs.

A Few Curricular Approaches to Avoid

In amusing language, Jones and Nimmo (1994) described some things that can go wrong with an early childhood curriculum, even at times, with the best of intentions.

• *The canned curriculum.* This often comes from a district or state and is designed to be teacher-proof. Unfortunately, it can't possibly fit every child, and alteration is not an option.

• *The enbalmed curriculum.* The teacher who has taught many years can be guilty of using this curriculum. The materials are old, perhaps faded and tattered, and practically can be taught in one's sleep. No regard is paid to the fact that the current year's children may be vastly different from those in previous years, that new content may be available, or that teaching in one's sleep may not be advantageous either to teacher or to children.

• *The accidental or unidentified curriculum.* For teachers who are content just to hang out with children, hope that learning will result from free play, and put no time or energy into planning, this is the curriculum that results. Typically, there are lots of good starting points, even interesting activities, but they never go anywhere or have any particular identity.

Curriculum-Based Assessment

Also called classroom-based assessment, curriculum-based assessment refers to procedures that teachers use to identify curriculum goals and objectives (assessment) and to monitor progress toward learning goals after teaching has occurred (evaluation). Curriculum-based assessment is tied directly to the curriculum content of the classroom and is a critical component of educational reform efforts that have produced specific grade level learning standards. The standards for each grade level form the framework for curriculum content, and classroom-based assessment and evaluation provide the mechanism for accountability that students are (or are not) meeting the academic standards set forth.

Curriculum-based assessment should not be confused with achievement testing or standardized testing. Curriculum-based assessment evaluates a child's learning against the classroom curriculum, whereas *standardized testing* compares a child's performance to the mean performance of a large group of same age peers. The use of standardized assessments with young children has been criticized roundly because the procedures for testing are not appropriate for young children, and the content of the assessments often has little or nothing to do with the content of classroom instruction. Curriculum-based assessment, on the other hand, is closely associated with children's learning and should be considered an important component of the teaching process.

NAEYC Curriculum Guidelines

The National Association for the Education of Young Children has devoted much of its energy to determining appropriate curriculum for youngsters' learning from birth to age 8. Beginning in 1987, they published position statements as a response to their concern with the nationally widespread trend toward pushed-down and watered-down curricula. Much progress has been made in the years since, but problems persist, because inappropriate curricula continue to be demanded by legislatures, requested by parents, and practiced by some caregivers and teachers.

There is an important underlying theme to the NAEYC's position on curriculum creation, and it reflects current opinion, observation, and research. It is that "in some respects, the curriculum strategies of many teachers today do not demand enough of children and in other ways demand too much of the wrong thing" (Bredecamp & Copple, 1997, p. 20). In other words, we have discovered in recent years that young children are capable of much more than we ever thought (e.g., self-direction, research using the scientific method), but we often inappropriately superimpose adult expectations on them (hours spent alone at desks, piles of worksheets). As you contemplate and design curriculum, keep in mind the following nine guidelines as well as the underlying theme just described.

1. Be sure to provide for all parts of the whole child: "physical, emotional, social, linguistic, aesthetic, cognitive."

2. Include content that is "socially relevant, intellectually engaging, and personally meaningful to children."

3. Build on "what children already know and are able to do," because this both consolidates their learning and fosters "their acquisition of new concepts and skills."

4. Help children make meaningful connections by providing cross-disciplinary learning. At times, focusing on a single subject is also appropriate.

5. Develop curriculum that promotes knowledge, understanding, processes, skills, and dispositions to continue learning.

6. Develop curriculum that has intellectual integrity and teaches children to use the "tools of inquiry of recognized disciplines in ways that are accessible and achievable for young children."

7. Be sure to support your children's home culture and language as well as to help them understand and participate in the culture of your program and the larger community.

8. Be sure that the goals of your curriculum are "realistic and attainable for most children in the designated age range for which they are designed."

9. If you use technology, be sure it is "physically and philosophically integrated in the classroom curriculum and teaching." (Bredecamp & Copple, 1997, pp. 20–21)

The basis of all curriculum design is children and their right to grow in all domains—intellectual, emotional, social, and physical. As you think about these guidelines and apply them to your own curriculum planning and implementation, keep in mind that they actually can make your task more enjoyable, because ultimately it will be more rewarding.

PLANNING THE CURRICULUM

As you first begin planning curriculum, you may find that the process seems quite involved. With practice, it should seem much less so. In the following sections, we offer practical explanations and ideas to get you on your way.

Planning Lessons and Activities

Although many people use the terms interchangeably, there are differences between lessons and activities (Price & Nelson, 1999). *Lessons* are more formal, require a teacher (even if that teacher is another child), have measurable objectives that the teacher intends the children to meet by the end of the lesson, and provide instruction on important skills and knowledge. *Activities*, on the other hand, leave children on their own to explore, practice, manipulate, and discover. The teacher does not necessarily lay out immediate objectives to be met, because children may return to the activities repeatedly over time. Activities can be entities on their own or they "may lead up to lessons, be part of lessons, follow up lessons, or extend lessons" (p. 8).

As an example of the ways in which lessons and activities can complement each other, consider a unit or theme in which primary grade children learn about transportation. A sample lesson plan for primary grades, which is included further on in the chapter, outlines one way to approach planning for the unit's opening. Because the learning experience is teacher directed, possesses objectives to be met by the end of the experience, and imparts specific knowledge, it can be defined as a lesson. However, at the end of the lesson is a final direction that puts the lesson's materials into a follow-up activity center. Thus, the activity will provide a chance for children to cement their lesson learning with independent exploration and experimentation.

Lessons work best when they are carefully planned and orchestrated. For this reason, objectives are always as specific as possible in terms of their outcomes, teaching procedures are sequential and closely related to the objectives, and there is some form of evaluation to ensure that the teaching actually led to the objectives being accomplished.

Activities work best when planned for a block of time in which children can choose from among materials and experiences, work with friends or opt to be on their own, and try new things or revisit old. Some of the materials and activities, such as centers or water tables, will remain available for long periods, perhaps for an entire school year. Others will stay only as long as they relate to a current theme of interest.

The younger children are, the more their learning should take place through activities rather than lessons. Infants, toddlers, and preschoolers do not learn as well through the more formal approaches. Kindergarten is often the time when the transition begins to be made toward more experiences with lessons, although this is also the time when ambitious educators sometimes force too much formality too soon. Even in the primary grades, there should be a good balance between the two. In any case, you need to have clear learning objectives whether you are using activities or lessons.

Adaptations and Modifications for Children With Special Needs

The children in your classrooms always will have skills and abilities that cover a range in every developmental domain and each subject area. Some students will struggle with social skills and be ahead of the group in academics, others will be skilled in math but challenged by reading, and yet others will be eligible for special services. Your job as a teacher of young children is to be as creative as possible in teaching the curriculum to whatever children you have in class. Usually this means having a variety of strategies for delivering curriculum content. Following are a few general principles that should provide a framework for adaptations, accommodations, and modifications in curriculum for children who are learning faster or slower than the rest of the group.

Maintain Responsibility for Learning Outcomes of Every Child

It is tempting to refer children to special education or gifted and talented programs and let specialists take the major responsibility for eligible students' teaching and learning. The regular curriculum, however, is almost always the focus of specialized instruction, and all children need to feel a sense of belonging with their peers. Specialists can provide individual tutorial work to supplement classroom instruction, offer support during delivery of the regular curriculum, and serve as consultants as you adapt and modify curriculum for students with special needs, but you should continue to see yourself as the teacher for all the children in your class. It is tragic when a regular classroom teacher is not even aware of the IEP goals for students in the class, because chances are good that many opportunities arise during each day for instruction on those goals.

Not all children who struggle academically or socially or both will meet eligibility criteria for special services, so it is also to your benefit to have strategies for adapting the curriculum for a range of students. A few students will be so advanced or delayed compared to their peers that different curriculum goals will be appropriate; however, making actual modifications in the curriculum content should not be undertaken lightly. For example, primary students with developmental disabilities should switch to a "functional" academic curriculum, such as learning sight words instead of reading, only after all available instructional strategies have been exhausted and the consequences of abandoning the regular academic curriculum have been considered. Similarly, sending a second-grade student to the fifth grade during math time should be considered only if all other avenues of delivering appropriate math instruction in the regular classroom have been attempted. Modifying the regular curriculum sometimes can be accomplished by prioritizing objectives for a unit of study. Letter sounds, for instance, are much more essential to know for reading than are letter names or the alphabet song. While the rest of the class is working on extension or nonessential activities, students who need extra instruction on critical objectives might receive specialized instruction in the classroom or in a resource room. The classroom teacher should be responsible for balancing supplemental instruction time with less demanding, less structured activities, so that children who need specialized instruction also have opportunities for less structured times during the day.

Check for Prerequisite Skills

Sometimes children have difficulties learning new skills and acquiring new knowledge if they have gaps in their earlier learning. It is a good practice to identify the important skills students need in order to master new learning and to check to see if all students in fact are in possession of the prerequisite information. In an integrated curriculum, this means checking across developmental domains and subject areas. If you are designing a graphing activity as part of a social studies lesson on families, for example, children need to know basic math concepts and skills as well as concepts and terms about families in order to benefit from instruction.

Children who lack prerequisite skills need instruction on those skills before going ahead with new information. Gifted students who demonstrate the knowledge and skills contained in lesson objectives before instruction also will need special accommodations in order to learn anything from the lesson. Special services personnel are good resources for providing supplemental instruction on prerequisite skills and identifying strategies for extending learning objectives.

Break Curriculum Goals Into Smaller Steps

For students who have difficulty learning, it often helps to break lesson goals into smaller steps and provide additional prompts and cues. For example, you might reduce the number of spelling words you give a child each week or be more explicit about each step of an important social skill such as lining up for lunch. If your direction to the group is, "Line up for lunch," you might want to be sure that the little girl who gets distracted between circle and the lunch line each day hears at least three separate directions: "Put your work away." "Get your lunchbox off the shelf." "Go stand in line at the door." In another situation, in preschool, you may expect certain children to learn one shape at time, whereas others are mastering circle, square, and triangle all at once.

Provide for Repetition

Children with special learning needs often benefit from repeated practice, because it takes them longer to learn something new. Making sure that the classroom provides multiple opportunities for using new knowledge and skills in a number of activities and centers can facilitate acquisition of new skills. The same activities that provide chances for independent exploration, extension, and experimentation for most of the class can be important times for you to reinforce skill acquisition with hands-on learning opportunities for those who need extra practice.

Plan for Generalization

Generalization is required anytime children are expected to apply a skill outside the setting in which teaching occurs. For example, preschoolers often need to be reminded where the bathroom is in each new place you go, or you can expect accidents. Children with cognitive delays may have particular difficulty with generalization, often demonstrating that they have learned something new in the classroom but are having trouble using the new skill in centers or on the playground. Whereas most children can apply what they learn about lining up for lunch to lining up for the bus, some youngsters may need additional instruction in each new setting. You can expect that they will learn more quickly in each new setting.

One primary advantage of emergent and integrated curricula in preschool and primary settings is that new information and skills are presented and taught in the same environments in which they are used by young children in their daily lives. For example, teaching writing skills in note taking and record keeping in science and social studies as well as during language arts makes it easier for children to understand the actual uses of writing throughout the day. And having writing utensils and paper available in centers offers additional opportunities for children to learn generalized application of writing to daily activities.

Identify Specialists and Technology Resources

Children who are eligible for special education have special education teachers and therapists assigned to teach and monitor IEP goals. These people are valuable resources for teaching the regular curriculum, both to eligible students and to others who can benefit from adaptations and modifications. Be proactive in asking questions, presenting concerns, and resolving confusion about children who receive special education services, and invite specialists to become familiar with your curriculum. Brainstorm ideas for integrating instruction of IEP goals and objectives into the regular curriculum, and make suggestions about what students need to know to be successful in the classroom.

There has been a virtual explosion of adaptive and assistive technology in the last few years, and specialists often have access to lending libraries of specialized devices. Technology can provide access to the regular curriculum, support instruction, and allow students to have alternative modes of communication. Subsequent chapters on subject-area curriculum present ideas for working with students with identified disabilities. Specific suggestions all arise from these general principles:

- Maintain responsibility for learning outcomes of all students.
- Check for prerequisite skills and break curriculum goals into smaller steps.
- Provide opportunities for repetition and plan for generalization across many classroom activities.
- Be proactive in use of available specialists and technology.

Some Basic Formats for Planning

In the first months, even years, of your teaching, you will be helped by writing down several elements and components of each lesson or activity you plan to teach: your goals and objectives, how you will evaluate your success in achieving them, the actual content of the activity or lesson, the teaching procedures you will use, the materials you will need, and variations that take into account the needs of children who don't fit the general mold. Doing all this for every moment of the day would take far too long, but it is a good idea to plan this way for the more important learning events. Even highly experienced teachers return at times to such formal and complex planning formats. They make us think through, at the deepest levels, why we believe that a particular content is important, what we really want our children to achieve, and whether or not we are succeeding in reaching every child.

Different forms of lessons and activities call for slightly different planning formats, and two examples are provided later in the chapter. Here, we define and explain the terms found in the forms. (You will not see every term in every form.)

Title

Some teachers enjoy inventing titles that are creative, whereas others prefer something more utilitarian. Either way, be sure that the title is descriptive enough that you will recall immediately what the content is when you refer to the plan in the future.

Subject(s)

This refers to the academic subjects or disciplines represented in the lesson or activity. It is usually helpful to list the most important one first. For preprimary or prekindergarten years, it is usually preferable to focus on learning domains rather than on academic subjects.

Domain(s)

Domains refer to each aspect of a child's development and are usually defined as cognitive, social, emotional, and physical. As well, language and aesthetics are sometimes listed separately. In a lesson or activity plan, the domains that are to be enhanced

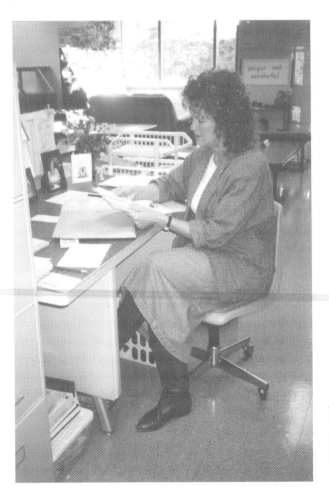

Although experienced teachers are able to do some of their planning mentally, even they spend much time writing down lessons and activities for their children.

by the experience are listed. It is preferable to think in terms of domains rather than subjects when planning for younger children. (This may well be preferable for the primary grades also, but few teachers have this luxury.)

Goals and Objectives

Curriculum *goals* are similar to goals in other walks of life. They are simply the ultimate aim of whatever you are doing. In the case of curriculum, however, the definition is characterized by nonspecificity: curriculum goals represent the overall purposes of a unit, project, or entire program. For example, if you just have purchased new classroom materials, your overall goal might be for every child to try them out before the end of the week.

Curriculum *objectives* are more specific and more precise. They can be identified as actual behaviors that will be accomplished by a portion of the curriculum. In the case of the new classroom materials, one objective might be that each child will learn to use the hammer and nails safely.

When planning a curriculum, it is important that goals and objectives relate to all domains of children's learning: intellectual, social, emotional, and physical. Figure 1.1 shows how this might work in three different curricular plans.

Figure 1.1 presents three quite different examples of the kinds of curriculum goals and objectives you might find yourself planning. If you read through them carefully, you should note a similarity between them: In each case, the first objective relates to intellectual growth; the second, to social growth; the third, to emotional growth; and the fourth, to physical growth. Still, it is difficult, even when dealing with precise objectives to avoid some overlap. In real life, the four learning domains cannot

Goal: Every child will experiment with new classroom materials by the end of the week.
  Objective: Each child will design and create at least one product of choice at the woodworking table.
  Objective: Each child will participate in two or more small group games.
  Objective: Each child will have an opportunity to work with a favorite new material at least twice.
  Objective: Each child will learn and demonstrate the ability to use the hammer and nails safely.
Goal: Children will appreciate literature through use of the library corner.
  Objective: Each child will identify at least two books at his or her level and read them.
  Objective: Children will understand and obey the rule that all books must be returned to the shelves when finished.
  Objective: Each child will demonstrate an enjoyment of literature by being able to choose at least one favorite book.
  Objective: Children will balance more active experiences with relaxation by spending at least a few minutes each day in the library corner.
Goal: Children will be exposed to classical music and composers throughout the year.
  Objective: Each child will learn about the life of at least one composer.
  Objective: In small cooperative groups, children will choreograph dances to ballet music.
  Objective: Children will demonstrate self-reliance by composing brief individual songs.
  Objective: Children will participate daily in free movement to classical music.

FIG. 1.1. Examples of goals and objectives.

always be) separated completely. For example, the third objective in the classical music curriculum is intended to demonstrate learning in the emotional domain, but it advances cognitive learning as well. Can you find others that might overlap?

In Fig. 1.1, the sample goals and objectives are curriculum oriented (new materials, literature, classical music). This is not the only way to assign them. It is also possible to develop them in terms of the learning domains. Some examples of goals in each domain might be:

- *Intellectual goals*
  Children will learn by solving problems.
  Children will appreciate poetry.
  Children will enjoy and welcome intellectual challenges.

- *Social goals*
  Children will learn to work in small groups.
  Children will learn to respect each other's property.
  Children will assume responsibility for care of the classroom.

- *Emotional goals*
  Children will learn to work independently with confidence.
  Children will be able to persist when work is difficult.
  Children will appreciate and trust their peers and teacher.

- *Physical goals*
  Children will have desirable health habits.
  Children will increase in both fine and gross motor control.
  Children will have a balance of active and restful experiences.

Materials

As you plan children's activities within each unit or project or portion of the day, you will need, of course, to go beyond goals and objectives and into the specifics of what will happen and the materials you will use. It is recommended that you include every bit of material that will be needed and that you do so in list form. In this way, if you are in a hurry or a bit nervous about the upcoming experience, you can survey the list quickly and you won't forget anything. Know too that the younger the children are, the less leeway you have for groping around for something or trying to explain why you are wandering the room while everyone begins to fidget and perhaps wander after you, or in the opposite direction.

With experience, you may find that one particular version, or brand, of a material works better than another. You will want to include this comment on your list for future reference.

Time

Beginning teachers tend to greatly over- or underestimate the time that a project will take. It takes some practice and a continually developing understanding of a particular group of children to estimate with some accuracy. As you plan a lesson or activity, confer with an experienced teacher about the time you think it will take. Once the experience is completed, make notes on your planning form for future reference.

Procedure

This section describes exactly what will happen during the activity or lesson. For planning purposes, it can be divided into three independent segments, although in practice, they flow together as one:

1. *Opening.* This introduces the children to the learning experience. It engages their interest, lets them know as much as necessary about what is to come, and gives the teacher time to observe and deal with any initial management problems. In addition, it can be coupled with an assessment of children's understanding so that adjustments can be made for the rest of the lesson and in subsequent activities.
2. *Body.* This is the main content and experience of the lesson or activity. It will probably require the most time of the three steps.
3. *Close.* Wrapping up the learning includes coming to closure, reviewing what has been learned, thinking about what is interesting, important, and scheduled to be learned next.

As you write out the steps in the procedure, you will need to decide for yourself how much detail works for you. Some beginning teachers find comfort in writing absolutely everything out and keeping the directions near at hand in case they get nervous and forget something. Others just like a brief checklist that refreshes their memory. The difference between the two approaches can be demonstrated in the two lesson openings that follow.

Example 1

1. Have children sit in circle.
2. Get attention with "criss-cross applesauce."
3. Ask: "If you can tell us what an opossum looks like, raise your hand."

Example 2

1. Children in circle.
2. Have someone describe an opossum.

In the first case, the beginning teacher makes sure that management details won't be forgotten and that wording will be optimal. In the second, the teacher has enough confidence that she assumes such details. Although this is a brief sample from a much longer procedural section, you can see clearly that the first approach takes twice as much space. Only you can decide how much detail you need. Some experimentation should prove helpful.

Assessment

Before beginning any lesson or activity, it is important to assess where the children are in their understanding and interest. It may not be possible or necessary to do so with detailed accuracy for every child but having a general idea is important. You might want to begin with an informal pretest. Asking children to raise their hands if they can define opossum is one example. Note here that it will not work to say, "Raise your hand if you know what an opossum is." Most children will want to be part of the "in group" and will raise their hands even if they have never even heard the word before. Letting them know that raising their hands may well lead to a request for a definition often will ensure more honesty. Older students can write down everything they know about opossums.

Another form of assessment is the teacher's observation of a previous lesson or activity. For example, perhaps the class has been energetically memorizing addition tables, but it has become apparent that many of the children are having trouble using their knowledge within the context of real life. Having made this assessment, the teacher decides to create a series of lessons that provide the children with practical applications of their learning, such as adding boys and girls each morning to determine how many are present.

In the example of opossums, the assessment is a part of the actual lesson and appears as a first step in the procedure. In the second example, the assessment has been done in advance and probably won't appear on the planning form. For generic skills such as letter sounds or math facts, it is worthwhile at the beginning of the year to use a more structured pretest, such as a worksheet, that you would expect children to be able to complete by the end of a lesson or unit.

Evaluation

You will want to know if a lesson or activity was successful so that you can plan for future experiences knowledgeably. First, you must define successful. To do this, look back at your objectives to determine what you wanted to accomplish. The evaluation always—repeat *always*—should be based on the objectives. (Has a teacher or professor ever given you a test that seemed to have nothing to do with what you learned in class or with what was in the textbook? That teacher did not base the evaluation on the objectives. If you have had this experience, you can readily see why doing so is important.)

Your objectives will refer to children's behavioral outcomes, but it is not only the children you will be evaluating. First, you must evaluate the lesson itself: Was it too brief or too long? Was it too shallow or too deep in its coverage? Was it too easy or over the children's heads? Did it mesh well with other activities currently going on?

Second, you must evaluate yourself: Was the lesson a favorite of yours but not of interest to the children? Were you sufficiently prepared? Were you so prepared that there was no room for spontaneity—and it mattered? Did you take time to listen to the children's input, or were you so driven by the planning format that it was a lesson for you and not for them?

Third, you must evaluate the children. Notice that the experience and the teacher are evaluated first, because these two factors determine the children's responses. It would be unfair to evaluate the children without first taking the other two elements strongly into account. Thus, as you evaluate the children, be sure to ask yourself first about the lesson design and about your own role in achieving overall success or lack of it.

The means you use to evaluate the success of the lesson, your part in it, and the children's performance can range from informal observation, to spot checks of ongoing work, to standardized tests. Five examples that work well with young children are listed here.

1. *Behavioral observation.* Watch children to see if they are participating or not, are able to achieve the objectives or not. Behavioral observation can be informal or formal. *Informal observation* is a basic component in teaching young children, should be daily and continual, and is used for both assessment and evaluation. It is important to realize that some children participate by watching happily while others are not engaged unless their whole bodies are involved. Furthermore, some children will be more able to reach a higher level of participation than others. Thus, informal observation, usually including brief notes to yourself, is a successful evaluation tool only when a teacher knows the children intimately.

Formal observation includes careful documentation designed to inform future curriculum planning.

Formal observation includes systematic recording of data and is more structured and generally related to research or evaluation of a particular child. Formal observation, with its careful documentation, is used mainly when teachers record observations on checklists as part of lesson evaluation.

2. *Journal writing and pictures.* As soon as children are old enough to begin drawing and writing, they can keep journals of their experiences. Teachers should expect no more than a sentence or two for some time, with more enthusiasm generally expressed about creating pictures of learning events. The journal can be a collection of stories and pictures that the class keeps together, or it can be one that each child keeps privately. In either case, the teacher can evaluate both words and pictures as a way to discover what children learned and found important.

3. *Follow-up activities and lessons.* If learning experiences are linked, sequential, or related, then some of them actually can serve as evaluation activities for previous experiences. For example, those earlier questions about opossums might have been an introduction to a story and video about the animals. A follow-up activity might be to have the children create clay opossum figures situated in an authentic site created from assorted materials that you supply. The results of this art activity will tell you how well the children attained an understanding of the information provided in the story and video. (You should also be prepared for some unexpected creativity as children adapt adult reality to their own. One second-grade teacher was a bit surprised to watch clay figures of Native Americans sprout mermaid fins, a nostalgic sidetrip to a favorite first-grade topic for some of the girls in the class. Such flights of fancy do not necessarily indicate that the children haven't learned what the teacher intended and evaluations should take this into consideration.) Having clear learning objectives will help you sort misinformation from extraneous details.

4. *Oral examinations.* Young children not yet literate are attuned to oral interaction. Even youngsters who are learning to read are, to a great extent, still part of a preliterate society. Asking them to tell you what they have learned or are learning can be a powerful method of evaluation. Where possible, avoid questions that lead to basic "yes" or "no" answers. If this is all you get, try saying, "Can you tell me more about that?" You still may get very little, but with practice, you will learn ways to help each child express himself or herself more fully.

5. *Demonstrations.* Just as children who are learning to read are still preliterate in some ways, so the youngest children who are just learning to talk have trouble expressing themselves orally. Thus, a request from you to "Show me what you've learned" may yield an effective response. Demonstrations can make use of dancing and other movement; miming or imitations; or art media such as tempera, crayon, and clay.

Simplifications

When you plan an activity or lesson for an entire class, a subgroup, or an individual, you must consider that some children will have difficulty attaining your objectives and that it is your responsibility to make the learning worthwhile for them. To

In planning curriculum, teachers must take into consideration the varying skill levels of the children in such activities as cutting with scissors.

plan simplifications knowledgeably, you will need to know the individual children in your center or class.

To demonstrate this point, we can return to the opossum learning experiences. Suppose the children are kindergartners, and being about 5 years old, some of them will have mastered cutting and some will not. Thus, the materials laid out for creating opossum habitats could create problems that lead to a lack of enthusiasm, even refusal to participate. Your evaluation might then indicate that several youngsters didn't understand the story and video when, in actuality, they simply were stymied in demonstrating their learning by their less-developed coordination. Showing them some careful tearing techniques could easily solve the problem, as would having pre-cut shapes from which they could create their habitats. In any case, it is the knowledge of habitats rather than cutting that you are evaluating for this lesson.

Part of the job description for people working in early childhood settings includes the need to teach basic life skills to individuals. Dozens of competencies from holding a spoon, to bouncing and throwing a ball, to cleaning up a puzzle may need to be taught by a caregiver or teacher. Different youngsters require a variety of teaching approaches to learn these skills, and it is good to begin now to collect an assortment of methods for simplifying. Tying shoes with the "rabbit ears" technique or putting on a coat by laying it on the floor then flipping it over the head are two examples. (See the end of this chapter for an activity to help you get started on your collection.)

Extensions of Learning

Just as there will be children who need simplifications to make their learning meaningful, there will be others who need more complexity, abstractness, and challenge. Teachers often forget these children, choosing simply to be pleased that they easily achieve the stated objectives and so can be praised and then ignored. Some may be sufficiently self-motivated to extend their learning on their own, but many highly capable children are not, or they are unable to figure out how to go about doing so. The result is that they don't achieve what they are capable of and may eventually turn off to school entirely. From the early years then, it is important to be aware of each child's special talents and capabilities and to encourage their development by providing extra challenges whenever appropriate. A child who quickly learns to walk on the balance beam while the rest of the group is still falling off can be taught some beginning tricks. A group of youngsters who easily classify a collection of plastic shapes according to color or shape can be encouraged to try the more complex skill of classifying by color and shape together. When most of your first graders struggle to write a single sentence or two, a few who can write whole stories should be encouraged to do so and be made aware of the basic beginning-middle-end story structure.

A word of caution: It is important to realize that a child might be highly capable in one area and need exceptional help in another. Never assume that a special intelligence in one area automatically translates into general ability or that slowness to understand one concept indicates a generally inadequate student.

Helpful Hints for Next Time

On your planning form, this section generally will remain blank until after you have taught a lesson at least once. What you write there will reflect what you learn from experience that will be useful to you in the future. Try to use this section for reflection every time you teach. It may include basic reminders for the ways a material is best used or a brand that works better than others. It might also incorporate adaptations you hadn't thought of for children with special needs, observations about pacing, or comments on the developmental appropriateness for a particular group of children.

The sample lesson plan and sample activity plan that follow provide examples of planning forms that can be used as they are or adapted to suit your teaching needs.

Sample Lesson Plan for Primary Grades

It is the **goal** of the following lesson that the children will be introduced to a new unit, Transportation, and look forward to it with enthusiasm. This particular introduction leads into their initial study of preindustrial modes of travel.

Title   How Can We Travel on Snow?   **Subject**   Social Studies

Objectives

1. Children will identify the physical similarities and differences between skis and snowshoes.
2. Children will describe the advantages and purposes of each mode of snow transport.

Materials

One pair cross-country skis
One pair snowshoes
One pair ski poles
One pair boots

Time   About 20 minutes

Procedure

Opening/Assessment

1. In whole group circle, teacher lays materials on floor.
2. Teacher asks children to identify and describe as they are able.
3. Teacher asks children to share any experiences using skis and snowshoes.

Body

4. Teacher asks individual children to explore materials and respond to questions about similar and different attributes of skis and snowshoes, then boots, then poles.
5. Teacher asks whole group to consider reasons for similar and different physical attributes. As hypotheses are presented, teacher or individual child demonstrates with materials. Teacher encourages further hypotheses.
6. As children begin to understand the different functions of the two types of equipment, the teacher leads the discussion toward an emphasis on ancient and pretechnological age skiing and snowshoeing as means of transportation.

Close

7. Teacher shares intent and topic of new unit of study. Children also are informed that the materials will be available in an activity center for independent exploration.

Evaluation

1. Teacher observes children at each step for enthusiasm and understanding and adjusts experience accordingly.
2. Teacher checks for understanding during each step through questioning and interaction with the materials.
3. Teacher observation of the follow-up activity center will include further informal questioning for understanding as well as encouragement of further exploration.

Sample Activity Plan for Preschool

The **goal** of this activity is to help children manipulate everyday fasteners that require the use of small motor skills. The introduction is essentially a **lesson**, but the focus is on turning the materials over to the children in the format of an **activity**.

Title Dressing Frames   **Domain** Physical

Materials

Set of wooden frames, each containing pieces of fabric with closures designed for practice:

buttons	zippers	safety pins
hooks and eyes	Velcro	snaps
buckles	laces	bows

Time

Introduction of each frame: 2 to 3 minutes

Informal and independent use after that

Procedure

1. Teacher gathers small group, facing same direction so that all can see.
2. Teacher chooses a frame to demonstrate. (Velcro is best for the first one, followed by snaps.)
3. Making sure to use the same method every time, teacher demonstrates once; invites a child to try; demonstrates again; invites another child to try, and so on.
4. Dressing frames are stored for children to work with during free-choice activity time.

Simplifications

If children have trouble with any of the fasteners, teacher can start the process and turn it over to them to finish.

Extensions of Learning

When a dressing frame becomes easily done, the actual piece of clothing can be substituted. Dolls wearing clothing with fasteners can be included in the collection, and children can also be asked to help younger children with various fasteners.

Making the Formats Your Own

These two plans are offered as samples of what you might try. As formats, they both have worked for others, but you might want to make modifications, depending on the age of the children, the kinds of lessons and activities in which you engage, and the degree of specificity you need to be comfortable. For example, in the second plan, you actually might want to write out the procedural details for each dressing frame: "To release pins, press them together with both thumbs while holding opposite bar with fingers. Hold fabric down with left hand and pull each pin out with right hand. Close each pin and lay it on table" and so forth. Although these instructions would be overkill for many teachers, they might remind others of the need to be consistent to which the original plan only alludes.

Planning the Daily Schedule

So far, we have described methods for creating individual activity and lesson plans. Of course, these must be placed in the context of the larger day. In this section, we present an overview of the elements of the day that you need to take into consideration for your curricular planning. A good place to begin is with your goals and objectives, because these should underlie the entire day, even if they all are not formally written down as were the sample lesson plan and activity plan here. On-the-spot objectives may be created informally whenever you need them. For example, when you see a child spilling milk again, you may think, "Tommy spills from that pitcher every day and has begun to think of himself as clumsy. Today I'll give him the blue pitcher and fill it just halfway. He can then be successful, feel better about himself, and have an easier time learning to pour the right way." Likewise, goals may be planned for a week, a day, or even a part of the day when the need arises. Perhaps the morning has been a contentious one, with children seeming to pick fights for no reason. You determine that many of them are tired after a long weekend and decide that for the rest of the day, the goal will be to have positive social interaction among all the children. You then redesign your planned schedule to make that happen. One approach would be to provide a longer, more relaxing afternoon snack time, during which you will converse quietly with the children rather than use the time to prepare activities, as you usually do. Your objective might be for the children to talk quietly and pleasantly with each other.

Although some goals and objectives are written and others simply are noted mentally, it is important that you do have them. They give structure and meaning to the day and guidance to your planning, both short and long term. Each day will be different in some respects, taking into account children's changing needs, interests, and abilities, but there still should be structure and stability to the schedule. Children feel more confident and secure when they know what comes next and can count on a basic rhythm in their daily routine. At different times of the year you may find it advantageous to make a major change or two, but this should be discussed and planned for with the children. For example, at the beginning of the year, you may want to begin the day with a structured activity followed by a free-choice activity time. Later in the year, the children may feel more comfortable and energized by coming into a classroom that is already prepared for its free-choice time. The descriptions of the following components of the day should be considered as guidelines, keeping in mind that flexibility is always necessary.

Arrival Time

The activities associated with arrival time should remain fairly stable so that children feel comfortable and secure when beginning their day. If changes are made during the year, be sure children are prepared for them. Arrival time provides an opportunity for the children to settle into the rhythm of the day and for you to have one-on-one interaction with each child. This is often a good time for children to choose freely from among quieter table toys and games. In the primary grades, the school may have expectations, such as roll call and lunch money collection or ceremonies, such as the salute to the flag. Much of this time can be wasted if children spend it waiting around for the daily requirements to be over with. Thus, in the primary grades, quiet games are also a good place to start the day. Furthermore, primary children can be trained to collect the lunch money, check their own names on the roll, and interrupt their games quietly when the schoolwide pledge begins.

Indoor Activity Time

This portion of the day will look quite different depending on the age of the children, the time of year, and the current curricular interests, but there are some similarities. For all groups at all times, this is a period of open movement, when children can work individually or in small groups and choose their own activities. Your role is to circulate among the children observing, encouraging, interacting, and helping them plan, make decisions, and formulate questions to answer. Because the children will be moving freely, planning for activity time includes providing enough activities so that there are always extras to choose from. Sometimes most of the activities will pertain to a unit or theme and will have been carefully planned with written-out goals and objectives. At other times, the materials will have been chosen from among those readily available. These should be selected to provide a balance between challenging and basic, active and quiet.

The beginning and ending of activity time both should be planned. Simply turning children loose at the beginning is an invitation to chaos. Children will need instructions before they start, even if just a quiet reminder as to how activity time should begin. Children who are learning to read often will enjoy the challenge of printed instructions at activity centers. Cleanup time is made easier if there is a rule that children put materials away as soon as they have finished using them. Then, when the activity time is over, the cleanup will take far less time, and there will be fewer instances in which children try to figure out who messed up what. Even toddlers can help with cleanup, particularly if adults work beside them, explaining what is happening and how it is being done. From about age 4, children generally are able to establish a set routine that is followed each day. That final bit of planning for activity time to be sure that enough time is allowed for adequate cleanup helps to keep the day running smoothly.

Whether your children are with you half a day or all day, a well-planned activity time is essential for intellectual, social, emotional, and physical development. If the children are present for the full day, a second activity time should take place in the afternoon after nap or rest. For preprimary children, this may be an outdoor play time, a walk around the neighborhood, or exploration of materials that weren't used in the morning. For primary children, the afternoon activity is another work period, but intensive intellectual work may be too much. This is especially true if the weather is very hot or if it is a major holiday period.

Outdoor Activity Time

Many children (and seemingly most caregivers and teachers) prefer being indoors, but there are others who work, play, and learn best outdoors. If there are enough adults to provide supervision, outdoor activities can take place concurrently with indoor activity time. Materials can be specific to outdoor learning or they simply can be indoor materials temporarily moved outside. When such an alternative is offered, not only the children who generally prefer the outdoors are served; others who need a bit of fresh air, a respite from studying, or a chance to move their bodies for a while have an extra opportunity to participate.

In most centers and schools, however, there is one specified outdoor period when the entire class has an opportunity to play. The reason may be that there are not enough adults to provide indoor–outdoor supervision at the same time, outdoor experiences are viewed by adults as less worthy, the adults prefer to be indoors, or no one is aware of the value of being outside. Traditionally, outdoor time is scheduled right after the morning activity or study time, after lunch, after nap, or just before it is time to go home. No matter how busy your schedule is or how many expectations are placed on you, you should include plenty of outdoor time. A change of scenery, an opportunity to use different muscles, to stretch a bit, and to be in the fresh air are all important to young children. Being outside also offers opportunities to learn important physical skills.

Perhaps most important, particularly in kindergarten and the primary grades, youngsters who seem unable to concentrate on their indoor work or who are tired or unhappy often are helped by being outdoors, thus making the indoor atmosphere more positive after the outdoor activity period. Because its attributes are all so positive, outdoor time should not be planned as a reward for good indoor behavior but as an important integral part of the day. We might even make a stronger argument that given the observation that many young children do not learn easily indoors in sedentary fashion, preventing their outdoor time until they finish their class work is almost abusive. It takes away the possibility that they can be as successful in their academic learning as other children in the class.

Lunchtime and Snacks

Depending on the age of the children and on the length of the day, you may have one, two, or perhaps no snacks each day. For toddlers, the snack works best if an assistant can prepare it out of the children's view and have them enter the snack area with the food immediately available. If this is impossible, it should be prepared as completely as possible in advance. By the time children are 3 years old, they are usually able to pour from a small pitcher and clean up after themselves. This makes it possible to incorporate a snack center into the activity time. You will need to plan this carefully with the children, making sure there are clear instructions about how many crackers or pieces of fruit each child is permitted to take, how many children may eat at one time, and what the cleanup process is. The first few days you try this, there may be one or two children who take too much, and there will always be occasional spills. The benefit of the snack center is the independent behavior and social interactions it fosters.

Lunchtime is at its best when children can eat together in small groups, serving themselves family style. Helpful adults can teach them the most efficient ways to serve from a large dish to their own smaller ones, the best ways to use their utensils, and simple first steps in good manners. Sometimes, lunchtime in public schools is a grim period, when discipline is maintained by permitting no child to talk or a chaotic period in which the noise and mess build. One elementary school turned around the behavior in its lunchroom by renaming it a restaurant. The food personnel and the principal shifted the long rows of tables into smaller clusters and then covered them with tablecloths (old sheets dyed in pleasing colors) and jars of fresh flowers. Attractive menus were posted and mellow music was piped in. The children knew in advance that changes were coming to the lunchroom, but they were given no new or stern rules of behavior. The changed atmosphere, however, altered the children's behavior immediately, and the improvement was permanent. If lunchtime in your school is unpleasant, you might consider some changes of this sort.

Ending the Day

Whether children are with you half a day or all day, you should allow enough time to impart a feeling of closure and some understanding of what to expect the following day. A whole-group gathering to discuss the day's events can help children recap their learning, evaluate activities, and determine how they can be improved. This meeting also provides an opportunity for children to help plan upcoming events and activities. Although much of the planning is your responsibility, children should be a part of it, too. The closing discussion is a good time to look both backward and forward, making plans that fit the flow of events and children's development. This discussion can be carried forward to the following morning if needed, and another planning session held before activity time begins.

Whatever the day has been like, it is important to end it with a positive feeling. Children should go home feeling comfortable about returning the next day, and they should come back the following morning feeling positive and prepared for what is to come. They will feel happiest if they have had some part in making the plans.

CREATING THE CURRICULUM

When learning is meaningful to children, they accept it more enthusiastically, are better able to make connections to other learnings, and retain it longer. Several approaches can be used to enhance meaningfulness, one of which is to involve the children in creating their curriculum. Group planning at the beginning and end of the day is an important step in this direction. Participation in this activity provides children with the intellectual stimulation of considering what learning is important for them, experiences in negotiation and positive social interaction, enhanced self-esteem as they realize their views are respected and used, and the opportunity to practice decision-making skills.

Meaningfulness is also enhanced when the teacher is flexible enough to permit spontaneity in the curriculum. A good curriculum and an atmosphere of receptivity should stimulate children's curiosity about the world. Curiosity, in turn, leads to questions of some importance as well as momentary whimsies, either of which may need exploration to answer satisfactorily. The flexible teacher stands ready to alter or enhance the curriculum to take into account children's changing interests.

A third way of making learning meaningful is to create a curriculum organized around themes of current interest rather than around traditional classroom subjects. This is the method of the Reggio Emilia schools and of the project approach briefly described earlier. (For a fuller accounting of both, see *Early Childhood Education: Yesterday, Today, and Tomorrow*, also in this series.) Historically, integrating the curriculum based on children's interests has been an acceptable approach in the preschool years but only intermittently accepted in the primary grades, where accountability requirements rather than children's actual needs often drive the curriculum. In recent years, however, as the connection between meaningfulness and learning has become more widely accepted, the use of interdisciplinary themes and projects has become more widespread in kindergartens and primary classrooms. A very few teachers at this level are able to place this approach to curriculum development at the core of what they do, whereas most find that they can delve deeply into thematic learning and projects only on occasion. More fortunate, generally, are the teachers of younger children, who have fewer constrictions on their teaching and can generate thematic learning projects most of the time.

Research on child development and learning indicates that the best way to serve the educational needs of children in the early years is to integrate the curriculum (Bredecamp & Copple, 1997; Hart, Burts, & Charlesworth, 1997). In the following sections, we provide two practical ways to achieve this integration, one at the toddler or preschool level, the other for the primary grades. In the first example, the emphasis is not on curricular subjects but on developmental domains, just as was the case with the sample activity plan provided earlier. In the second example, primary grade curriculum pays homage to the usual need for a focus on the disciplines while showing how these can be integrated for more meaningful learning (see the activity plan described earlier).

Older Toddlers and Young Preschoolers

To get you started on planning that fills more of the day or week than do individual lessons and activities, we present a theme that is commonly used in centers and preschools. Very young children are just beginning to learn about colors, and some preschool programs choose to study them in depth. The traditional model is to choose "the color of the week" and wrap much or most of the curriculum around its theme. This may make structural sense to adult planners, but younger children—especially toddlers—often find little sense in segmenting their learning into week-long units. In the case of colors, it may be that there is a color that is a great favorite on which the children would like to focus or, just as likely, a color they would be happy to abandon after a day or two. Related to this is the possibility that a set of activities is more or less popular than others, or there is a holiday break that the children find distracting.

Another concern with the "color of the week" model is that activities sometimes are chosen for no other reason than that they offer an opportunity to emphasize a particular week's color. Dinosaurs, which have little meaning to toddlers, other than their ability to attack and say "grr," may be introduced simply because their models come in green (or brown). Preschoolers, who find themselves learning to sing "You Are My Sunshine" for the single "yellow" week and never again, wonder whatever happened to that perfectly good song. In both these cases, adult theme structuring has gotten in the way of children's need for conceptual growth.

Basically, there is nothing wrong with teaching children colors in a way that integrates domains and activities. For the adult planner, the important thing is to determine what concepts, in addition to the concept of color, will be the focus of learning. Are dinosaurs really necessary in the toddler room? Not likely, and eliminating them will also eliminate one more behavioral concern. Is there anything wrong with introducing "You Are My Sunshine" during a study of yellow? Of course not, but its meaning easily could be expanded to a better understanding of friendship, certainly an ongoing theme of the preschool curriculum. In other words, as you plan a theme such as colors, avoid choosing activities simply because they are colorful. Think about the broader goals of your center or classroom. Once you have done that, it will be easier to choose and create activities and lessons that make a real contribution toward children's development.

There are many things to think about during planning, but the sequence of steps can actually be quite basic:

Step 1: Choose the broad goals

Some examples of broad goals that would apply to an entire study of colors might include

1. Children will understand differences among the three primary colors (cognitive).
2. Children will appreciate the beauty of differing colors (emotional).
3. Children will begin to learn about working together (social).
4. Children will participate in and enjoy movement experiences (physical, emotional).

Step 2: Divide the unit or theme into logical segments and plan each one

For these very young children, dividing the theme into individual colors makes sense. You might create enough activities for one week per color, remaining flexible enough to move on to the next color if interest flags, or to add activities if interest is high. For our purposes, we will focus on a segment devoted to the color yellow.

Step 3: Make a list of activities and create a curriculum web

Some of the activities that might work well in a study of yellow would be

1. Write a note home to parents requesting donations of materials and reinforcement of learning. Before sending the note, read it to the children, and have them "decorate" it using a yellow marker.
2. Make butter.
3. Tie yellow ribbons on each child's wrist each day.
4. Find yellow in picture books.
5. Teacher wears something yellow each day, and children identify it.
6. Make instant vanilla pudding with yellow food coloring added.
7. Have a bouquet of different colored flowers, some of them yellow. Each child chooses one yellow flower to put in an individual pot.
8. Plant marigold, zinnia, or other easy-to-grow seeds with yellow flowers. Place the empty packages on sticks and plant them at the end of each row as identifying markers.
9. When children wear yellow, ask other children to identify it.
10. Using any appropriate music, children dance freely trying to keep yellow balloons aloft, or trailing yellow streamers.

As you plan your unit, creating a *curriculum web* will give you a visual idea of what the coming weeks will be like. In the center of the web you will place the theme title. Each major area of study within this theme will have its own radial line, in this case, one that belongs to the color yellow. From each line will radiate smaller lines in which you write the activities you have chosen. Those that are similar in focus, such as cooking or clothing-related activities, will be clustered. By doing this, you can see if there is a focus that has too many activities or is underrepresented. In Fig. 1.2, we see that the color yellow has its strongest focus on clothing-related activities, whereas only one activity uses movement. The plans for the other colors should take this imbalance into account.

Primary Children

Curriculum planning for younger children generally avoids focusing on the subject disciplines, but the opposite is true in the primary grades and often in kindergarten. Although the older children still learn most naturally according to themes of interest, the academic demands of these years ensure that subject disciplines will be an important part of planning. In that regard, the integrity of each discipline should be respected by identifying and explaining the disciplines to the children. Failure to do so may lead to confusion for the children or to an embarrassing teaching experience, such as that of one second-grade teacher. Earlier in this chapter, we recounted the experience of the second-grade girls who went from making clay figures of Native Americans to nostalgic mer-

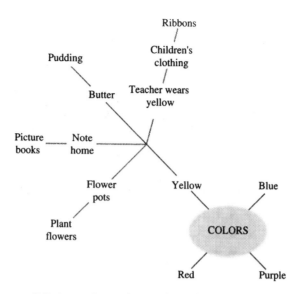

FIG. 1.2.   Curriculum web—theme of interest.

maids. The original intent of their teacher was to have the class create an authentic early Indian village of the New England region as part of a study centered on Pilgrims and Thanksgiving. Everywhere throughout the room there was evidence of their study, including whole villages made from clay. One morning, the principal dropped in, bringing with her the district superintendent. After looking around the classroom for a few minutes, the superintendent said to a group of children, "I see you do lots of social studies in here." The children looked puzzled and turned to the teacher for help. "Social studies?" they asked. "What's that?" After that, the teacher identified the disciplines for the children, who found them quite interesting and spent the rest of the year enjoyably sorting them out on their own each time a new theme was introduced.

Another example of curriculum integration involved a third-grade teacher who wanted to take advantage of the fact that her school was situated in a neighborhood in which school, homes, church, and shopping were all within close walking distance. She knew that the children had studied the community in the first grade, because it was a focus of their state-mandated social studies text. She believed, however, that further study of the topic could focus on new sites and issues and make use of the third graders' more mature capabilities. The enthusiasm with which the children tackled this "old" topic demonstrated to the teacher that she hadn't been wrong. Her role, then, was to make the children's study sufficiently challenging while reinforcing their earlier learnings.

Although this was primarily a social studies project, the teacher integrated other areas of the curriculum where it was advantageous. Some of the activities she chose were:

1. Interviews with employees, owners, ministers, and priests about their job responsibilities and reasons for choosing their careers. Small teams were assigned to do each interview, and their findings were placed in a class book.

2. Writing personal letters to the children's parents, then tracing each step of the letters' delivery through the postal system. The children then created a wall diagram showing the entire process and also wrote an accompanying explanation.

3. Devoting another wall to a gradually evolving community map. The first entries were based on their walks to various places. Later, the children used an easy-to-read realtor's map to fill in the places they hadn't visited.

4. Hikes to determine the outer reaches of their mapping territory. The children decided that whatever street was 15 minutes from their school in each direction would be the "frontier."

5. Spur-of-the-moment song compositions to make the hikes seem shorter.

6. A litter patrol activity that grew from children's concerns about an otherwise attractive "pocket" park. They weighed the sacks of litter and estimated the cubic feet, then wrote a letter to the editor of the local weekly newspaper asking fellow citizens to cooperate in keeping the area clean.

7. A trip to the park after the litter was cleaned up. Children drew crayon pictures of their favorite scenes.

8. Individual journals in which children wrote about their own responses to each of the activities.

When the teacher made the curriculum web, she divided activities among the subject disciplines. Figure 1.3 shows what these eight activities looked like when webbed.

Just a brief look at this web makes it apparent that this unit is totally lacking in science activities, and that math and art are underrepresented. You will also note that it is possible for some activities to appear in more than one discipline (litter patrol) and for others to fit only within social studies (the wall map). These observations can alert you to under- and overrepresentation in the academic curriculum. It may not be necessary

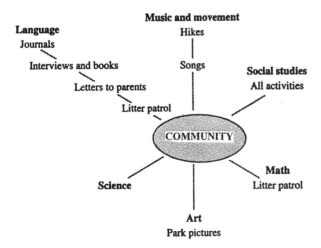

FIG. 1.3.   Curriculum web—subject disciplines.

or important to include science in the community unit for instance, but seeing that empty space on the web can remind you that science should be a focus at another time.

Another way to determine if there is under- or overrepresentation is to check whether each of the developmental areas or domains has been attended to. For this, another type of web can be created. It also contains the disciplines, but has an additional focus on human development.

This second web (Figure 1.4) illustrates that all developmental domains have been considered in some way. This type of web is less common than the first one but deserves consideration if you take seriously your mission to educate the whole child.

This chapter has provided an introduction to ways of looking at and creating curriculum for young children. The bias of the authors, as well as of most educators involved in early childhood, is toward integration of adult-defined subject matter into child-defined themes or topics of interest. Nevertheless, it is important to preserve the integrity of the various disciplines so that teachers can be aware of just what it is they are integrating and thus help children achieve the academic learning that is expected of them. As you read each of the following chapters, pay close attention both to the descriptions of what is included in each discipline as applied to young children and to the ways in which the discipline can also be made more meaningful as part of an integrated curriculum.

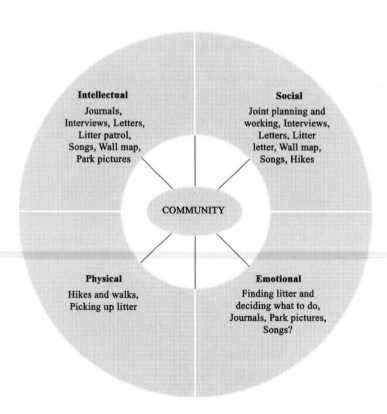

FIG. 1.4.   Curriculum web—developmental domains.

EXTENDING YOUR LEARNING

1. Observe an activity in a child-care center or classroom, then create a lesson plan for it according to your choice of instructions in this chapter. Share the plan with the teacher, and discuss whether you have correctly analyzed the plan's components.

2. Choose one age level, and plan a 1-day curriculum. Use a real classroom if it is available to you. Choose 3 or 4 activities for making lesson plans. Then, for the whole day, web the domains of development as in Figure 1.4. Adjust the activities to provide better balance if necessary.

3. Observe a single child for 20 to 30 minutes, using a clipboard or notebook. Using a pen of a second color, analyze what you have seen. Then analyze your observation capabilities. Where did you succeed? What needs improvement?

4. Interview a teacher to learn how he or she extends the curriculum for children who are more capable. Are they just given more work? Are their learning methods different? Are they provided with texts from the next higher grade? If so, does the teacher coordinate this decision with the teacher of the following year?

VOCABULARY

Adaptive or Assistive Technology. Any hardware, software, computer access, or adaptive equipment that allows students with special needs to participate more fully in home, school, and community activities.

Assessment. The collection and recording of evidence related to children's school progress. Methods of data collection may be formal (standardized) or informal. In conjunction with evaluation, assessment is used in curricular decision making.

Curriculum. The content of what is learned. In a school setting, it includes the list of subjects that are studied.

Developmental Domains. The aspects that make up the whole child and that develop with age and experience, typically cognitive, social, emotional, and physical.

Emergent Curriculum. Curriculum that is not prescribed by teachers or other authorities but grows from the students' own interests.

Evaluation. Interpretation and analysis of data gained through the assessment process. Judgments are made of the data's quality and value. In conjunction with assessment, evaluation is used in curricular decision making.

Goals. The ultimate and overall aims of a curriculum.

Individualized Educational Plans. Often referred to as IEPs, these plans are created by small teams of adult educators and specialists to meet the needs of specific at-risk children. Goals and objectives may be written for any of the developmental domains.

Integrated Curriculum.   Curriculum that incorporates more than one academic subject at a time. It can be prescribed, emergent, or a combination.

Methodology.   When applied to teaching, this term refers to the variety of ways in which the curriculum is delivered to students.

Objectives.   Specific behaviors that are to be accomplished by a single portion of the curriculum, usually a lesson or activity.

Project Approach.   An in-depth study of a topic chosen by children in negotiation with the teacher.

Pushed Down or Watered Down Curriculum.   Curriculum that has been taken from upper grades and adapted for use by younger children.

Thematic Curriculum.   An integrated curriculum created around a single theme or concept.

INTERNET RESOURCES

Web sites provide much useful information for educators and we list some here that pertain to the topics covered in this chapter. The addresses of Web sites can also change, however, and new ones are continually added. Thus, this list should be considered as a first step in your acquisition of a larger and ever-changing collection.

Early Childhood Education Online
   www.ume.maine.edu/~cofed/eceol

Early Childhood Special Education Thematic Units
   www.sbcss.K12.ca.us/sbcss/specialeducation/ecthematic/index.html

The Gateway to Educational Materials
   www.thegateway.org

Resource Center/Hall of Early Childhood Education
   http://tenet.edu/academia/earlychild.html

References

Bredecamp, S. (1997). In Hart, C., Burts, D., & Charlesworth, R. (Eds.), *Integrated curriculum and developmentally appropriate practice*. Albany: State University of New York Press.

Bredecamp, S., & Copple, C. (1997). *Developmentally appropriate practice in early childhood programs: Revised edition*. Washington, DC: National Association for the Education of Young Children.

Edwards, C., Gandini, L., & Forman, G. (Eds.). (1993). *The hundred languages of children: The Reggio Emilia approach to early childhood education*. Norwood, NJ: Ablex.

Hart, C., Burts, D., & Charlesworth, R. (Eds.). (1997). *Integrated curriculum and developmentally appropriate practice*. Albany, NY: State University of New York Press.

Jones, E. (1970). In Dittmann, L. (Ed.), *Curriculum is what happens*. Washington, DC: National Association for the Education of Young Children.

Jones, E. (1999). An emergent curriculum expert offers this afterthought. *Young Children, 54*(4), 16.

Jones, E., & Nimmo, J. (1994). *Emergent curriculum*. Washington, DC: National Association for the Education of Young Children.

Katz, L., & Chard, S. (1989). *Engaging children's minds: The project approach*. Norwood, NJ: Ablex.

Kostelnik, M., Soderman, A., & Whiren, A. (1999). *Developmentally appropriate curriculum: Best practices in early childhood education*. Upper Saddle River, NJ: Merrill.

Price, K., & Nelson, K. (1999). *Daily planning for today's classroom*. Belmont, CA: Wadsworth.

Unks, G. (1995). Three nations' curricula: Policy implications for U.S. curriculum reform. In A. Ornstein & L. Behar (Eds.), *Contemporary issues in curriculum*. Boston: Allyn & Bacon.

2

LANGUAGE AND LITERACY:
SPEAKING, WRITING, AND READING

*Education is not a race. A child who learns to read at age three has in no way
"won" over a child who learns to read at age six or seven.*

David Elkind

▼ *Chapter Objectives*

After reading this chapter, you should be able to:

- ▼ Describe today's views of teaching language and literacy skills.
- ▼ Explain some useful techniques for teaching language and literacy skills.
- ▼ Recognize ways that literacy activities can be incorporated throughout the curriculum.
- ▼ Explain some of the ways in which the structure of Standard English presents challenges to native speakers and immigrants as well.

As you think about and apply chapter content on your own, you should be able to:

- ▼ Plan language and literacy experiences in relation to children's physical, social and moral, and cognitive development.
- ▼ Plan language and literacy activities taking into account the needs of individual children, including a variety of cultural backgrounds.

A major part of being human is the variety of ways in which we communicate: by speaking or signing, by writing to and for others, and by reading what others have written. Skilled communication underlies most successful human interaction, whereas failed communication can lead to unpleasant misunderstandings, rifts within families, botched business dealings, even war. No wonder that parents, schools, communities, and nations place great importance on children's language learning. Historically, parents have seen to their children's learning of spoken language, whereas schools have been responsible for the teaching of reading and writing. In recent years, however, the lines between school and home have become blurred. On the positive side, educational research has shown that there is much to learn from home-style language and reading instruction. Less happily, more and more children are arriving—and leaving—school with inadequate communication skills. As research continues and knowledge expands, philosophies of language teaching and learning come in conflict with each other. The result can be very different-looking educational settings.

To demonstrate what is happening in the schools, we describe two recent language-learning episodes. They took place on opposite sides of the United States and represent very different ways of thinking about how young children learn language.

EPISODE 1: RAISING THE TEST SCORES

Eastside Elementary School is one of two schools located in a small and rather poor southern town. The principal is dedicated to proving that "his" children can perform as well as those who live in the wealthier areas nearby. To further that ambition, he spends much time studying the scores the children achieve on their standardized tests. His approach to learning is what he likes to call "good old-fashioned," meaning that an observer in the school would find children and teachers, at all grade levels, facing each other in formal rows and engaged in drill, practice, and direct instruction. This highly regimented approach to teaching and learning seems to pay off because, on standardized tests, the children at Eastside regularly outscore the children on the other side of town.

All Eastside's teachers, with the exception of an occasional kindergarten teacher, have embraced the "good old-fashioned" approach to teaching and proudly share the children's test scores with parents and visitors. Not long ago, the principal analyzed the kindergarten scores and noted that the most rigidly prescriptive teacher seemed to produce children with the highest language scores. The differences in the scores were not statistically significant; that is, they were so small that a researcher probably could attribute them to chance. But the principal argued that the differences were testimony to the superiority of the most prescriptive teacher and immediately ordered the other two kindergarten teachers to emulate her teaching methods. One teacher agreed to the change; the other asked for and received a transfer.

The next year all three kindergarten classes focused on reading readiness skills. They followed the guidelines of the county-adopted basal readers, with close attention to detail. Rarely was a prescribed activity omitted, and suggested sequences were followed carefully. The teaching methodology was a combination of teacher directed lessons and follow-up seatwork. For example, if the children were studying the letter m, the teacher might lead them in naming all the objects they could think of that started with that sound. These would be listed on the board and the m's underlined. The teacher would then show the children a series of attractive pictures and ask them to find objects within the pictures that began with the m sound. Related seatwork would consist of worksheets con-

taining a number of pictures, some of them possessing names beginning with m. *The children would be instructed to color the* m *pictures and leave the others blank. Since the follow-up tests in the basal reading series and the questions in the standardized tests both emphasized such finite skills as these, the children were well trained to perform at a high level on such tests. At the end of the year, all three classes performed almost identically. A researcher, however, might argue that the performances were almost identical before the cross-class consistency was required.*

This prescriptive approach to teaching, with its highly directive instruction complemented by independent practice, has been common in the United States in one form or another since our earliest schools. Episode 2 describes a type of classroom that also has existed since earliest times, but it demonstrates another way of teaching language and literacy skills, as well as a different relationship between teacher and children and among the children themselves.

EPISODE 2: WHOLE LANGUAGE, WHOLE CHILD

Shady Grove School is located in a working-class neighborhood in the Pacific Northwest. The building shares with Eastside the same standard school architecture of the 1970s, but the teaching and learning atmosphere is quite different. The principal of Shady Grove has long been fascinated by approaches to language and literacy instruction that build on children's own interests and needs. In earlier years, these approaches were called *language experience*; the more recent and expanded versions have been called *whole language*. (You will encounter these terms again further on in the chapter.) The principal has encouraged her teachers to experiment with whole language ideas in which there is less emphasis on drills and worksheets and more on learning the necessary skills in the context of meaningful experiences. Assessment is more likely to be done through analysis of portfolio collections of children's work than through standardized tests. To see how all this works in practice, consider the following description of a single hour in one third-grade class.

The third graders have been studying generational histories within their own families. They have interviewed older relatives and are now bringing to class interesting artifacts that have historic meaning to their families. The session begins when the teacher briefly explains the day's project, then models for the children what she expects them to do. First, a student teacher from the local university shares a sample of lace that has been in her family for over 100 years. As she does this, the teacher takes brief notes on a large index card. Next, the teacher shares the notes with the children and explains that she has just modeled what the children will be doing in pairs. She explains that the person who has taken the notes will then share with the class what he or she has learned from the owner of the artifact. The teacher proceeds to model this final behavior.

The children seem to understand immediately what it is they are to do. They are permitted to pair up with anyone they like, and this is done quickly. The results, however, are not uniform. Quite a few children model the teacher and student teacher almost perfectly, asking pointed and appropriate questions, skillfully sharing artifacts, and taking concise and focused notes. Other children are distracted by the novelty of the artifacts and forget to take notes. When they do, the process seems difficult for them, although they have had the experience before. The teacher reminds them that note taking does not require perfect spelling or penmanship and that it is all right to draw a picture if a word is too hard to spell.

The children respond to the announcement with renewed confidence, and no one hangs on the teacher asking for help in getting things right. One child, concerned that her toy carousel horse might not be described adequately, dictates the notes to her partner. "Write that it's blue and green and red," she commands; then, "Now write down that it was my grandma's." There is one deaf child in the class, and a full-time interpreter explains as necessary both to him and to his partner. Two children receive special education service, and halfway through the hour a special-ist enters to work with them. She helps them to focus on the note taking and to write down a few words that will help them make their presentation. The room hums with activity as children work in their pairs, and the teacher and student teacher float among them, giving help where it seems needed, briefly checking in on pairs who are doing fine on their own.

With 10 minutes to spare before lunch, the first three pairs share their partners' artifacts with the class. They are almost uniformly successful in following the model established by the teacher and student teacher 45 minutes before. In just one case, a child has trouble reading her notes. The teacher chooses not to intervene and the child's partner provides sufficient and uncritical help so that the presentation proceeds satisfactorily. After each presentation, the entire class applauds. When the teacher promises that there will be time later in the afternoon for more presentations, the children reluctantly agree to leave for lunch.

These two episodes differ greatly in their view and treatment of young children. In the Eastside classrooms, each teacher is clearly the authority figure (although only the children may think so, given the overshadowing presence of the principal). At Shady Grove, the teacher is a leader but allows the children to participate in decision making. The children are often permitted to choose with whom they will work, their performances are permitted to vary, and everyone is expected to be supportive of one another's presentations. Although teachers in both schools are fond of their children, the relationships are somewhat different. At Eastside, the children stay quietly in their seats unless given permission to talk or leave. At Shady Grove, children must obtain permission to leave the room, but they are otherwise free to move about and talk as they wish unless someone (not necessarily the teacher) has the floor.

The underlying assumption of how children learn is quite different in these two settings. At Eastside, learning is viewed as something that happens from the outside in; teachers are the knowledge givers and children the recipients. Good teaching hap-pens when the children prove themselves on classroom quizzes and standardized tests. At Shady Grove, learning is viewed as something that happens from the inside out. Teachers facilitate learning in such a way that children engage in self-directed and self-chosen activities. Good teaching happens when the children remain enthusi-astic about language and literacy, choosing on their own to learn more.

The view of the way children learn to read is quite different in the two settings as well. Eastside follows the traditional philosophy that reading readiness skills, such as letter recognition and letter sounds, should be learned first and that reading will then follow with greater ease. Kindergarten and the early weeks of first grade are desig-nated the reading readiness time, and true reading becomes appropriate after that. Conversely, the teachers at Shady Grove believe that literacy emerges over a long period of time, possibly beginning at birth. Fluent reading is a major step in the process, but it shouldn't be separated out in such a way that there is first a series of readiness skills and then reading itself. Rather, many interrelated experiences—dif-ferent for each child—lead to literacy.

Both ways of viewing children's learning of language and reading have their roots in history and theory. In this and subsequent chapters, we show that today's various opinions about education are not recent inventions but ideas that have evolved over centuries.

PERSPECTIVES ON HISTORY AND THEORY

We may never learn how and when humans began to use words in their oral communication, but the written record is somewhat clearer. From cave pictures that represented events in people's lives communication progressed to two basic systems of writing. One is logographic and makes use of shorthand pictures, each one of which represents a word. Chinese characters are today's most widespread example of logographic communication, although the Sumerians of ancient Mesopotamia are thought to be the originators of the idea (Adams, 1990). Although a literate Chinese needs to learn between 4,000 and 5,000 characters, the Chinese have stood by their difficult and complex system (although they are currently simplifying it for the computer age.) In the Middle East, however, alterations were made when writers started using symbols that represented syllables in words that couldn't be pictured. Later, symbols were used to represent initial consonants, and these were passed from language to language. Eventually, some of these symbols reached the Greeks, who, it is believed, misunderstood some of those they found unpronounceable, confusing them for vowels. In this way, the alphabetic system was created, an invention as important to social history as to language development. No matter what the language, its alphabet has fewer than 50 symbols to learn, thus making reading available to almost anyone at any level of society. Conversely, learning thousands of characters is an activity reserved for those who have the leisure time to invest—that is, the elite.

In English we use an alphabet system—one that is far from perfect. As you think about teaching young children to read and write, consider the problems our language presents as expressed in this poem fragment:

I take it you already know
Of tough and bough and cough and dough?
Others may stumble but not you,
On hiccough, thorough, laugh and through. (Adams, 1990, p. 20)

Other languages may provide fewer alphabetic stumbling blocks than English, but all contain irregularities or exceptions. Furthermore, an alphabet system of any type is inherently more abstract than early picture writing. Thus, moving children beyond their early inclinations to communicate by pictures and into an alphabetic system takes some sort of teaching. *How* children can best be taught is the argument of centuries.

Early Views of Teaching

Jan Komensky (1592–1670), a bishop in the Moravian church, is most commonly known by his Latinized name, John Comenius. This forward-looking religious figure and educator believed that learning should be enjoyable to children, that children need concrete objects to make new ideas meaningful, and that the first language of school should be children's native language. Comenius was responding to his contemporaries' preference for teaching in Latin, but today's research is beginning to show that children can read a second language most easily if they learn in their own language first. His view that learning should be enjoyable and concrete led educators in very different directions from the dominant practices of his day.

The English philosopher John Locke (1632–1704) was best known for his advanced thinking about democratic forms of government. Like Comenius, he also wrote on education, and like Comenius, he believed that children should enjoy learning and that teachers should make use of concrete objects. Locke, you will recall, viewed children's minds as blank slates to be written on by adults. Thus, in his view, a child's learning to read comes from external sources, such as adult teachers, who impart their knowledge in some form of direct teaching and provide rewards for successful learning. In this century, Locke's philosophical heirs are usually considered to be the behaviorists, who propose providing rewards for good effort and who break learning into a chain of manageable pieces. Each piece is linked to the next until the fullest possible understanding eventually is reached. Skillful teaching includes knowing when a learner has been pushed too far along the chain, and perhaps cutting back to the nearest manageable piece. Learning to read and write from this philosophical viewpoint suggests working from the parts to the whole, or from learning letters and sounds to the actual acts of reading and writing. Drill and practice are viewed as necessary to mastering the pieces, so that, in time, reading and writing will be skillful and fluent. Episode 1 at the beginning of the chapter presents a modern-day example of this philosophy of teaching. Teaching goals are clear, disciplined practice is provided, and in the end, the children have achieved the levels of competency that their teachers set for them.

Jean Jacques Rousseau (1712–1778), born in Switzerland but later a French citizen, echoed and expanded on Locke's views of democracy. (The French Revolution of 1789 was inspired, in part, by Rousseau's writings.) Although he, like Locke, wrote extensively on education, his views reflected European society's changing views of infants and young children. Where Locke saw youngsters as blank slates to be written on, Rousseau pictured them as inherently good beings preprogrammed for development much as a plant is. Just the right amount of watering and fertilizing makes a plant grow successfully to maturity just as the right amount of nurturing and education make a child reach his or her potential. This view led Rousseau to argue that young children should not be pushed to learn. In his view, reading and writing will happen when the children are ready and interested. A few of his contemporaries experimented with this sort of education for their children, eventually bemoaning the fact of the children's continued illiteracy—as well as their undisciplined behavior. Rousseau's philosophical heirs in this century are those who continue arguing against pushing children, although their views aren't usually so extreme as his.

The 20th and 21st Centuries

One notable attempt at a Rousseau-like atmosphere was Summerhill school, founded in England in the middle of the 20th century by A. S. Neill (1960). In this school, children were never pushed to read. Neill observed that, as soon as a real need or interest arose, most children would learn to read quickly and with little frustration. Neill was even willing to wait until the high school years for this to occur.

The American Arnold Gesell (1880–1961) and his maturationist philosophy provided a slightly different twist on the Rousseau tradition. To a maturationist, children are ready to read when they have achieved the intellectual level of a "normal" 6-year-old (more specifically, a 6.2-year-old). Since children achieve this level at different times, the teacher must observe individual progress closely so that a child isn't pushed too far too soon. Before the time when reading can be introduced successfully, reading readiness activities are appropriate. Here, the Rousseau-like philosophy may be replaced by Locke-like goal-oriented activities in which information is presented in pieces. Phonics games, for example, might help children approach readiness.

Because developments across the centuries can take so many turns, Rousseau's legacy leads to different models of reading. In the broadest terms, a Rousseau-inspired reading curriculum would look more like Episode 2 at the beginning of the chapter, with its emphasis on letting children choose the friends they work with, employing flexible grouping and timing, and promoting reading and writing as a natural activity that fits into whatever else is happening. In a maturationist interpretation, however, the pace of learning has a Rousseau-like naturalness, but the teaching methodology may be more reminiscent of Locke's goal orientation. Another critical difference is the view of reading itself. A maturationist believes there is a prereading period in which special reading readiness activities prepare a child for the real reading ahead. Inherent in the earlier Rousseau philosophy is the view that reading development is all of a piece, that early experiences with language are as much a part of learning to read as the eventual act itself. Thus, when the child is ready to read, it may appear to happen suddenly and spontaneously, when in actuality, the child's whole life experience has been leading to the glorious moment.

The development of reading and writing instruction in this country has not followed the Locke-Rousseau dichotomy exclusively by any means. A variety of factors also have influenced the picture. In Colonial times, for example, Bible study was the most important reason for learning to read. During this period a two-step teaching methodology prevailed that was a simplified version of that in Episode 1: Teach the phonetic and alphabetic codes, and then have students read (Adams, 1990). Until the middle of the 19th century, when more varied reading materials became available, this approach to reading remained fairly constant. As a way to get around the boredom of the repetitive practice required of their teaching system, educational leaders began recommending that children learn meaningful words first and the phonetic–alphabetic rules later. It took patience to convince teachers and parents that this new approach would work, but the method finally gained acceptance in the second quarter of the 20th century, coming to be called the *look–say approach*. The teaching of phonics was not dispensed with entirely, but it was provided only gradually; children spent most of their time trying to memorize unfamiliar words to add to their vocabularies.

Although the look–say method was not the only one used in the United States during this time, it was common enough that a critical 1955 book called *Why Johnny Can't Read* rang a bell with the mainstream culture as well as with educators and legislators, even becoming a best seller. In this critique of reading instruction, Rudolph Flesch decried the look–say system, arguing that the only children who could read well were those who were able to intuit the alphabetic and phonic systems. He maintained that in a democratic society every child should be able to read well, and that meant increasing instruction in phonics.

Much research followed the publication of Flesch's book, and to a great extent, his argument was borne out: Children who had early instruction in phonics became better readers. Yet teaching methods focused on phonics can become just as rigid and inadequate as those focused on looking and saying. Eventually, two camps emerged, each adamantly opposed to the other, making it difficult to combine the best of each method in a rational way.

In the 1940s, the idea of a *language experience approach* emerged, but it didn't begin taking hold until the 1960s. As its name implies, the approach seeks to tie reading and writing to real-life experiences. Children were provided with many experiences in and out of the classroom: field trips; group activities in science, social studies, and math; discussions and storytelling; drama, music, and art. Each experience was recorded on charts and lists, magazines and newsletters, and in child-generated books that became classroom reading material. However, language experience tended to become routinized over time, losing some of its early excitement and popularity (Goodman, 1989).

Meanwhile, a similar but expanded approach was stirring interest. In New Zealand, the writing, research, and teaching of Sylvia Ashton Warner, Marie Clay, and Don Holdaway led to literature-based reading programs in which children were immersed in trade books and magazines rather than in formal school-oriented readers. Additionally, teachers would produce oversized "Big Books" of children's favorite stories and give them repeated readings. Since New Zealand's education system was influenced by John Dewey, it is not surprising that this new approach gained favor in this country as well. Dewey (1859–1952) was born and educated in Vermont, then studied and taught history and philosophy. As a professor at the University of Chicago, he established one of the first-ever laboratory schools. Based on his view of democratic principles, even the "subprimary" classes were designed to be a microcosm of society. Dewey believed the curriculum should be integrated rather than taught in isolated segments; that children should be involved in their own learning, grappling with real problems; and that reading, writing, and oral expression are tools for expressing what has been learned in these real experiences.

As well, the views of the Swiss Jean Piaget (1896–1980) lent support to the New Zealand approach. Piaget argued that although there was something to be said for both the nature (Rousseau) and nurture (Locke) views of development, a third explanation also was possible. With input from both the environment and their biology, Piaget argued, children actually construct their own knowledge. Thus, Piaget's view of self-constructed knowledge provided additional support for an approach in which children are more self-selecting in what they read, tell, or write about.

In the United States, however, official support of the move away from basal readers and programmed instruction was lacking. In its place, teacher support groups were created, the first and best known being Teachers Applying Whole Language (TAWL). The term *whole language* emerged in the 1970s from various sources. As Yetta Goodman (1989), one of the early and continuing leaders in the movement, explained:

> The early users of the term were not consciously naming a new belief system or movement. We were talking about some new ideas about language, about teachers and learners, and what these meant in terms of implementation, and we needed new language to express our new meanings. (p. 115)

Ken Goodman (1992), Yetta's husband and another major leader in the movement, added that it was the Canadians who popularized the term: "They needed a term to differentiate their developing educational philosophy, programs, and practice from the skill–drill, text–test model they saw in U.S. schools" (p. 195).

Some critics of whole language argue that it is nothing more than an updated language experience methodology, but whole language proponents answer that whereas it shares the same basic tenets, it is in actuality much more. For example, whole language relies less on a teacher as producer of charts, lists, and so forth and hands over much of the writing activity to the children. This approach is based on research showing that children learn to write by writing and that imperfect spelling is a useful stage in their development. Whereas language experience tended to give writing duties to the teacher until children were able to write with some skill, whole language proponents believe that invented spellings are both permissible and useful learning tools (Routman, 1988; Wilde, 1989).

The teachers at Shady Grove School base their teaching on the principles of whole language, although in the best tradition of this approach, they put their own interpretation on the principles in order to meet the specific needs of their classes. For example, whole language enthusiasts generally shun standardized tests of any sort, but the Shady Grove teachers make use of placement tests to help them divide the children into various groupings for different projects. In addition to letting the children choose their partners, groups are sometimes made up of children with similar skills and reading attainment or, at other times, with children whose differences complement each other.

Although the principal supports their experimentations with the whole language approach, the teachers at Shady Grove are well aware that there is considerable skepticism on the part of other teachers around town. This skepticism has spread throughout the United States as children in whole language programs have failed to perform well on standardized tests of reading attainment. Hard questions have been asked in recent years: Are the tests asking the wrong questions? Is the method itself responsible for low scores, or could it be teachers' interpretations of the method? Should we return to drill-for-skill phonics teaching? If we do, will children grow up capable of but hating reading?

As teachers, researchers, parents, and legislators began to look for answers, proponents for one method or the other pointed to "scientific evidence" that their view was the one, true way. Thus emerged what became known in the 1990s as the "reading wars." Cooler heads began to suggest that a truce be called, that, just perhaps, it was possible that no single technique can be best for all children, and all approaches to reading instruction have strengths and ideas that can be used. As one writer who argued for compromise said:

> We must avoid either/or positions that reject out of hand the possibility of blending and blind us to the value of different perspectives. Advocacy of systematic direct instruction does not mean that indirect instruction is considered of no value. On the other hand, advocacy of whole language does not mean that children are left alone in a state of benign neglect. . . . If bridges are to be built, we need to think in terms of a continuum rather than a dichotomy. (Spiegel, 1992, p. 38)

Although the 1990s saw continued progress in such attempts at blending and acceptance of approaches, the reading wars also continued. Speaking of the "rancorous public debate over beginning reading instruction" that included "overstating, exaggerating, and maybe even creating evidence," a research scientist and member of the International Reading Association's (IRA) board of directors suggested that we ask "for copies of the five most compelling studies that support" any particular assertion and then examine them "carefully for what was really demonstrated" (Allington, 1997, pp. 15–16).

As Allington wrote this plea, a major review of reading and language research sponsored by the National Research Council (a subgroup of the National Academy of Sciences), was being finalized. Calling themselves the Committee on the Prevention of Reading Difficulties in Young Children, a group of scholars read and analyzed studies both major and minor, quantitative and qualitative, and published their results in a major book called *Preventing Reading Difficulties in Young Children* (Snow, Burns, & Griffin, 1998a). Typically referred to as "the Snow report" after Catherine Snow, the group's chair, the book immediately attained widespread fame and quickly underwent repeated printings. Here, it seemed, was an excellent review of a huge body of research, undertaken by members from both sides of the war, with potential for excellent directions for teaching, as well as for an end to the reading wars.

A summary of the major findings and recommendations from the committee, first for younger children, then for those in the primary grades follows (Snow, Burns, & Griffin, 1998b).

For preschool and kindergarten:

- Motivation to read begins in the preschool years as does the collection of reading skills that will be needed in later years. Thus, language experiences in these early years are of critical importance.
- Child-care settings available to parents of limited economic means often provide impoverished language and literacy environments. This must be changed.
- All preschool programs, including those designed as interventions for children at risk of reading failure, should provide programs that support cognitive, language, and social development as well.
- Kindergarten programs should stimulate verbal interaction and vocabulary growth. In addition, they must provide plenty of talk about books while encouraging skills with sound structure, knowledge about print, and "familiarity with the basic purposes and mechanisms of reading" (p. 6).

For the primary grades:

- To promote fluency, classrooms should contain a good collection of well-written books at the children's comfort level of reading.
- Explicit instruction must be provided to help beginning readers with spelling and sound conventions, sight recognition of common words, independent reading, and reading aloud.
- From the beginning, children should learn such skills as summarizing the main idea, predicting upcoming text, making inferences, and monitoring their reading for misunderstandings.
- Writing should begin as soon as children learn some letters. Invented spelling should be accepted at the same time instruction is provided in conventional spelling. Writing activities should be provided regularly at all levels.
- In-school reading activities should be provided daily and have two goals: to support independent reading at children's comfort level and to provide support for reading that is somewhat more difficult, so that children's skills will advance.
- Independent reading outside school should be fostered through daily homework, summer reading lists, parent and community involvement, and assistance from librarians.

By the third printing, the report's creators were becoming concerned with some people's interpretations and use of their findings. They emphasized what they saw as "the core message concerning reading instruction, that reading instruction *integrate* attention to the alphabetic principle with attention to the construction of meaning and opportunities to develop fluency" (Snow, Burns, & Griffin, 1998a, p. vii). They did not intend, the committee stated, to imply that reading methods simply were to be balanced between phonics and whole language—that there should just be "a little of this and a little of that". Instead,

> "Integration" means precisely that the opportunities to learn these two aspects of skilled reading should be going on at the same time, in the context of the same activities, and that the choice of instructional activities should be part of an overall, coherent approach to supporting literacy development, not a haphazard selection from unrelated, though varied, activities. (p. viii)

The focus of the committee's research was on studies of learning to read, but it should be apparent through reading their recommendations that oral language and writing are part of the learning process as well. Although the nation's attention currently is focused on the seemingly intractable problem of reading, it is only through attention to all the forms of human communication that this problem can begin to be solved.

Subsequent to publication of the Snow report, James Paul Gee (1999) reflected on its findings and reinterpreted the data from a view that took into account the social and cultural aspects of learning to read. Arguing that the Snow committee was negligent in focusing primarily on such issues as phonological awareness, decoding, word recognition, and comprehension, Gee pointed out the relationships inherent among reading, poverty, racism, and culture. These social issues, he said, are not separate from learning to read, nor are they mere "background noise." If we choose to ignore them Gee predicted:

> We will soon face another and new "crisis": elementary, middle school, and high school classrooms will be filled with children who have successfully passed basic reading tests by the third grade and yet cannot use language (oral or written) to learn, to master content, to work in the new economy, or to think critically about social and political affairs. (p. 358)

Gee then took some of the findings in the report and redirected their meaning using his sociocultural framework. For example, he draws our attention to the report's mention that such things as vocabulary and the ability to engage in verbal interactions are important to reading success and that these verbal abilities are enhanced by family, cognitively challenging talk and texts in school, and sustained studies in both oral and written language. Thus, children who come from verbally supportive families and who attend schools where "school language" is taught and supported have a natural advantage in all forms of communication. The committee's mere mention of all this should have been expanded with an indepth analysis, Gee argued.

The field of literacy education today may well be at a crossroads. The reading wars may become a thing of the past, as the best of several philosophies are combined and integrated for more effective teaching approaches. In addition, as issues of diversity continue to be important to the creation of our programs for young children, we need to take into account their relationship to the development of communication skills (reading, speaking, writing). As you observe and work in classrooms, talk with teachers about their views on language development and teaching. Try out some of their ideas with children, note the results, and begin to develop the philosophy that works best for you in the situations in which you find yourself.

PERSPECTIVES ON DEVELOPMENT

The distinctive language capabilities of humans remain somewhat of a mystery in terms of how language is learned, although emerging brain research is beginning to offer some hope of understanding. Meanwhile, theories and philosophies continue to provide interpretations, explanations, and guidelines for teaching. Following are descriptions of the major views.

Theories of Language Acquisition

The behaviorists, whose roots lie in John Locke's blank slate theory of learning, argue that adults provide the language model and children learn by listening to and imitating them. Positive reinforcement from those same adults encourages children to continue their development. Although this theory must be considered incomplete (Morrow, 1993), it does have practical value. Young children frequently parrot the words, phrases, poems, and songs they hear around them, even though they often lack the cognition and vocabulary to reproduce everything accurately. When that occurs, they simply substitute a similar-sounding word or phrase that has meaning to them. One midwestern child, trying to sing "God Bless America," apparently could not conceive of an "ocean white with foam" and substituted "to the ocean's telephone." A Japanese 2-year-old sang every verse of "My Darling Clementine" although she didn't understand a word of English. Her amused parents, who had taught it to her, noted that she occasionally lapsed into a Japanese word when she forgot the English sound. Two years later, when the child was enrolled in an English-language nursery school, it became apparent that her imitation was developing into some minimal understanding. Between the ages of 2 and 4, the child had continued to sing the song everywhere she went, largely because of the positive attention she received both publicly and privately.

Punishment or lack of reinforcement can also affect children's language development. A child who is continually told to be quiet or to "shut up" is likely to do just that, particularly if the words are said in a negative tone of voice. Unfortunately, much language learning takes place through practice, and this child loses out on important developmental opportunities. The same is true for children whose parents rarely speak. Such environmental deprivation in the early years can have lifelong negative implications.

Maturationists view language learning in the tradition of Rousseau: Children are preprogrammed for innate development. As children observe their social environments, they begin to understand how language works. They begin to intuit naturally the necessary rules and conventions of their native language and begin to communicate intelligibly. Children need to hear language in order to understand it, but adult instruction is not essential, because cognitive maturation leads naturally to language functioning. Children naturally experiment with and test the linguistic rules that govern the language around them. As they generate more complex language, children unconsciously create a more complex rule system.

To constructivists, language is both genetically determined and environmentally influenced. In the biological sense, humans have the ability to communicate through language. Young children make use of this ability as they respond to the sounds in their environment. Two theoretical researchers in this field, Piaget and Lev Vygotsky, have greatly influenced today's views of how children learn language.

According to Piaget, children's first words—or their approximations—are egocentric, centered on their own interests and actions. In the early years, their communication relates to those things they experience through the senses. Furthermore, young children believe that those who communicate with them perceive and understand things in the same way that they do. For instance, 3-year-old Peter received a baseball cap from his grandparents. Within a few days, they telephoned and asked him if he liked it. Instead of answering directly, he laid the phone down, ran to his room and put on the cap, ran back to the phone and, lifting it, asked, "Doesn't it look good on me?" As children move from preoperations to concrete operations, they begin to realize that others have perspectives that are different from their own. Linguistically, they begin using this knowledge to construct speech that takes into account the views of others. If Peter were 2 or 3 years older, he would understand that his distant grandparents couldn't see the cap on him and that it was his responsibility to inform them of how good it looked.

According to Vygotsky, infants begin to develop speech without understanding that its purpose is to communicate. Instead, they develop a kind of inner speech that only gradually becomes connected to external communication. It is the adults in their environment who encourage the transition from speech as a private toy to speech as a social tool. The first step in this transition process begins when babies begin to understand something of what adults say to them, even if they are largely unable to communicate in return. With repeated interactions, they begin to pick up and use adult meanings.

At 6 weeks old, Hayley began playing with the sound "da da" and soon noticed that it got the attention of the two primary adults in her life. In fact, they seemed quite excited by the sound, and she began using it simply to make them pay attention to her. It wasn't long before she realized that one of the adults was always the one to respond and that the second one would follow soon after saying, "ma ma." Some practice with both sounds made her realize that if she said "da da," the one with the beard approached and if she said "ma ma", the one with the curly hair did. In either case, the adult looked very happy to see her. This common sequence of early events in an infant's life nicely demonstrates Vygotsky's view, as does the follow-up step in which Hayley took the communication skill she had learned from her parents and expanded on it. From the beginning, she had differentiated Mama from Dada not only by appearance but in relation to her interest in mealtime. Thus, for a while, "ma ma" meant not only *mother*, but *milk* as well. Since she had but one word for two meanings, Hayley was forced to be creative about her tone of voice and body language to get what she wanted or needed at the moment. It is through such experiences that humans learn the art and skills of communication.

Linguistic Systems and Children's Language Development

Infants begin learning language by experimenting with every sound their mouths will make. At the same time, they begin mimicking the sounds they hear in their environment and eventually exclude any others. Before long, it becomes less possible to make the sounds not associated with their home language, although initially they had the potential for speaking any language in the world. By the end of kindergarten, most children have learned the basics of their native tongue. Doing so means that they have mastered five systems of language.

• *Phonology* is the system of language sounds. In English, there are 44 phonemes, or individual sounds. Infants begin by approximating the sounds they hear, perhaps dragging a "blankie" in one hand, carrying a "baba" of "mik" in the other. With practice and maturity, children learn the sounds that make up words, rules for combining sounds, proper articulation, and intonation patterns.

• *Morphology* deals with the internal structure and formation of words. For example, young children begin to learn that adding an s makes a word plural. Soon they generalize this rule even in incorrect ways, referring to men as "mans" or to a flock of sheep as "sheeps." Morphology also includes changes made to words to indicate different tenses, and again, children overgeneralize at first. "I goed" or "I sleeped" make good sense structurally but not culturally. By the end of kindergarten, children have figured out most of the basic exceptions to the rules.

• *Syntax* is the grammar of language, the system for placing words in phrases and turning phrases into sentences. Sentences take varying forms such as questions, comments, and exclamations, and children must learn the differences among these. Hayley's early "ma ma," used for two different purposes, gave way eventually to simple phrases, such as "Hayhee want mulk" or "Mama not home?" Eventually, her simple phrases developed into more complete, though still simple, sentences—"I don't like these eggs"—until just before her second birthday, Hayley's first complex sentence was uttered: "I'm in the garden with Mama, pulling weeds."

• *Semantics* is the system children must learn for giving meaning to words. In the beginning, words that are repeated over and over take on meaning for the infant, as long as the objects they represent are present at the same time. As preschoolers mature in their linguistic understanding, they can give more complex meanings to words but are still tied to their egocentric view of the world. When a kindergarten teacher asked her class to define the word *family*, one child said, "It's my mom, my cat, my dog, and me." Another answered, "Me, my daddy, my mommy, Gramma, and Billy." If the children were 1 or 2 years older, they most likely would give a generic definition rather than their egocentric ones.

• *Pragmatics* refers to the application of language to specific and cultural situations. The social interactions of a neighborhood, region, school, church, and so on help determine the accepted rules of communication. Children intuit many of the rules and are taught others by parents, school, and older siblings. Cultural changes can cause discomfort for children if they move or begin to attend school with children and teachers of different backgrounds. One teacher moved to a southern state after a lifetime in the North. In the first hour of the first day of class she found herself saying heatedly to three different children, "Don't you 'ma'am' me!" when they answered "Yes, ma'am" to her questions. When the third child burst into tears, it finally occurred to the teacher that in her own nervousness at being new, she hadn't picked up on the polite culture of her young children and had caused them much discomfort. In the same town nearby was a private school that had recently become integrated after years as a Whites-only school. Black children as young as 4 years old quickly learned to speak Standard English in the classroom, but on the playground, their speech patterns changed depending on the race and culture of the children they played with.

Phonology, morphology, syntax, semantics, and pragmatics are all elements of linguistics that young children need to learn to communicate successfully. Given a supportive environment and normal maturation, success is generally ensured. Because not all children have these advantages, it is good for teachers to be aware of each element, its role in language development, and its importance to communication.

DIVERSITY AMONG CHILDREN

Children with disabilities, like all children, will learn language and literacy skills at different rates. As a classroom teacher, you can provide a language rich environment for all students and work with speech pathologists, occupational and physical therapists, special educators, and parents to identify adaptive equipment and specialized instructional techniques. Regardless of their skill levels, all children should have plentiful opportunities to engage in conversation, hear other people talk and read, and express themselves through speaking, drawing, writing, or any combination of these. Chances are good that any adaptations, modifications, accommodations, assistive technology, or specialized instruction that helps a child with a developmental delay or disability also will be useful for other students in the class who are challenged by learning to speak, read, and write.

Curriculum Considerations for Children With Special Needs

Early childhood educators are frequently involved in the identification and remediation of problems in children's language and communication skills. If you suspect a child is having difficulty learning language, review the information at the beginning of this section about the five elements of language, and try to make an initial distinction between problems in phonology, morphology, semantics, syntax, and pragmatics. A 3-year-old child who seems to comprehend the spoken word as well as peers but is unintelligible when she speaks may be delayed in acquiring control over production of speech sounds (phonology), a problem that might resolve over the course of the next year but also might require speech therapy for articulation in primary school. The language problems of a 6-year-old who speaks clearly but uses three- to four-word sentences with limited vocabulary and has trouble following simple directions and has a limited grasp of word meanings (semantics). Some of the special needs that are related to language and literacy are discussed in the following sections.

Sensory Impairments

Children who cannot see well often learn to speak without much difficulty but are likely to have trouble reading print. Large print books, keyboards, and high-contrast instructional materials are helpful for some children whose vision is corrected with glasses. Those who are blind will often learn to read Braille, a tactile system of raised dots that represent letters and numbers. Thermal pens and heat-sensitive paper provide raised images that allow children to feel graphic designs and other visual displays. The opportunity for hands-on learning experiences is especially important for young children with visual impairments, and teachers should take care to remember to let these youngsters hold and manipulate objects that are shown to the rest of the class. Current computer technology includes speech input and output devices, the former allowing students to "type" by talking at the computer and the latter "reading" aloud whatever is on the screen. Speech output programs are available that scan written materials and read them; others "read" Internet screens and Web sites.

Children who cannot hear well do not receive the linguistic input necessary for typical language development. Whenever a child fails to start talking between the ages 1 and 2, his or her hearing should be tested. Children with hearing impairments often will wear hearing aides or use FM devices to help them hear better in the classroom. Increasingly, young children with certain types of hearing impairments are being referred for cochlear implants, a surgical procedure that imbeds a tiny device in the ear that allows children to hear sounds.

Children who are deaf will usually learn a manual language, most often American Sign Language (ASL), and will come to class with interpreters. The teacher should remember to look at and talk to the child rather than to the interpreter. ASL is a bona fide language with unique rules for semantics, morphemes, and syntax, so children who express themselves using ASL are learning to read and write English as a second language. Learning to read is doubly difficult for children who cannot hear the phonic code associated with the printed word. There is a story book series that shows hand signs along with written words, based on a system of manual communication that uses Standard English syntax. Although it is helpful to see the signs and the words together, teachers should keep in mind that ASL and Standard English are two separate languages.

Cognitive Impairments

Language is essentially a symbolic system of communication, and young children with cognitive delays often have trouble with the abstract nature of the verbal expression. Youngsters with cognitive delays and mental retardation also have problems remembering vocabulary, sequencing words for creating complex sentences, making discriminations between words that sound alike, and translating ideas into words. Sign language is commonly used to teach vocabulary and word order to preschool children with cognitive delays, because the signs are more concrete than the fleeting sounds of the spoken word. Children with cognitive delays often learn language and literacy skills more slowly than their peers and need more practice to master basic competencies. Language and literacy goals may be addressed in the regular classroom and through supplemental instruction individually or in resource room settings. Children with significant cognitive delays may learn to recognize "sight words" critical for daily living activities rather than learning to read and write by learning the written code of the language.

Physical Impairments

Children with physical impairments may need support or accommodations for the movement components of language and literacy. Conditions such as cerebral palsy can affect the speech mechanism and render a child's speech unintelligible, regardless of how well he or she has learned language. A number of programmable assistive communication devices from very simple to quite complex are available on the market today that allow youngsters to express themselves understandably.

Children with physical impairments who learn to read may need assistance with holding books and turning pages. Special grips for writing utensils are helpful for some children, and others who speak clearly can use the computer for writing—typing on regular or adapted keyboards, using head pointers to type, or using speech input programs.

Cultural Considerations

If all children arrived in their classrooms with equal access to language skills, teaching undoubtedly would be easier but certainly not so interesting. One of the challenges facing today's teachers of young children is the fact that children arrive speaking different dialects and, with increasing frequency, different languages. Some come from families in which they are read and talked to daily; others may never have seen a book and rarely communicate with family members. Still other children may have language delays for varying reasons of health or mental capacity. The teacher's responsibility and challenge is to try to meet all their needs.

If you teach in an area where there is more than one culture or race, you may find that some of the children in your class speak a dialect that is different than what you usually hear. It is important to realize that a dialect is not simply deficient Standard English but a way of speaking that has its own consistent vocabulary, morphology, and syntax, all of which the dialect-speaking child must learn, just as other children learn Standard English. The northern teacher who had to accept being called ma'am was almost as startled to hear one child ask another, just before recess, "Are you fixin' to go out?" To which the other responded, "Uh huh. I'm either gonna jump rope with Peggy Jane or play tag with the boys, one." One what? the teacher wondered. And fixin'? The elements of the local dialect that were new for this teacher included vocabulary ("fixing" rather than planning or preparing), morphology ("fixin'" with its lack of a final /g/, although this is common to many cultures), and syntactic ("or play tag with the boys, one"). In this case, the dialect was a regional one. Other dialects belong to social classes or ethnic groups. Although the northern teacher's southern career got off to a rocky start, by the second or third day she came to understand that her own dialect was not necessarily superior, even though it was the one most commonly heard on national television news.

Teachers must walk a tightrope between valuing children's home dialects and introducing them to Standard English. There is no reason children can't learn to be "bilingual," as the Black children in the private school demonstrated. But first they must recognize that there are different ways to talk. As they learn to read stories in Standard English, and as they continue to hear them, some children will automatically pick up on the differences. Additional learning can be fostered by reading stories that are written in dialect and discussing the differences with the class. Inviting a guest speaker with an unfamiliar dialect, then discussing his or her speech, further heightens awareness. (Be sure, however, that the speaker knows what will happen and agrees to it.)

The United States is experiencing an immigration wave in which a high percentage of the incoming children speak languages, such as Japanese or Vietnamese, that have little or no relation to English. Furthermore, these may not be languages that any of us traditionally learn to speak in school. These two facts alone make comfortable assimilation difficult. Add to them a situation in which a large urban area might have more than two dozen languages represented in its school population, and the situation becomes a challenge for everyone.

It is commonly assumed that through play, younger children easily absorb the dominant language of their peers. This, however, is not necessarily the case (Logan, 1990). If there are others around who speak their native language, the children may choose to play only with them, reserving their contact with English for the formal, teacher-directed experiences. Furthermore, they come from a variety of backgrounds, just as the native speakers do, and may have a learning deficit in their native language that impairs their ability to pick up a second language. For children who can find no one in the center or school who can understand them, the situation may well be frightening.

A teacher's role is to be sensitive and supportive. Underlying all teaching techniques and interventions should be a respect for each child's own language and culture. You can help new children in a variety of ways:

- Arrange with the principal or director to meet with new children and their parents before they join the classroom. This provides an opportunity to make the child feel comfortable and to inform the teacher of the extent that linguistic intervention might be necessary.

- Prepare the class for the new child once the meeting is held. Role play in which the children are placed in a foreign situation in which no one understands them can be helpful. A follow-up discussion of ways to make the new child feel welcome is useful, particularly if moderation is stressed. (Sometimes a class goes overboard in their enthusiasm, making the new child feel overwhelmed and subsequently confused about how to behave.)

- Invite the child's parents or others from the same culture to share artifacts, games, dances, and stories from the culture. The class can be taught some basics of the language. If the new child is permitted to be the language teacher, self-esteem and respect are fostered.

- Identify other students who speak the new child's native language, and create a buddy system.

- Use flexible grouping to place non-English speakers with native speakers to work on projects. Provide guidance to the group in assigning non-native speakers to jobs that require a level of English that is challenging but still manageable.

- Avoid placing non-English speakers in isolated groups or excluding them from activities because you assume they won't understand. Much language learning takes place through observation and listening. At the same time, if there is more than one child who speaks the same language, be sure that there are informal times when these children can relax and communicate with each other if they so choose.

- Make full use of available resources for interpreters and for English as a Second Language (ESL) instruction.

Finally, it is good to keep in mind what Gonzales-Mena (cited in Morrow, 1993) said concerning the help teachers can give children who are learning English:

- Children are eager to learn English when there is an openness and an acceptance of them, their cultures, and their native languages.
- Language should be taught as part of the total integrated curriculum, not as an isolated subject area.
- Because children learn through their senses and through physical activity, they will learn language best when they can examine and explore real objects and act out new expressions. Pictures can help, but action provides a stronger imprint.

Giftedness

Frequently, children who talk more easily than others and read fluently with little instruction are ignored in favor of attention to children experiencing more difficulties. In actuality, many of these gifted children learn best if provided considerable independence. There is a difference, however, between leaving a child alone because you are too busy to pay attention to him or her and leaving the child alone because it is part of a well-thought-out plan of encouragement.

Children who have a talent for early reading also enjoy being read to. Furthermore, they can read to very small groups of their friends or to younger children. One kindergarten teacher trained his early readers to read stories to the class just as he did: holding each new page up so that everyone could see the pictures, permitting children to ask questions and make comments, and leading a brief discussion at the end. At least three other children, inspired by and perhaps envious of their friends' leadership opportunities, began making heroic efforts at learning to read so that they, too, could read to the class. In varying degrees, all three were successful.

Children who can read early, and others who are on the verge, are frequently capable of very interesting composition, although their handwriting may not yet be competent. These children can be introduced to the computer keyboard or to small plastic or cardboard letters. Dictation is always a good approach, but the computer or letters provide the independence a creative child may sometimes prefer.

In the primary grades, gifted readers and writers may become interested in pursuing a research topic in great depth. A teacher who facilitates this kind of learning goes a long way toward fostering the greatest learning for these children. Due to time constraints, in-depth research must sometimes be done at the expense of other activities. It is up to you as the teacher to decide if another activity is sufficiently important that the research enthusiast must participate. If this is not the case, then you should inform the child of the choice to be made, let the child decide which to do, and then respect the child's decision. (Respecting the decision may seem obvious, but all too frequently teachers present the options and then convey by their facial expressions or body language that they really would prefer that the child join the larger group. It is important to give options only if you are willing to live gracefully with the child's choice.)

FOCUS ON LANGUAGE AND LITERACY: SYSTEMATIC ELEMENTS OF COMMUNICATION

Language, by definition, is a system of sounds that are used to communicate orally or in written form. Infants are not born knowing any of the systematic elements of communication, but they begin to learn them almost immediately, as their parents and other caregivers repond in differing ways to their cries, gurgles, and coos. As young children, they learn the additional systems of reading and writing. At each step of the way, from infancy onward, the quality of children's oral and literacy production is influenced by the quality of interaction with significant others, a point brought out in the discussion of the Snow report and emphasized in Gee's response to it.

Traditionally and historically, the teaching of English language communication skills was approached by focusing on oral language, writing, and reading experiences separately. Research and the development of the whole language approach in recent decades, however, have provided a more enlightened view of language learning as an integrated activity in which oral language, writing, and reading interact with and complement one another. In the following sections, we briefly separate these skills for explanatory purposes and then discuss them collectively, as they occur in natural communication.

Oral Language

Quality early oral language experiences foster competent language development, whereas a lack of experiences almost certainly impedes progress. Earlier, we saw how the infant Hayley experimented with "da da," first as a sound to play around with, then as a way to get attention from her parents, and finally to specifically call her father to her. Consider what would have happened if her parents had not responded as they did, if they had been inattentive, didn't care, or were too busy just surviving in a more difficult world. It might have been a very long time before Hayley learned that her playful noises actually could be used for communication. Now, multiply that situation by repeated missed opportunities for quality interactions, and you can understand how delays in oral language development can come about, even to infants born with no biological risk factors.

Additionally, reading and writing are systematic activities, and the more a young child experiences oral language as a system, the easier it will be to acquire new skills. Furthermore, richness in oral expression translates into more creative writing and more comprehension in reading.

Infants

In their first months, infants communicate by crying when they are in distress, by smiling and vocalizing to initiate social contact, and by babbling and laughing. Eventually, they begin to combine their various babbles, carry on private monologues when alone and listen to the conversations of others. Between 8 and 18 months, they can create long babbled sentences as well as some clear words. Babies begin to understand quite a bit more than they can articulate and can point out named objects and people. The National Association for the Education of Young Children (NAEYC) recommends a number of appropriate practices for caregivers based on observation and research. They suggest that caregivers (Bredecamp & Copple, 1997):

- Engage in many one-to-one, face-to-face interactions with infants, speaking in a pleasant, soothing voice.
- Hold and carry infants frequently, talking to them before, during, and after moving them around.
- Talk while engaging in routines such as diaper changing, feeding, and changing clothes. They should explain what will happen, what is happening, and what will happen next.
- Respond to and imitate the sounds infants make. These should be respected as the beginnings of communication.
- Respond quickly, soothingly, and tenderly to signs of distress.
- Talk, sing, and read to infants frequently. (pp. 72–73)

Toddlers

Toddlers and 2-year-olds continually build their vocabulary, perhaps reaching a total of 200 words, which they begin to combine for increasingly skillful communication. Toward the end of this period compound sentences that include nouns, verbs, adjectives, and adverbs begin to appear. Toddlers and 2-year-olds can explain the use of many household items, recount the events of the day, and begin to play pretend games, using fantasy in their accompanying language. NAEYC suggests that caregivers:

- Continue frequent one-to-one, face-to-face conversations.
- Let toddlers initiate language, and continue the communication, waiting patiently for the sometimes slow and awkward responses.
- Label and name objects, describe events, and reflect feelings such that children have opportunities to learn new vocabulary.
- Sing, do fingerplays, act out simple stories, and tell stories on a flannelboard or magnetic board, letting the children manipulate the figures. (Bredecamp & Copple, 1997, pp. 81–84)

Preschoolers

Preschool children not only continue rapid language development, they fairly explode to a new level as vocabularies grow to 8,000 to 14,000 words by age 6. Their enthusiasm for vocabulary expansion includes a desire to get the names of things right. One well-meaning father, not wanting to confuse his child with too many technical words one day said to her, "Look up there at that noisy airplane!" and the 4-year-old responded with great disdain, "Don't you know that's a helitopter?"

At first, younger preschoolers may not care much for group participation, prefer to talk rather than listen, and often ask questions they already know the anwers to. This trait is at times annoying to adults, particularly when the word "why" appears so

As children gain confidence in their oral communication, they can take leadership of class discussions (with or without the assistance of a visiting dog!).

repetitiously, but understanding caregivers and teachers recognize that children do this to start a conversation or to practice answering questions themselves.

Children who are learning a second language at home during these years are at a great advantage for growing up speaking as native speakers do "within the context of a trusting, ongoing relationship with a fluent speaker of that language" (Bredecamp & Copple, 1997, p. 104). Thus, caregivers and preschool teachers should be both supportive of the talents such children bring and encouraging of the role the family plays. Additionally, they should take care not to denigrate bilingual children when they make mistakes due to mixing their two languages anymore than they would criticize the errors that monolingual children make.

Throughout the preschool years, children's communication becomes phenomenally more adept as they gain greater skills, particularly with the aid of the adults in their lives. NAEYC suggests that caregivers and teachers:

• Talk with children all day long, speaking clearly and listening to their responses.

• Encourage children to describe their ideas, projects, and products.

- Provide plenty of social experiences and opportunities for conversation.
- Include dramatic play, block building, and other collaborative activities.
- Incorporate experiences in which children learn to both talk to and listen to their peers. (Bredecamp & Copple, 1997, pp. 110–127)

Primary Children

Primary children not only have acquired most of their adult grammar but also attain a vocabulary of about 20,000 words. Mainly, this development occurs as children participate in speaking and listening, but it is also due to several years of television watching and to their reading and writing experiences in school. Also responsible is a better understanding of part–whole relationships in which children learn that words can be pulled apart and pieces of them applied to create other words. For example, "tri" indicates three of something, so a child who plays the triangle in music class is not surprised to see three corners, is delighted when her tricycle is outgrown, and begins to understand that "bi" indicates two of something when she graduates to her new bicycle.

Bilingual and multilingual children continue to be at an advantage for learning to speak as natives do and to have advantages in general cognitive, language, and literacy development (Bredecamp & Copple, 1997). It is important that the school encourage the home language and not try to stifle it in favor of English only. The latter approach can lead to *semilingualism*, in which neither language is spoken or read proficiently.

Primary children learn much through verbal interaction, just as they did when they were younger. To their recently achieved sentence structure, they are ready to add negotiation, cooperation, and other social skills that require a more mature understanding of self and other. NAEYC suggests that teachers:

- Provide opportunities for learning in small heterogeneous groups in which children's opinions, planning, and decisions are important.
- Use whole-group meetings and discussions that promote not only oral language skills but social–emotional development.
- Engage in reciprocal discussions, and pose intellectually challenging questions that take children seriously.
- Read books to the children that contain a modest amount of new vocabulary, which is both read in context and discussed for meaning.
- Provide generous amounts of time for children to interact with each other using a wide variety of interesting materials and activities. (Bredecamp & Copple, 1997, pp. 157–172)

Writing

A number of researchers have tried to observe and describe some sort of stage development in early childhood writing, but no one has succeeded completely (Morrow, 1993), and it may well be that there is no fixed sequence to be observed (Clay, 1998).

Some of the steps that parents, caregivers, and teachers observe on the way to competent writing include drawing pictures to tell a story or communicate, scribbling in a format that looks like cursive writing and may move from left to right, imitating letter forms, stringing actual letters together randomly, placing letters together to make words, using invented spelling, and, finally, producing words that resemble adult writing.

Drawing on broad-based research with young children, Lesley Morrow (1993, pp. 234–236) suggested that the following elements pertain to early writing acquisition:

- "Children's early literacy experiences are embedded in the familiar situations and real-life experiences of family and community." Many families don't realize how much writing is a part of their lives and that the young children in the family observe and copy such activities as writing one another notes, making grocery lists, and sending holiday greetings. It appears that young children learn much about writing in this fashion, even across cultures and classes.
- "As a process, early writing development is characterized by children's moving from playfully making marks on paper, through communicating messages on paper, to making texts as artifacts." At first, children don't care about the product of their mark making, losing interest in it once they are tired of writing. Once they learn that the symbols have meaning, interest in the product grows.
- "Children learn the uses of written language before they learn the forms." Observers of scribbling children have noted that the children seem to know what their writing is for before they know what the conventional forms are.
- "Children's writing develops through constant invention and reinvention of the forms of written language." When preschool children learn to write, it is through experimentation not through direct teaching. As they observe, model, and interact with others more literate than they, children develop increasingly recognizable symbolic representation.
- "Children need to work independently on the functions and form of writing that they have experienced through interactions with literate others." When children are given time to invent, experiment, rehearse, and explore writing on their own, competent writing emerges.

Because children as young as 2 years old demonstrate an understanding of the function of writing when they begin making marks on paper, both caregivers and teachers should be alert to opportunities to enhance development. When we speak of providing writing experiences for young children, we are not talking about handwriting drills or copying single letters over and over. Although the development of coordination to achieve these skills is important, we focus here on writing's relationship to reading, its encouragement of the awareness and understanding of letter–sound relationships, letter formation, word and sentence structure, story structure, and so on. Here, from Marie Clay (1998), long one of the world's best-known proponents of writing as an integral part of reading acquisition, are some important reasons to provide writing experiences for young children:

- Writing fosters slow analysis. Even though children might learn to speak and read quickly, the muscular nature of writing slows things down, thus encouraging more thought about what is happening. "The slow production of writing provides the young learner with time and opportunity to observe visual things about printed language that were not previously noticed, and to observe organizational and sequential features of printed language" (p. 138).

- Writing highlights letter forms, sequences, and clusters. When children write each letter and place letters in clusters to form words and in words to form complete thoughts, they are forced to begin recognizing and learning these conventions.

- Writing encourages children to switch back and forth between different sources of information in print. "Writing can foster reading competence and vice versa if the learner becomes aware of the reciprocal nature of these acts. Reading and writing can be learned concurrently and interrelatedly" (p. 138).

- Writing can provide cognitive advantages. As young children develop their own theories about the printed word and what it means to them personally, they benefit from every form of literacy education available to them. Learning new bits of information through writing adds to children's store of cognitive knowledge about the reading and writing processes.

Additional reasons for providing plenty of writing experiences are given by two literacy educators as they offer suggestions to help children who find reading difficult (Rasinski & Padak, 2000):

- Children learn what it is that writers do when they create stories and books, thus helping them see "the authors behind what they read and perhaps understand their purposes and processes" (p. 193).

- When children write a lot, they are forced to read a lot as they reread their drafts, share their finished products with others, and read what their classmates have written.

When children become aware of the functions of print and begin to make some standard letters and invent spellings, a number of activities and teaching approaches become possible. A writing center can be established and filled with tools appropriate to the children's age and development. Colored markers make a popular first writing tool. Paper of different sizes, some of it folded to make greeting cards, can be introduced and changed as children's interests change. Word banks can be kept for each child in his or her private envelope. Each envelope contains index cards with one favorite or important word written on each. Often these are names of relatives, pets, and good friends that the child can refer to during writing sessions. Journal writing permits children to reflect on the day and on their private feelings. It helps if the teacher models this activity the first few days, writing and then reading the entry aloud. The teacher's journal can be kept in a public place where children can examine it for format or ideas.

Choosing some writing to publish involves more formality and perfection than writing in journals, jotting notes, or keeping lists. When a story or expository piece is deemed interesting or important enough for publication, it goes through a series of systematic steps to completion. This is as true in the classroom as in professional life. Calkins (1986) suggested five steps that have been adopted or adapted over the years: prewriting (brainstorming to generate ideas); drafting (the first attempt at writing); conferencing (reflecting on the draft and discussing it with a peer or teacher to determine possible changes); revising (making the changes for a second draft); and editing (making minor changes in punctuation, spelling, grammar, etc.). Publication outlets are only limited by one's imagination: minibooks for the class collection or school library, newsletters home, reports and other papers posted on walls for visitors to read, and gift stories to accompany handmade greeting cards are some. Writing experiences can also be integrated into dramatic play centers: taking orders in restaurants, writing prescriptions at the doctor's office, writing letters at the office, taking down addresses before going to put out a fire, and so forth.

Reading

The spread of compulsory education in the early 20th century produced a need to determine which students were ready to advance to the next grade, to enter a program or graduate from it, and even to begin reading. The idea of standardized testing was conceived just before World War I, and by the 1920s, standardized tests were being used by schools to determine which children were ready for formal reading instruction. Thus, the concept of *reading readiness* arose and, with it, a definition of this skill, which categorized children as first preliterate, then ready to begin formal reading instruction, then literate. The tests were used to diagnose specifically lacking skills, thus providing teachers with some guidance about which children were not yet ready to learn (Pearson & Stallman, 1994). Research has demonstrated that in schools in which prereading skills are taught in kindergarten and formal reading in first grade there is a high correlation between adequate readiness skills and success in formal reading (Snow, Burns, & Griffin, 1998a).

The idea of reading readiness coincides well with the maturationist philosophy described in the history and theory section of this chapter. In keeping with that philosophy, the thinking was that if a child's reading skills could be identified according to a norm of 6.2 years, then the precise moment of readiness for formal instruction also could be identified. The use of reading readiness scores retained its popularity for decades, until educators and researchers responsible for the evolution of the whole language theory argued that there should not be a pedagogical division between kindergarten prereading and first-grade formal reading. Instead, they countered, literacy capabilities begin to develop in infancy and should be regarded as progressing along the lines of a continuum of *emergent* or emerging *literacy*. When we consider literacy acquisition in this way, we value and respect children's attempts at reading from infancy, when a book is something to chew; through the toddler years, when youngsters might talk to a book's pictures; and into the preschool years, when they might hold a finger on the book's words and pretend to read or identify a favorite fast-food restaurant sign. The concept of emergent literacy fits less well with the maturationist theory than it does with constructivism (Scott, Hiebert, & Anderson, 1994), in which children's attempts at reading are seen as a series of emerging skills, facilitated by caregivers and teachers.

Vygotsky's (1962) view that children construct their own literacy learning with the assistance of adults and more advanced peers and Jerome Bruner's (Boyle & Peregoy, 1990) extension of this concept of scaffolding provide some direction for teachers' support of children's attempts at learning to read. *Scaffolding* refers to the ways in which adults elaborate and expand on children's language attempts, thus facilitating their growth to a higher level.

Reading stories to young children is an example of scaffolding in that it introduces children to language and story patterns that will be useful later, when they begin reading and writing on their own. Reading aloud to children is one of the most useful ways of introducing them to the act of reading, and one of the most effective tools seems to be predictable books. These are books that have repeated phrases, obvious cues in the text, or pictures that help children make sense of the story (Conlon, 1992). Reading the same book again and again may not appeal to the adult reader, but this technique seems to encourage reading as children become more and more familiar

The continuum of emergent literacy begins in infancy when being surrounded by literature means something quite different than it will in a very few years.

Children's emergent literacy is encouraged when adults provide scaffolding experiences such as one-on-one assistance with reading.

with the text. Adult readers should also permit children to ask questions, discuss the plot, join in on familiar words and phrases, and share related personal experiences.

A reading-rich environment that includes the presence of print in many forms is an important part of reading development. There should be labels, lists, signs, charts, posters, restaurant menus, notepads, stamps and envelopes, and greeting cards in addition to a good collection of picture books, poetry, informational books, and Big Books (Freeman & Hatch, 1989). Language experience activities in which children dictate words and stories help them see firsthand how stories are written and read.

As children begin to get the idea of reading, opportunities will present themselves to facilitate skill building in specific areas. These skill-building opportunities usually are generated by children on a need-to-know basis, and they generally occur in the context of a meaningful experience. Although the method of teaching the needed skill may be direct instruction, skill building today is unlike that of earlier years when instruction was given out of context. In other words, skills that were once taught in isolation for their own sake now more often are taught as part of an attempt at meaningful, real-life communication. One example of an important skill area is the *alphabetic principle*. Before the evolution of language experience and whole language teaching approaches, the alphabet was generally taught for its own sake, usually before reading instruction began. Often, each letter was given its own week, and activities were designed to highlight it. This practice still is popular in many preschools and kindergartens, but research has shown that such in-depth teaching is not necessary (Reutzel, 1992). Once children begin to understand the alphabetic principle by learning a few letters, they generalize to others without further training. As children learn to read, more of the alphabet is revealed to them naturally. Observant teachers will note which letters are unfamiliar or difficult for specific children, and then provide learning experiences. Alphabet activities can include an alphabet center stocked with magnetic letters, puzzles, sandpaper letters, games, chalkboards, tracing papers, and stencils for informal exploration. Alphabet books, songs, chants, and poetry provide natural means toward learning alphabetic order.

Two related examples of necessary skills are phonological and phonemic awareness. Phonology, one of the five systems of language mentioned earlier, refers to the overall speech sounds of a language, and a child who possesses phonological awareness can use, even play with, sounds and hear speech patterns such as rhymes and syllables within words. Within phonology are *phonemes*, specific sounds as they are connected to alphabetic symbols. Children with phonemic awareness have an understanding of written language essential to reading in an alphabetic system. English is tricky to learn in this regard, however, because words are spelled not just on the basis of their sounds but on their historical origins, and there are quite a few of these. For example, /ph/ to represent the /f/ sound indicates a Greek origin. Historically, writers of English have chosen to retain such linguistic connections rather than to create spellings based simply on sound–letter connections as is done in languages such as Spanish in which you can count on the /f/ sound always being spelled with an f. For instance, in this paragraph, we have used the words *phonology* and *phonemes*, and to them we might add *phonograph*, *telephone*, and *microphone*, all based on the Greek word for *sound*. And let us not forget *phonetic* and *phonics*, the first an adjective referring to speech sounds and their production, the second to reading instruction that teaches children through acquainting them with the sounds and letters that go together.

Although this chapter has separated oral language, writing, and reading for discussion purposes, it is important to remember that they are really parts of an inseparable whole as directly experienced by children. Figure 2.1 gives examples of how these pieces all fit together at different ages, although normally developing children's programs might well differ from the ages the figure designates. This figure is based on the work of various researchers as reviewed in the writing of Snow and colleagues (1998a), Bredecamp and Copple (1997), and a joint position statement on learning to read and write from the International Reading Association and the NAEYC (NAEYC, 1998). Keep in mind that some children learn to read by themselves before they enter kindergarten, and others require explicit instruction on specific skills such as phonemic and phonological awareness.

LANGUAGE AND LITERACY ACTIVITIES ACROSS THE CURRICULUM

As infants and young children learn to communicate their interests, needs, desires, and feelings, they do so in every aspect of their lives. Language is not just learned for its own sake but because it is an integral part of the child's world. This point makes

Birth to 18 Months

- Vocalizes; smiles; cries to express interest, initiate social contact, express pain or distress.
- Babbles using sounds from many languages, then eliminates those not heard in the environment.
- Connects babbles into longer and longer strings or "sentences."
- Looks at picture books with increasing interest and in increasingly conventional ways.
- Points to objects in books.
- Makes marks on paper (and the nearby territory), then looks at them to see what has been created.

18 Months to 3 Years

- Replaces vocalizing by enjoyment of nonsense word play and rhyming.
- Increases speaking vocabulary to about 200 words.
- Combines words, eventually into compound sentences.
- May begin to distinguish between drawing and writing, even making letterlike forms.
- Understands that pictures in books are symbols for real objects.
- Labels objects in books.
- Comments on characters in books.

3- and 4-Year-Olds

- Expands vocabulary from about 2,000 words to as many as 6,000.
- Lengthens sentences from three or four words to five or six.
- Has difficulty with the pronunciation of some words.
- Asks *who*, *what*, *where*, *when*, *how*, and *why* questions but at first has difficulty responding to them, especially *why*, *how*, or *when*.
- Can tell or retell a simple story but may forget its point, get events out of order, or just focus on its favorite parts.
- Enjoys rhyming games.
- Knows that alphabet letters have their own names, and can identify some of them.
- Recognizes familiar environmental print, such as stop signs and names of fast food restaurants.
- Learns that it is the print, not the pictures, that is read in stories.
- Can connect information in a story to events in real life.
- Writes (scribbles) messages on paper.
- May begin attending to beginning or rhyming sounds.

5-Year-Olds (Kindergarten)

- Makes use of new vocabulary and more complex grammatical constructions in speech.
- Increases vocabulary from about 5,000 to 8,000 words.
- Takes turns in conversation and interrupts less frequently.
- Can recite simple poems, remember many songs, and repeat lines of dialogue from movies or TV shows.

FIG. 2.1. Milestones in children's language development.

- Listens intently to stories told or read by teacher or caregiver.
- Can tell and retell stories keeping sequence of events straight.
- "Reads" familiar stories, not necessarily verbatim.
- Recognizes some words by sight.
- Understands that the sequence of letters in a word represents the sequence of sounds.
- Begins to write letters and some familiar words.
- Uses phonemic awareness and alphabetic knowledge to invent spellings.
- Builds a list of conventionally spelled words.
- Can write most letters, own first and last names, first names of friends.

6- to 7-Year-Olds (First and Second Grade)

- Learns words at a rate of up to 20 per day, if the environment provides language-related support.
- Becomes aware that words can have multiple meanings.
- Gains and uses greater control of language to think and to influence others' thinking.
- Develops humor that values jokes, puns, tongue twisters, and riddles.
- Demonstrates fluency in speech and grammatical construction, but struggles with some complexities such as the passive voice.
- Uses phonetic knowledge to invent spellings while knowledge of conventional spelling grows.
- Can revise and edit own writing with assistance.
- Learns to attend to spelling, mechanics, and presentation for final written products.
- Makes transition from emergent to real reading.
- Reads aloud with accuracy and comprehension if text is designed appropriately for age and time of school year.
- Can use strategies such as rereading, predicting, questioning, contextualizing when comprehension doesn't work.
- Predicts what will happen next in stories.
- Reads and understands both fiction and nonfiction if it is designed appropriately for grade and age.

8-Year-Olds (Third Grade)

- Increases vocabulary to approximately 20,000 words.
- Begins to understand most complex constructions, including the passive voice.
- Can read for enjoyment.
- Reads aloud with fluency if text is designed appropriately for age.
- Reads chapter books independently.
- Can summarize main points in a reading.
- Can use roots, prefixes, and suffixes to infer word meanings.
- Can independently review own work for spelling, mechanics, and presentation.
- Can write in a variety of formats such as stories, reports, and literature responses.

FIG. 2.1. *(Continued)*

a strong argument against compartmentalizing and decontextualizing language learning experiences in centers and classrooms.

The following ideas and activities are suggested ways in which language and literacy can be an integral part of the entire curriculum. To incorporate them, and others you add on your own, is as much an attitude as it is careful planning.

Math

1. Create "story problems" from everyday activities. These can be conversations carried on about naturally occurring events: deciding how many napkins are needed for a snack table, counting children in line, counting the number present, and figuring out how many are absent. The problems also can be more hypothetical as the children grow older and are aware of mathematical processes. "What would happen if . . . ?" questions can be created for almost any occasion.

2. Create story problems in conjunction with short stories you write for the children to read independently or in pairs. These can be integrated into the body of the story or added at the end.

3. When children learn new math processes, they can write about them in their journals or in letters to take home to their parents. As they describe what they have learned, they reinforce the math learning while expanding their writing and critical thinking skills.

4. Cut up paperback versions of favorite stories and place the pictures of the plots' sequence of events on cards. Number the cards on the back, or write the ordinal numbers. Children tell the stories to each other and place the cards in order. They check their accuracy by turning the cards over and reading the numbers. Children can also recreate the story, placing the cards out of their original order. If desired, they can then turn the cards over and renumber them in their new order.

Social Studies

5. When children are having difficulty interacting successfully with others, provide them with direct instruction in oral communication skills. Help them with brief phrases that are likely to win them more friends. "Gimme the trike!" for example, can be replaced by, "Will you let me use the trike when you're finished?"

6. As children enter in the morning, hand them index cards on which are map outlines of a country or state (these can be drawn freehand with a marker). There should be duplicates of each small map so that children will end up with partners. Children first find their country or state on the class map or globe and then find their partner; or they first find their partners and search together for their country or state. The children remain partners for the rest of the morning or the day. (Children as young as 4 years old can do this if the drawings and maps are very clear. Older children can write the geographic names within the outlines.)

7. Place "coffee table books" of interesting places in a center for informal perusal. Help advanced readers read the captions under pictures they find interesting. Or write a few brief sentences yourself about some of the most interesting pictures and place the paper in the appropriate page for children to discover and read. Children who are not yet ready to read enjoy hearing stories about interesting places. Generally, these should be factual rather than fanciful so that children can first sort out the reality of unfamiliar places.

Science

8. Any science experiment that involves equipment can benefit from labeling. Make a label with the name of each piece of equipment and tape it on. If the item is to be put away, make a matching label in its proper place. Even children who aren't quite ready to read can match labels and put equipment away properly.

9. After any observational experience, such as a nature walk in the woods or a session outdoors looking at insects, have children dictate everything they recall observing. Write their ideas on a chart. Stretch the experience by putting aside time to reobserve very soon afterward. Take the experience chart with you and try to add more observations.

10. Primary children can keep journals or write "lab reports" of their experiments in science. These can be free-form or can have a more formal format, using printed questions with spaces for answers. Some suggestions:

- List the steps you took in the experiment.
- What is one important thing you learned?
- Draw a picture of the most interesting part of the experiment.

Creative Arts

11. Whenever children learn a new letter, part of speech, punctuation mark, or word, have them act it out in some way. Letters, for example, can be made with the whole body or parts of it; they can dance on the wind; they can be frozen in space and then melted to the floor.

12. Favorite stories can and should be acted out whenever possible. This can be done formally, in play form, with children playing parts, or it can be done informally as you read the story to the children. With a minimum of rules (e.g., no noise as you move), children can become active participants in the reading or telling of a story.

13. Use music experiences to play with various kinds of sounds. Let children substitute words and nonsense syllables for the original ones. Make up whole new verses or try singing the verse from one song to the tune of another.

14. If you are singing or humming while holding an infant, repeat the same words to the same tunes rather than being inventive. The child will eventually grasp the patterns of sound and learn to expect them.

15. Whenever possible, let children tell you about the pictures they are drawing, but don't force the issue. Sometimes children enjoy dictating stories about what they have done, but at other times they prefer to let the picture tell its own story. Respect their artistry and ask permission first.

EXTENDING YOUR LEARNING

1. Review the two episodes that opened this chapter. Which one more nearly describes the experiences you had in your first years of school? In what ways are your memories positive or negative? Compare your experiences and memories with other students in your class.

2. Interview two or three children about television shows they enjoy. As children use program-related words that you believe they may not actually understand, ask for their definitions. Informally discuss the dictionary definitions with them while making note of their own first interpretations.

3. Model enthusiasm for reading by keeping a book with you to read at odd moments. If you are working with children, share a bit about your book with them, telling them what you like about it and a little about the characters. If they are interested, read a short section to the children, paraphrasing where necessary to help their understanding.

4. Model enthusiasm for writing by keeping a journal of what happens in your center or school. Choose events that can be shared with the children, then do share.

5. Begin a collection of books that you can take with you into your teaching career. This can be expensive, of course, so become an avid visitor at garage sales, buying only those volumes that are in nearly perfect condition and at little cost. Another source may be your city library's occasional book sale.

6. Go back to the integrated language activities at the end of the chapter. Choose one activity, and write a lesson plan using the outline in chapter 1. Be specific about your learning objectives.

VOCABULARY

American Sign Language.   A method of communication, using hand signals, that does not exactly match the structure and spelling of standard English, but possesses its own unique structure and rules.

Constructivism.   The theory that humans develop in accord with their given biology, their response to the environment, and through their own self-construction as these interact. Language development is both genetically determined and environmentally influenced.

Emergent Literacy.   The view that learning to read can begin as early as infancy and includes all learning experiences related to books, signs, and other experiences with the printed word.

Language Experience.   An approach to teaching beginning reading that provides children with rich experiences that are then written about using labels and other simple text.

Maturationism.   The theory that humans develop in an orderly and predetermined fashion, although at different rates. Language develops as children observe their social environments and intuit rules and conventions.

Morpheme.   The smallest meaningful unit or form in a language.

Morphology.   The internal structure and formation of words.

Phonemes.   Specific sounds as they are connected to alphabetic symbols.

Phonology.   The system of sounds of any given language.

Semilingualism.   An ability to communicate in a language with a lack of proficiency.

Standard English.   The English language as spoken or written in accordance with rules created and maintained by the academic establishment.

Syntax.   The grammar of any language.

Whole Language.   An approach to teaching reading that rejects programmed basal readers in favor of real literature, values children's inventive ways of writing and spelling, and teaches phonics skills on an as-needed basis rather than in a programmed sequence.

INTERNET RESOURCES

Web sites provide much useful information for educators and we list some here that pertain to the topics covered in this chapter. The addresses of Web sites can also change, however, and new ones are continually added. Thus, this list should be considered as a first step in your acquisition of a larger and ever-changing collection.

International Reading Association
   www.reading.org

National Council of Teachers of English
   www.ncte.org

References

Adams, M. (1990). *Beginning to read: Thinking and learning about print.* Cambridge, MA: MIT Press.
Allington, R. (1997, August–September). Overselling phonics. *Reading Today*, pp. 15–16.
Boyle, O., & Peregoy, S. (1990). Literacy scaffolds: Strategies for first- and second-language readers and writers. *The Reading Teacher, 44*(3), 194–200.

Bredecamp, S., & Copple, C. (1997). *Developmentally appropriate practice in early childhood programs*. Washington, DC: National Association for the Education of Young Children.

Calkins, L. (1986). *The art of reaching writing*. Exeter, NH: Heinemann.

Chomsky, N. (1965). *Aspects of a theory of syntax*. Cambridge, MA: MIT Press.

Clay, M. (1991). *Becoming literate: The construction of inner control*. Auckland, New Zealand: Heinemann.

Clay, M. (1998). *By different paths to common outcomes*. York, ME: Stenhouse.

Conlon, A. (1992). Giving Mrs. Jones a hand: Making group storytime more pleasurable and meaningful for young children. *Young Children, 47*(3), 14–18.

Flesch, Rudolph (1955). *Why Johnny can't read*. New York: Harper.

Freeman, E., & Hatch, J. A. (1989). Emergent literacy: Reconceptualizing kindergarten practice. *Childhood Education, 66*(1), 21–24.

Gee, J. (1999). Critical issues: Reading and the new literacy studies: Reframing the National Academy of Science's report on reading. *Journal of Literacy in Reading, 31*(3), 355–374.

Goodman, K. (1992). I didn't found whole language. *The Reading Teacher, 46*(3), 188–199.

Goodman, Y. (1989). Roots of the whole-language movement. *The Elementary School Journal, 90*(2), 113–127.

International Reading Association & the National Association for the Education of Young Children. (1998). Learning to read and write: Developmentally appropriate practices for young children. *Young Children, 53*(4), 30–46. Author.

Logan, T. (1990). Controlling involvement: A naturalistic study of peer interaction in a bilingual, bicultural preschool. Unpublished doctoral dissertation, University of Florida.

Morrow, L. (1993). *Literacy development in the early years*. Boston: Allyn & Bacon.

National Association for the Education of Young Children (NAEYC). (1998). Learning to read and write: Developmentally appropriate practices for young children. *Young Children, 53*(4), 30–46. Author.

Neill, A. (1960). *Summerhill*. New York: Hart.

Pearson, P., & Stallman, A. (1994). Resistance, complacency, and reform in reading assessment. In F. Lehr & J. Osborn (Eds.), *Reading, language, and literacy: Instruction for the twenty-first century*. Hillsdale, NJ: Lawrence Erlbaum Associates.

Rasinski, T., & Padak, N. (2000). *Effective reading strategies: Teaching children who find reading difficult*. Upper Saddle River, NJ: Merrill.

Reutzel, R. (1992). Breaking the letter-a-week tradition. *Childhood Education, 69*(1), 20–23.

Routman, R. (1988). *Transitions: From literature to literacy*. Portsmouth, NH: Heinemann.

Scott, J., Hiebert, E., & Anderson, R. (1994). Research as we approach the millennium: Beyond becoming a nation of readers. In *Reading, language, and literacy: Instruction for the twenty-first century*. Hillsdale, NJ: Lawrence Erlbaum Associates.

Snow, C., Burns, M., & Griffin, P. (Eds.) (1998a). *Preventing reading difficulties in young children*. Washington, DC: National Academy Press.

Snow, C., Burns, M., & Griffin, P. (1998b). *Preventing reading difficulties in young children: Executive summary*. Washington, DC: National Academy of Sciences.

Spiegel, D. (1992). Blending whole language and systematic direct instruction. *The Reading Teacher, 46*(1), 38–44.

Vygotsky, L. (1962). *Thought and language*. New York: Wiley.

Wilde, S. (1989). Looking at invented spelling: A kidwatcher's guide to spelling. In K. Goodman, Y. Goodman, & W. Hood (Eds.), *The whole language evaluation book*. Portsmouth, NH: Heinemann.

3

MATHEMATICS: HOW MUCH, HOW MANY, WHAT SIZE, WHAT SHAPE

Many of us were not taught as we now wish our students to be taught. We are lacking role models for how good math education should be conducted. . . . Can we be the teachers we never had?

Joyce Baron

▼ Chapter Objectives

When you finish reading this chapter, you should be able to:

- ▼ Explain research-based positions and standards from national organizations.
- ▼ Describe the mathematical capabilities of young children based on their developmental levels.
- ▼ Explain ways in which mathematical learning can be incorporated throughout the early childhood curriculum.
- ▼ Have an increased awareness of natural mathematics experiences in daily life from which children can learn.

As you think about and apply chapter content on your own, you should be able to:

- ▼ Plan mathematics activities in relation to children's physical, social, and cognitive development.
- ▼ Plan mathematics activities taking into account the needs of individual children.
- ▼ Incorporate mathematics activities into all areas of the curriculum.

The field of mathematics includes an array of subfields, skills, and systems, many of which are appropriate for study in some form by young children. Among the more commonly taught topics are classification; seriation; counting; numeration; measurement; geometry; graphing; and arithmetic (addition, subtraction, multiplication, and division). Even without instruction, very young children intuit mathematical principles. When Matt was 2 years old, the lunch he liked best was a small cup of soup surrounded by a small sandwich cut into four triangles. This usually proved too much for him, however, and he regularly left one of the sandwich pieces, which his mother then ate. One day, feeling quite hungry, his mother ate "her" section of the sandwich before Matt walked in the kitchen, then spread the other three pieces out to fill the plate. (She, like you, had read about Piaget's experiments showing that young children believe that there are more objects when the objects fill a larger space.) As Matt sat down, however, he looked concerned, then faintly outraged. "Where's de udder one?" he demanded. Whether it was his understanding of number or of spatial relationships or both that prompted Matt's reaction, it was clear to his mother that his mathematical ability had outdone her attempt to circumvent it.

Another 2-year-old began to demonstrate what her day-care teacher considered slightly strange behavior. Annie would be intensely engaged in carrying various dolls and stuffed animals around to different chairs and baby carriages. Suddenly she would stop, survey the entire collection, and begin a walking and pointing survey that separated toys into like groups. For instance, walking purposefully from one side of the room to the other, she would pass by a series of stuffed animals, pointing and saying loudly, "Bear . . . bear . . . bear . . ." or Dog . . . dog . . . dog. . . ." The teacher told Annie's mother, who had been noticing the same behavior at home. "Yes," she said, "yesterday I watched her walk around the living and dining rooms saying, 'Chair . . . chair . . . chair . . . chair . . . ,' and right after that, she did the same thing with tables." Suddenly, the two of them looked at each other and realized what was happening: Annie was learning classification, one of the most important mathematical concepts for young children to grasp.

Matt and Annie appeared to their mothers and the day-care teacher suddenly to have acquired mathematical skills that hadn't been apparent before. In actuality, they had begun to think mathematically during infancy (National Council of Teachers of Mathematics [NCTM], 2000). Such mathematical thinking happens quite naturally from the beginning of life, but adults in children's lives can foster optimal development while maintaining an informal approach to learning, at least until the primary grades. Even then, a more playful approach remains the most effective one, for most children, for much academic learning. One way to think of informal mathematics is "as analogous to the child's spontaneous speech. Just as everyone learns to talk, and spoken language is the foundation for reading, so everyone develops an informal mathematics" (Ginsburg & Baron, 1993, p. 3).

Whether children begin to learn mathematical concepts in the first months of life, or whether their awareness starts with the missing piece of a sandwich, there are many ways in which the real world can bring informal math learning to young children. Children need to play with mathematical concepts just as they do with language, although this view has not been widely held in this country. Nevertheless, it may be that a lack of informal and playful mathematical experiences is one cause for the poor performance of U.S. children on international mathematics tests.

In recent years, cross-national mathematics tests have demonstrated that children in the United States fall further behind the children in many other countries the longer they stay in school. Yet, when they first enter preschool or kindergarten, U.S. children arrive with the same possibilities for growth as do children in other countries. Furthermore, these disturbing results happen despite the dedicated efforts of countless teachers to provide their children with sufficient mathematical learning. In this chapter, we explore some of the ways in which young children can be turned on to mathematics and tuned in to real understanding. We begin with a description of one teacher–researcher's experience with first graders. What she learned from them may provide some clues as to what may be going wrong in U.S. schools and what might be done to turn them around.

THREE WAYS OF LOOKING AT ARITHMETIC:
ONE TEACHER'S EXPERIENCE

Suzanne Colvin was an early childhood teacher of considerable experience as well as a graduate student interested in the ways young children learn mathematical concepts. For her primary doctoral research, she decided to explore the ways that first graders learn to add and subtract. Suzanne wondered why most of the children were able to memorize the required addition and subtraction facts but didn't seem to have a clear understanding of what they were doing. Story problems were difficult for almost everyone. The school principal and the three first-grade teachers shared Suzanne's concern and agreed on a cooperative plan that they hoped might lead to some answers.

Suzanne's plan was to teach math to all three classes, focusing specifically on the introduction of addition and subtraction, for a period of 7 weeks. To be sure that all three classes started out on an equal footing, she administered readiness tests to every child. Because the classes had already been divided according to age, sex, and entrance test scores, Suzanne wasn't surprised to learn that the three classes were just about equal in their readiness to begin addition and subtraction. A few children were eliminated from the study. Those who already knew how to add and subtract or weren't ready to learn were given specialized activities by their own teachers while Suzanne worked with the other children. Suzanne then planned three completely different teaching approaches for the three classes. To find out how successful each one was, she gave tests to all the children before her instruction started. After 7 weeks, she gave everyone the same tests again to see what improvement had been made. Then, to check on the permanence of the learning, she went back once again, after 4 more weeks, and gave the children similar tests.

The three teaching approaches represented different philosophies of how children learn mathematics. The first approach Suzanne called traditional. *The children in the traditional class were taught according to the instructions in the commercial textbook that had been adopted by the school system. The text was organized along the lines of the traditional U.S. approach to teaching addition and subtraction: First, the children are given facts, or number sentences, to learn. Then, to help them learn the facts and apply them to real situations, story problems are presented that make use of the just-learned facts. This first approach was the one the school had been using for some years, probably because it conveniently coincided with the approach taken by the text publisher.*

The second approach reversed this process. First, the children were presented with story problems, which they discussed, drew, or role played. The stories were those that related to the children's own lives or were interesting to them in some way. Once they had, as a group, figured out the answers, Suzanne showed them how to represent the problems and their answers using written symbols. Because she immediately followed up the story discussions with information about symbols, Suzanne called this approach immediate.

The third approach resembled the second more than the first. The children in this class also were presented with story problems before symbols. In this case, however, the children didn't learn about symbols until the sixth week. Instead, they spent 5 weeks discussing and acting out many mathematical story problems in a totally informal way. Because the symbols weren't presented to the children until the last 2 weeks of the project, Suzanne called this approach delayed.

As she began teaching the children, one of the first differences Suzanne noticed among the groups was their attitude toward story problems. The immediate and delayed classes seemed to enjoy the stories and spent considerable time discussing different ways to solve them, but the traditional class seemed to have no interest in them at all. For them, getting right answers to the addition and subtraction problems was all important and the stories merely a distraction, barriers to quick attainment of the facts. It was not surprising when, in the posttest, this group was the only one of the three that made no progress in solving story problems. The children in all three groups had performed inadequately in the pretest, generally guessing at possible answers rather than trying to figure them out. After 7 weeks, the immediate and delayed groups tackled the stories with confidence and interest; the traditional group continued with guesswork.

The tests also required the children to work with story problems and number sentences together. For example, Suzanne might say, "I have two blocks and you have three. That's five altogether. Can you write a number sentence that shows what we just did?" Or, conversely, she might show them the number sentence and ask them to make up a story to go with it. After 7 weeks, the immediate group did best in writing number stories to go with the sentences, but after 4 weeks of extra practice, the delayed group did just as well. The traditional group never did catch up. When it came to inventing stories to go with the number sentences, the delayed group did best after 7 weeks, and the immediate group caught up with them after another 4 weeks. Again, the traditional group did poorly.

Since the traditional group spent so much time practicing addition and subtraction facts, Suzanne thought that this might be where they would outperform the other two groups. However, after 7 weeks, the immediate group outperformed the others, whereas after another 4 weeks, everyone was about the same in this area.

Other testing showed that the immediate and delayed groups understood arithmetic symbols better than the traditional group, even though the traditional children spent more time studying them. And subtraction was harder for everyone than addition was.

For Suzanne, the conclusions to be drawn for teaching were obvious. Although all three approaches eventually helped children answer addition and subtraction problems with equal correctness, the traditional approach was far less effective in helping children to understand what was going on or apply those memorized numbers in meaningful ways. Continual, daily exposure to story problems appeared to Suzanne to be the most beneficial approach to take with young children. She also began to wonder if it was really appropriate to introduce children to subtraction quite so soon.

The questions raised by Suzanne and the questions and answers that grew out of her experience with the three classes reflect some of those that have, for many years, framed the debates about mathematics education. For example, one way to divide approaches to instruction and learning is between "top-down" and "bottom-up" (Charlesworth, 1997). Suppose the teacher wishes the class to see the ways in which the number 16 can be divided. A *top-down method* of teaching would be to provide a worksheet of problems, possibly containing an instruction to write each one several times, with this followed by a quiz the next day. Suzanne's traditional approach would fit this description. A *bottom-up method* of teaching would be to divide a class into small groups, each with 16 counters representing cupcakes. Each group would "invite" 2 children to a party, then 4, 8, and 16. In each case, the groups must figure out how many cupcakes each child would get. Depending on their level of understanding and recording capabilities, the groups would write out their answers, draw pictures, or simply show and tell. This bottom-up method of teaching is most akin to Colvin's delayed approach. As we saw, it was her most successful, a result that should make us think about which of the two basic methods of instruction we want to incorporate most into our math programs for young children.

Another way of dividing math learning is through experiences that are naturalistic, informal, or structured (Charlesworth & Lind, 1999). *Naturalistic experiences* happen spontaneously in the course of everyday life. Matt's sandwich trauma and Annie's toy classification fit this definition. *Informal experiences* occur when the teacher senses that a teachable moment is at hand. Suppose one group of the children dividing 16 "cookies" seemed to be finding the solutions extremely easy and began using the counters to play tiddledywinks. The teacher, passing by, might realize that their off-task behavior was due less to naughtiness than to boredom and give them a larger number of "cookies" to divide. *Structured experiences* are those lessons or activities that are preplanned. These can be with individuals, small or large groups, or an entire class. Suzanne's work with first graders can be divided into top-down and bottom-up methods of teaching, but all the experiences were carefully structured to accomplish her well-planned goals. More often, structured experiences tend to be concentrated in formal methods of teaching. A quick example shows how one young child, in a very few minutes, understood and responded to two approaches.

> Alissa, a new first grader, was shown the expression 3 + 2 = ? and asked, "How much is 3 plus 2?" She squirmed in her seat and finally confessed, "I haven't learned that yet." Asked how much three pennies and two more pennies are altogether, Alissa quickly put up three fingers on her left hand and two fingers on her right hand, counted the fingers, and responded cheerfully, "Five!"

The debates of recent decades that consider top-down and bottom-up approaches and compare the learning that comes from naturalistic, informal, and structured experiences are based on many centuries of theorizing, practice, and—in more recent times—research. The following section provides a brief overview.

PERSPECTIVES ON HISTORY AND THEORY

Throughout history, mathematical concepts and systems have been developed in response to real-life problems. For example, the zero, which was conceived of by the Babylonians around 700 B.C., by the Mayans about 400 A.D., and by the Hindus about 800 A.D., first was used to fill a column of numbers in which there were none desired. For example, an 8 and a 3 next to each other is 83; but if you want the number to read 803 and you put something between the 8 and 3 (other than empty space), it is more likely to be read accurately. Another example of early applied mathematics is demonstrated in the Egyptian development of simple arithmetic and geometry so that boundary markers in the fields could be reset after the annual spring flooding of the Nile (Baroody, 1987). When it comes to counting, tallying, or thinking about numerical quantity in general, the human physiological fact of 10 fingers and 10 toes has led in all mathematical cultures to some sort of decimal system.

History's early focus on applied mathematics is a viewpoint we would do well to remember today. A few hundred years ago, a university student was considered educated if he could use his fingers to do simple operations of arithmetic (Baroody, 1987); now we expect the same of elementary school children. The amount of mathematical knowledge expected of children today has become so extensive and complex that it is easy to forget that solving real-life problems is the ultimate goal of mathematical learning. The first graders in Suzanne Colvin's classes demonstrated the effectiveness of tying instruction to meaningful situations.

More than 300 years ago, John Comenius (1896/1633) pointed out that young children might be taught to count but that it takes longer for them to understand what the numbers mean. Today, classroom research such as Suzanne Colvin's demonstrates that young children need to be given meaningful situations first and then numbers that represent various components and relationships within the situations.

The influences of Locke (1964) and Rousseau (Boyd, 1914) are felt today as well. Locke shared a popular view of the time that the world was a fixed, mechanical system with a body of knowledge for all to learn. When he applied this view to education, Locke described the teaching and learning process as writing this world of knowledge on the blank-slate mind of the child. In this century, Locke's view continues to be popular. It is especially popular in mathematics, where it can be more easily argued that at least at the early levels, there is a body of knowledge for children to learn.

B. F. Skinner, who applied this view to a philosophy of behaviorism, referred to mathematics as "one of the drill subjects." Whereas Locke recommended entertaining games to teach arithmetic facts, Skinner developed teaching machines and accompanying drills, precursors of today's computerized math drills. Although such drills are still considered useful for teaching basic skills to those who are easily distracted by the content of stories or who have difficulty extracting facts from a story or activity, there are critics of this approach to mathematics learning. One of these critics has argued that it has failed to provide a powerful explanation of more complex forms of learning and thinking, such as memorizing meaningful information or problem solving. This approach has, in particular, been unable to provide a sound description of the complexities involved in school learning, like the meaningful learning of the basic combinations or solving word problems (Baroody, 1987, p. 13).

Rousseau's views of how children learn were quite different, reflecting his preference for natural learning in a supportive environment. During the late eighteenth century as today, this view argues for real-life, informal mathematics learning. While this approach is more closely aligned to current thinking about the way children learn than is the Locke/Skinner approach, it can have the undesired effect of giving children so little guidance that they learn almost nothing at all.

The view that seems most suitable for young children at this point in our history is that inspired by cognitive theorists, primary among them Jean Piaget. Three types of knowledge were identified by Piaget (Kamii and Joseph, 1989), all of which are needed for understanding mathematics. The first is empirical or *physical knowledge*, which means being able to relate to the physical world. For example, before a child can count marbles by dropping them into a jar, she needs to know how to hold a marble and that it will fall downward when dropped.

The second type is *logicomathematical knowledge* and concerns relationships as created by the child. Perhaps a young child holds a large red marble in one hand and a small blue marble in the other. If he simply feels their weight and sees their colors, his knowledge is physical (or empirical). But if he notes the differences and similarities between the two, he has mentally created relationships.

The third type of knowledge is *social knowledge*, which is arbitrary and designed by people. For example, naming numbers *one*, *two*, and *three* is social knowledge, because in another society, the numbers might be *ichi*, *ni*, *san* or *uno*, *dos*, *tres*. (Keep in mind, however, that the real understanding of what these numbers mean belongs to logicomathematical knowledge.)

Constance Kamii (Kamii & DeClark, 1985), a Piagetian researcher, has spent many years studying the mathematical learning of young children. After analyzing teaching techniques, the views of math educators, and U.S. math textbooks, she has concluded that our educational system often confuses these three kinds of knowledge. Educators tend to provide children with plenty of manipulatives, assuming that they will internalize mathematical understanding simply from this physical experience. Or educators ignore the manipulatives and focus instead on pencil-and-paper activities aimed at teaching the names of numbers and various mathematical terms, assuming that this social knowledge will be internalized as real math learning. Something is missing from both approaches, said Kamii:

> Traditionally, mathematics educators have not made the distinction among the three kinds of knowledge and believe that arithmetic must be internalized from objects (as if it were physical knowledge) and people (as if it were social knowledge). They overlook the most important part of arithmetic, which is logico-mathematical knowledge. (p. 13)

In the Piagetian tradition, Kamii argued that "children should reinvent arithmetic." Only by constructing their own knowledge can children really understand mathematical concepts. When they permit children to learn in this fashion, adults may find that they are introducing some concepts too early while putting others off too long. Kamii's research led her to conclude, as Suzanne did, that first graders often find subtraction too difficult. Kamii argued for saving it until later, when it can be learned quickly and easily. She also pointed to studies in which place value is mastered by about 50% of fourth graders and 23% of a group of second graders. Yet place value and regrouping are regularly expected of second graders!

As an example of what children can do earlier than expected, Kamii and colleague (1985) pointed to their discovery (or reinvention) of negative numbers, a concept that doesn't even appear in elementary math textbooks. Based on her experiences with young children, Kamii argued that it is important to let children think for themselves and invent their own mathematical systems. With Piaget, she believes that children will understand much more, developing a better cognitive foundation as well as self-confidence:

> Children who are confident will learn more in the long run than those who have been taught in ways that make them distrust their own thinking. . . . Children who are excited about explaining their own ideas will go much farther in the long run than those who can only follow somebody else's rules and respond to unfamiliar problems by saying, "I don't know how to do it because I haven't learned it in school yet." (p. 14)

In recent years, as the work of Lev Vygotsky has become increasingly popular throughout the early childhood community, his views also have been incorporated into the thinking of mathematics education researchers and writers. Piaget was primarily concerned with individual children constructing their own knowledge—and not being pushed inappropriately to learn more than they were ready for—whereas Vygotsky's sociocultural views emphasized the importance of knowledge construction aided by more mature peers and adults and of making sure children learned enough to reach their full potential. Now, along with educators from other academic disciplines, mathematicians have increasingly accepted the idea of compatibility of the two approaches. As one early childhood mathematics educator argued, "By combining both approaches mathematics educators can take into account the students' learning through meaningful tasks (constructivist theory) in schools that account for student diversity (sociocultural theory)" (Charlesworth, 1997, p. 55).

NCTM PRINCIPLES AND STANDARDS AND THE NAEYC POSITION

In 2000, the National Council of Teachers of Mathematics (NCTM) published for the first time a set of principles and standards addressing the educational needs of children from the preschool years and up. (A decade earlier, the original edition began with kindergarten.) Explaining this new coverage, the NCTM (2000) pointed to research showing that even infants can understand small numbers of objects, that preschoolers acquire surprisingly complex and sophisticated knowledge about number and geometry, and that quality learning experiences can enhance this development.

Defining the early childhood years as preschool through age 8, the NCTM (2000) describes this time as "one of profound developmental change. In no other grade band is the growth in mathematical knowledge so remarkable" (p. 105). Arguing that this fact demonstrates the need for quality early childhood mathematics programs, the NCTM said that these:

• Build on and extend children's intuitive and informal mathematics knowledge.

• Are grounded in knowledge of child development.

• Provide environments that encourage children to be active learners who are eager for new challenges.

- Develop a strong conceptual framework that provides anchoring for skills acquisition.
- Nurture and develop children's natural inclination to solve problems. (p. 105)

Echoing both Piaget's focus on individual self-construction of knowledge and Vygotsky's preference for self-construction with the frequent intervention of others, the NCTM (2000) went on to state that "young children are active, resourceful individuals who construct, modify, and integrate ideas by interacting with the physical world and with other children and adults" (p. 106). The organization reminds us too that "all children need adequate amounts of time and opportunities to develop, construct, test, and reflect upon their understanding of mathematics" (p. 106). The National Association for the Education of Young Children (NAEYC) shares the sentiment that rushing children through mounds of math work is never the route to true understanding.

The NAEYC, in its position statement regarding developmentally appropriate practices (DAP) (Bredecamp & Copple, 1997), arrived at views of teaching mathematics to young children that reflect those of Kamii, Piaget, Vygotsky, and the NCTM. Their position regarding infants, toddlers, and preschoolers is that mathematics should be part of the day's natural activities: counting children in the class or crackers for snacks, for example. For the primary grades they are more specific, identifying what is appropriate and inappropriate practice. Table 3.1 summarizes their guidelines.

The positions taken by the NCTM and NAEYC have informed the writing and content of this chapter. A series of nine standards for preschool through high school is also supplied by the NCTM (2000) with special applications for the early childhood years. These too are incorporated and referenced throughout this chapter. The next section shows how all phases of development have influence on how young children learn mathematics.

TABLE 3.1

Appropriate Mathematics in the Primary Grades (The NAEYC Position)

Appropriate Practice	Inappropriate Practice
Learning is through solving meaningful problems.	Math is taught only as a set of facts and skills to memorize.
Skills and problem solving are fostered through play, projects, and daily living.	Children have few opportunities for hands-on activities or small-group problem-solving activities.
Manipulatives and games are provided.	Only children who finish seat work are permitted to use manipulatives.
Manipulatives are carefully chosen for appropriateness to the targeted concepts and problem-solving skills.	Teachers assume that use of manipulatives alone is sufficient.
Math activities are integrated with other subjects and projects.	Math is integrated in other areas without systematic focus or engaged time to ensure acquisition of skills and concepts.

PERSPECTIVES ON DEVELOPMENT

Although we begin our discussion with cognitive development, it is important to realize that, as intellectual as the subject of mathematics might seem, social, affective, and physical development also enter in to a young child's learning. These are discussed in their turn.

Cognitive Development

In Piaget's (Piaget & Inhelder, 1969) theory of development, young children are intellectually tied to empirical evidence. During the preoperational stage between the preschool years and first or second grade, youngsters make sense of their world by their response to the physical environment around them. Additionally, because they generally center their attention on one thing at a time, comparisons between objects or ideas are difficult for them. Even when they are well into the elementary grades (the concrete operational stage), children need concrete objects to help them make connections and decenter their attention. At the same time, it is important for teachers to make sure that the manipulatives are directly related to the mathematical concept being taught. "Use of a manipulative just because it is available—but not appropriate for the concept—is as detrimental to student understanding as not using a manipulative at all" (Dougherty & Scott, 1993, p. 304). The NAEYC agrees with this position (see Table 3.1) and also with the need to use manipulatives. Such objects remain an important part of children's move toward logicomathematical understanding. Several areas of learning are affected by these developmental phenomena.

As an example, children have trouble conserving objects or number until their thinking approaches the concrete operational stage. Conservation tasks are particularly difficult if the objects used in teaching bear little relevance or meaning in the daily experience of young children. In general, preoperational children focus their attention on a single interesting attribute, such as the shininess of some pennies but not others; the beautiful red shade of the wooden geometric shapes they work with; or the amount of space used up by the pennies or shapes. Piaget referred to such abstraction of physical properties as empirical or simple abstraction. Preoperational children cannot take the next step of reflective abstraction, which requires making a mental relationship between or among the objects. This mental reflective step is necessary for learning number concepts. The lack of it explains why preoperational children cannot understand that by spreading out a row of 10 pennies to fill a bigger space, the amount remains the same. Without the capability of reflective abstraction, children cannot operate on numbers unless they are related to physical objects directly in front of them. Because children throughout the primary grades are moving into but not necessarily safely harbored in concrete operations, mathematics teaching should take this into account.

Placing objects in a series according to size is difficult for children who focus on one thing at a time. You can ask preoperational children to choose the smallest and largest objects in a series. If they do this first, they can then place some of the remaining objects in order, but don't expect perfection until the stage of concrete operations has been reached. Seriation activities and materials provide an interesting challenge to children at the mature end of the preoperational stage then suddenly become boring once they have achieved a mathematical understanding of seriation. At that point, you might try giving the children several sets of seriation materials to coordinate into complex patterns.

Preoperational children also have difficulty with the order of numbers. You no doubt have heard a small child rote count, "One, 2, 3, 7, 10." If a child is given a group of objects and can count them fairly well, it may appear that he also understands ordering and counting fairly well. But if you interview the child carefully, you may find that he believes that the numbers he recites are actually names for the objects and might just as well be Sam, Joe, and Stephanie. Thus, even with the assistance of manipulative materials, the child has not yet learned the mathematical meaning of the numbers but can only focus on their socially determined names. This does not mean you should avoid giving preoperational children objects to count, but it does mean that you cannot force the mathematical understanding on them. Children will construct their learning on their own schedule, although they may require adult assistance in the form of more structure or instruction.

The same is true of classification. Because young children focus on one attribute at a time, it will be a while before they can classify objects in more complex ways. Geometric wooden shapes, for example, are popular classification materials that preoperational children enjoy grouping by a single attribute, such as color or size or shape. Teachers can encourage them to think of making more complex relationships, but understanding of such groupings as small green circles or large blue triangles is gained as the children learn more sophisticated skills for classification.

Clock time is usually a topic in early elementary mathematics texts, yet most children just recently have acquired the adult concept of what time is. Many children are about 9 years old before they can solve time problems on a logical rather than a trial-and-error basis. Throughout the primary grades, some children believe that when they move quickly the clock does the same. Much time may be spent in frustrating workbook exercises that have little real meaning to the children. Here is another case in which children may memorize the socially defined numbers but not have a good understanding of their meaning. During the primary years, it is best to use the clock in informal ways that relate to the life of the classroom. Children might make their own paper plate clocks, with hands made from tagboard and fastened with a brass paper fastener. They can then compare times to the classroom clock, set them ahead for upcoming events, or just explore them informally.

Social and Affective Development

Mathematics is one curricular area in which social learning theory (Bandura, 1963) can be applied to good effect. According to this theory, children learn behaviors and attitudes (both positive and negative) as they are modeled by adults. Because many children learn to dislike or fear mathematics at a fairly young age, it may be that teachers need to change their own attitudes toward this subject and convey more enthusiasm to the children. Just as you set an example of enthusiasm for literature, you can find ways to show your own interest in mathematical experiences. Let children see you use a yardstick to measure a new bulletin board, and talk about it aloud. Pace off game areas on the playground, counting your steps so that children can hear you. Have children help you count the milk money (and act as if you enjoy it). When you introduce new mathematics topics or discuss problems, do it with confidence and enthusiasm, just as you do for an interesting new story. Make mathematical exploration an exciting adventure for children by being excited yourself and by making math relevant to their lives.

Social interaction with the teacher is also important to the constructivist theories of Piaget and Vygotsky, but the focus is somewhat different than in the social learning theory. In constructivist theory, people are not considered the source of feedback for the development of logicomathematical knowledge; the child's internal thought processes account for this. Instead, the teacher's role is to cast doubt in children's minds about the adequacy of what they are thinking, or to help them consider on their own alternative ways of coming to desired answers. The teacher should remember that for young children the exact answer is rarely as important as the thinking process that produces a reasonable answer. In the constructivist view, the teacher needs to interact with the children, but optimal development takes place when there is less direct teaching and more encouragement and facilitation.

According to constructivist theory, social interaction with peers also is important to mathematical development. Conversely, social competence is aided by cognitive development, thus making peer interaction doubly effective. Egocentric young children feel no need to make sense when they talk to others. As they have social interactions, however, they begin to realize how necessary it is to engage in coherent communication, to avoid contradicting oneself, to reason logically, to make true statements, and to use words that will be understood by others. "The desire to 'make sense' and to exchange points of view with other people undergirds the child's growing ability to think logically" (Kamii & DeClark, 1985, p. 26).

Furthermore, having the opportunity to engage in peer dialogue has been shown to be effective in improving children's mathematical understanding. In one experiment (Kamii & DeClark, 1985), groups of three children were given juice and different shaped drinking glasses, then assigned the task of dividing the juice into equal quantities. With one child serving as pourer, all three of them debated the equality of amount between a glass that was short and wide and one that was tall and narrow. A replica of the first glass was offhandedly given to the children to use "if needed" after they had started their attempt at equality. This experiment is a version of a Piagetian conservation task, which tests children's ability to determine equality of liquid between differently shaped containers. In this study, in addition to several groups of three, there were an equal number of children who served as a control group and did not have the juice-pouring experience just described. When given a posttest, the children who had the juice-pouring experience had made significantly greater progress in being able to conserve liquid than had the children in the control group. There was carryover progress as well: The children who had the juice-pouring experience also improved significantly in other types of conservation tasks. This and other studies appear to demonstrate the benefits that come from providing children with opportunities to discuss and debate mathematical problems rather than assigning quiet, independent seatwork.

Physical Development

Infants and toddlers attain most of their cognitive learning through physically active experiences. Whereas quite a bit has been learned about very early language acquisition, studies of infants' mathematical development have been fewer. Nevertheless, it may be assumed that to begin learning mathematical concepts, some activity is essential. One-year-olds begin filling and dumping containers, providing early exploratory experiences with size and early concepts such as *one* and *many*.

Although physical development is not so closely tied to cognitive development as children get older, it still is of importance. For example, children become able to grasp a pencil at about 18 months but may continue experimenting with various grips until first grade. Because the adult three-fingered method of gripping isn't established for all children until about age 7, demanding that younger children engage in pencil-and-paper math activities is inappropriate for physical as well as cognitive and social reasons. Boys are more likely to develop their small motor functions later than girls, so they are at a special disadvantage when pencil-and-paper learning begins early. Yet it is entirely possible that you will see classes of 4-year-olds seated at tables, or even desks, struggling over math worksheets. Children this young not only have trouble grasping the pencil effectively but also need to move around more often and more extensively than is possible when engaged in worksheet learning. One seeming answer to the problem might be to give the children frequent recesses, but this solution does not address the inappropriateness of doing such activities in the first place.

In addition to making mathematics learning a natural part of the day, it also is possible to create activities that permit children to be physically active. Some of the teaching suggestions at the end of this chapter are designed with this goal in mind.

DIVERSITY AMONG CHILDREN

The NCTM is dedicated to ensuring that every child in America receives "an equitable *Standards*-based mathematics education" (NCTM, 1998, p. 10). The council's statement on what is meant by "every child" is a powerful one that can be applied to every area of the curriculum, and so we repeat it here:

> By "every child," we mean every child—no exceptions. We are particularly concerned about students who have been denied access to education opportunities for any reason, such as language, ethnicity, physical impairment, gender, socioeconomic status, and so on. We emphasize that "every child" includes—
>
> • learners of English as a second language and speakers of English as a first language;
> • members of underrepresented ethnic groups and members of well-represented groups;
> • students who are physically challenged and those who are not;

- females and males;
- students who live in poverty and those who do not;
- students who have not been successful and those who have been successful in school and in mathematics.

There are any number of ways to make the idealism inherent in this position statement practical.

When you approach the teaching of mathematics in an informal way, taking advantage of natural experiences, you have taken one important step toward providing each child with individually appropriate learning. Giving children the opportunity to reinvent mathematics on their own at their own pace is a second important step. A third step is to observe children with care. When you do this, you will be more able to reach, as the NCTM proposes, every child.

If your curriculum and attitude toward teaching are both flexible, and you permit children to develop at their own pace, it is possible that the other children will not be aware of the few who are having difficulties or who are progressing at an accelerated rate. Once you are aware of their developmental levels, you can provide materials and activities that meet their needs.

Of special interest in mathematics is the long-standing difference in performance between boys and girls. There is still some debate as to whether boys are genetically more capable of some mathematical understandings, such as spatial relationships, than are girls. Whether or not this proves to be the case, one continual problem for girls has been that they are not expected to do well, and teachers often make excuses for them, permitting them to escape permanently to the library corner. One approach that Piaget (1975) usually found to be successful in overcoming this tendency was to delay the use of numerical symbols until there had been considerable experience with stories and manipulatives—the same approach as that taken in Suzanne Colvin's third class. Using this approach, Piaget found that most of the reluctant girls eventually came to enjoy mathematics.

Curriculum Considerations for Children With Special Needs

Using Piaget's perspective on the three types of understanding and learning in mathematics makes it obvious that delays or disabilities in sensory, cognitive, physical, or social domains will have an impact on a child's ability to master early math concepts and skills. We will address considerations in designing math curricula for children with identified disabilities, as well as for those who are living in poverty, or come from diverse cultural backgrounds.

Sensory Impairments

Children who do not see well may lack knowledge of basic premath concepts, such as size and shape, that are dependent on visual experiences. They need access to curriculum materials that take the fullest advantage of their other sensory modalities, and hands-on activities are especially beneficial. For example, children who are blind or who have vision impairments may need extra verbal explanations and always benefit from tactile input for learning math concepts. They need to feel shapes and sizes to understand the concepts, because they aren't seeing what other children see, and more complex categories can be especially difficult. Try to imagine how you would classify vehicles into categories of planes, boats, and cars if you couldn't see pictures or objects. Think of all the other concepts involved in this classification task (air, water, land, wheels, wings, propellers). Enlarged print is required for some students to read math materials in the primary grades, and students who are blind may be learning Braille, which includes a number symbol system. You may be working closely with a vision specialist to make sure that children with vision impairments have access to all possible learning activities and materials for learning math. Parents are also excellent sources of information about prior learning and effective materials.

It is most likely that children who don't hear well or at all will miss out on verbal instructions and are heavily dependent on their vision to interpret the world around them. They may have strong prior experiences with premath concepts such as size and shape, but they are at risk for missing important directions or teaching in the classroom. Most students can listen to the teacher talk and at the same time examine materials, papers, models, objects, or manipulatives being presented for a lesson or activity visually. Children who have sign language interpreters in class have to switch their attention back and forth between the interpreter (for verbal input) and the materials being shown (for visual input). Directing your instructional delivery at the student and allowing a few extra seconds for him or her to look back and forth helps immensely and is probably advantageous for others in class who can benefit from extra time to process information. Computer software for teaching early math concepts is another resource for self-paced supplemental instruction.

Cognitive Impairments

Number concepts are not very concrete, and manipulating those concepts in operations such as addition and subtraction is an even more abstract activity. Young children with cognitive delays are especially at risk for learning rote counting or numeral labels without understanding the underlying concepts. They benefit greatly from the types of concrete, naturalistic, real-life experiences described throughout this chapter but also learn well with direct, supplemental instruction on basic math facts. Additional instructional time in the resource room or in the classroom, explicit instruction on concepts during naturalistic activities, and as much practice as possible with both hands-on and math fact experiences constitute the best approach to improve performance in math. At some point in the primary years, a more "functional" math curriculum might be considered for children with severe cognitive delays, for example teaching a "next dollar" strategy (rounding up from any amount of cents to the next dollar) instead of teaching money concepts. Replacing the regular math curriculum should be undertaken only if all other methods of effective instruction have proven unsuccessful.

Physical Impairments

For infants, toddlers, and preschoolers, a physical impairment can mean fewer meaningful activities moving through space or manipulating objects, which are important foundational skills for understanding concepts of size, shape, measurement, and counting. Providing a range of planned sensory experiences for young children with physical disabilities and labelling concepts at the same time promote early understanding of the physical world. Computer simulations often are more easily accessible to children whose movements are limited and can be very useful for supplemental practice. Computer use can replace actual physical experiences to best advantage if children have their own repertoire of experiences to relate to. For example, once a student who uses a wheelchair has personal experience with being pushed fast and slow, she will be able to make better use of computer simulations that address speed and distance. Primary school students with physical disabilities need to be seated comfortably and securely in the classroom so that they can participate in math lessons and activities without worrying about maintaining head control, sitting positions, or standing postures.

Cultural Considerations

The many daily applications of math concepts are socially and culturally determined, so children with cultural backgrounds that differ from the mainstream may not share the experiences that contribute to learning the math concepts typically taught in the early grades. Young children who grow up in families that organize work around the seasons or daylight hours also have different experiences with time and the calendar than those whose parents work a typical work week that matches the school week. For example, children's parents may work in the spring and summer, start the work week on Tuesdays, or use a different calendar altogether than the school uses. Children whose families have immigrated from subsistence cultures may have no concept of money and its uses. For children whose backgrounds differ from the teacher's, it is especially important to identify hands-on, real-life activities and materials that are meaningful for each child, or problems in the math curriculum may be identified as learning difficulties instead of teaching oversights.

Poverty

Children whose families struggle with chronic and severe poverty may have difficulties with the social applications of math and the math curriculum. Money, for example, is a very sensitive subject for children whose families have none, pay for groceries with food stamps, and receive monthly public assistance checks. Preschool teachers who use edible materials such as cornmeal, beans, and macaroni in the math curriculum for sorting, classifying, and other activities may not be able to maintain the attention of children who are hungry and focus on such items as food sources. Math is probably not occupying the minds of hungry children who are expected to handle food during math instruction.

Giftedness

Some young children show extra interest and excitement in mathematical concepts, and this is often manifested in unusual competence. The occasional kindergarten or primary child may resist using manipulatives, finding it more interesting and challenging to imagine them in his head or just look at them. (We once knew a 6-year-old whose fingers fairly quivered with the need to touch the manipulatives, but he explained that it wasn't what the big kids did, and he was highly successful in all his work.) Others may find inventive and unusual ways to figure out problems. It is good for these children to be able to explain and demonstrate their solutions for the rest of the class. Occasional others will learn and understand the solutions while the advanced child has an opportunity to think more deeply during the explanation.

FOCUS ON MATHEMATICS: CONCEPTS

Children begin their mathematical learning as infants. Babies in their cribs observe the space between the bars and, making an intuitive measurement, grab them accurately enough to pull themselves up. Playing with balls, they come to understand the shape of a sphere and what happens to it when it is pushed. As they shove a clothespin in a plastic bottle, or a geometric solid into the similarly shaped hole of a plastic ball, they intuit information about measurement. In early classification experiences they learn to differentiate clothing from food or toys and even to intuit addition and subtraction concepts.

Through their daily experiences, toddlers, preschoolers, and primary children also learn mathematics concepts in a natural way. When 2-year-old Matt demanded, "Where's de udder one?" he demonstrated intuitive counting and understanding of spatial relationships. When children share cookies or other snacks, they engage in division, even to the point of puzzling over what to do with the remainder when the sharing comes out uneven. If they decide to solve the problem by breaking up the cookies, they gain experience in fractional division. Real-life experiences such as these are essentially story problems in which some understanding of number is used to solve a problem situation.

Because daily life presents so many opportunities to learn mathematics in a natural way, and because such learning provides young children with the most meaningful and easily remembered mathematical understanding, teachers need to consider such possibilities as they create their curriculum. Mathematical learning for young children is much more than the traditional counting and arithmetic skills; it includes a variety of mathematical concepts.

Classification

Classification is the placing of objects or ideas into groups that are alike in some way. Teachers classify all day long as they put tired children down for naps and read stories to those who are awake; send the boys to one bathroom and the girls to another; give children who didn't have one yesterday a turn on the trikes and send everyone else to play on other equipment; select books for the library corner based on a particular theme and put the rest on an out-of-the-way shelf; spoon the applesauce into small cups and pour juice into larger ones; and send home the children whose parents have arrived and keep the others in the classroom. This list could almost be endless, yet, for the adult, such classification is so much a part of ordinary life that little or no conscious effort is involved.

For young children, classification cannot be taken for granted. Rather, they must develop their understanding of grouping according to like attributes. Their first attempts have little logic to them. A child might pull a red block from a group, *then* decide to put all the red blocks together . . . at least until he notices the stripe down the side of one block and then begins seeking other blocks with stripes. Sometimes, a child groups objects together for reasons that are not apparent to the adult observer, perhaps offering explanations of the decision that seem nonsensical. As children grow in their understanding of classification, they are able to group objects according to a single property, such as color, shape, or size. Still later, two or more properties can be coordinated, and ideas as well as objects can consciously be grouped.

The NCTM (2000) regards the ability to classify a critical one that has implications across much of mathematical learning. When children sort, classify, analyze simple patterns, and make predictions about them, they are creating a foundation for the learning of algebra. In addition, these activities provide the beginning of understandings of data and data analysis and of informed decision making. For example, the simple toddler activity of putting some groceries in the refrigerator and others on the shelf leads to an intuited understanding that things that feel cold should go one place while warmer objects go to the other. Before long, the mother can hand the child an object from the grocery bag and she will know where to put it, although she doesn't yet understand the abstract principles of temperature, refrigeration, or spoiling.

Teachers can provide numerous opportunities for children to learn classification skills. What is important is that the materials and activities relate to the developmental levels of the children, and that there are specific learning objectives.

Preschool children are still learning who they belong to and what belongs to them, what things are theirs and what things belong to others, where some objects belong and how they are used. Thus, belonging is an appropriate concept for learning to classify objects and to understand their relationships (Read & Patterson, 1980). Informal conversations can include such teacher comments as, "This is a book; it belongs inside," "This is Janey's stuffed dog; it belongs to her," and "The mop and the broom belong in the housekeeping corner."

Preschool children also benefit from experiences that focus on likenesses and differences. Interesting objects always should be available to sort. Variety should be provided based on children's changing interests or themes of study. If you have children who still explore objects by putting them in their mouths, be sure that the objects you choose are large enough to be safe and give extra attention to cleanliness. One popular source of objects is the natural environment surrounding the school or in a nearby park. Sticks, small rocks, and leaves can be brought into the classroom to be separated from each other. Then each of these groups can be regrouped according to the children's own definitions of sameness and difference. Big sticks might be separated from small ones and yellow leaves from green ones. Other ideas for sorting materials include:

- Squares of various types of fabric, all the same size.
- Buttons of different sizes and colors.
- Pairs of shoes to be matched or separated by color.
- Postcards with pictures that have some obvious similarities.
- Holiday greeting cards that have some obvious similarities.
- *Large* nuts, bolts, and screws.
- Seashells.
- Dramatic play props that are functionally related: dishes and utensils; dolls, bottles, and blankets; hats, vests, and shoes; wooden blocks, cardboard blocks, and foam blocks.

Kindergarten children and some 4-year-olds need time for informal sorting experiences, but are also ready for teacher questions and larger challenges. For example, a child sorting buttons might be asked, "Are all the gold buttons alike? Can you find a way to separate them again?" Try to let the children discover that some of the buttons have two holes and some have four rather than simply telling them to put one group in one pile and the second group in another.

Primary children continue to need experiences in classification. Commercial attribute blocks (plastic geometric pieces in varying sizes, thicknesses, and colors) provide numerous ways of grouping. In addition to physical attributes, numbers of objects within a set can be used to classify. A large jump rope can be placed around a group of children and the rest of the class challenged to create sets of equal size. Or children can work in pairs to challenge each other to create equal sets from boxes of materials such as buttons and small blocks.

Ordering (Seriation)

Sequencing objects from first to last is known as **seriation** or ordering. Going from first to last may involve increased height, darkening shades of a single color, increased width, and so on. In your daily life you may arrange bills in your wallet in order of their value or arrange drinking glasses in the cupboard according to size, activities that provide order in your life but little intellectual challenge. For young children, understanding seriation takes until the first, second, or even third grade to accomplish. Counting numbers can be considered seriation but only when a child has a true understanding of what the numbers mean. Before that, counting is simply a rote activity.

Preschool children begin learning to order objects by doing simple comparisons. A teacher can observe children putting dolls away and ask which one is largest and which is smallest. Then, moving to other children putting blocks away, the teacher might ask which is heaviest and lightest or which is longest and shortest. There are also commercial materials made specifically for classification. One material manufactured in varying forms by several companies is a long wooden block with a row of different-sized holes in its top. Into this fit cylinders (with knobs for handling) of increasing size. Preschool children engage in such fitting activities most easily if they fill the smallest and the largest holes first. From there, they typically find the proper holes by trial and error. The same is true if they try to order the cylinders correctly outside the wooden block. Although preschoolers eventually can get the cylinders in the right order, their trial-and-error method indicates that their sense of seriation is still in the beginning stage and does not yet include the ability to use logic rather than physical observation to achieve their goal.

Kindergarten children continue to enjoy seriation activities, and some will begin to order objects in a more logical way than trial and error. Many of the materials that are used for classification can be used for seriation as well. Shells or buttons, for example, can usually be ordered according to size and with some teacher preparation, a few can be ordered according to color variations. Abstract concepts that do not involve matching objects can be introduced, although children may not fully understand them. Examples include *before* and *after*; *yesterday*, *today*, and *tomorrow*; and the smaller ordinal numbers *first, second, third . . . tenth*.

Primary children can increase their ability to use ordinal numbers, particularly if teachers build practice into the normal flow of the day. When materials are passed out, they simply might be counted (cardinal numbers) one day but identified according to their order (ordinal numbers) the next. Similarly, as children stand in line, they can count off in cardinal numbers one time and ordinal numbers another. A primary child's understanding of seriation is such that he or she can arrange eight or more objects in ascending or descending order without resorting to trial and error. The child also understands that in a line of people arranged according to height, the second person is taller than the first and the third is taller than both the second and the first (Read & Patterson, 1980).

Counting

When adults or older children count, it is generally for the purpose of identifying how many objects or ideas are in a group or groups. For each number named, there is a single object or idea to match it. Counting with such one-to-one correspondence is known as rational counting. For very young children, consistent matching of object or idea to number name is not yet possible. They may be able to count, whether it is just a few numbers or many, but this skill is a memorized one known as rote counting. A child who counts by rote does not automatically associate objects or ideas with the numbers.

Preschool children "should develop the fundamental idea that the next number in the counting sequence is one more than the number just named. They connect cardinality with ordinality (number sequence) by comparing the results of counting" (NCTM, 2000, p. 110). Informal experiences in daily life such as counting pencils in a can, individual stairs to the next floor, number of children at a table, and the number of dolls in a baby carriage or blocks in a pile can go on continually. Songs, chants, and rhymes with numbers in them, such as "Five Little Monkeys," "When I Was the

Age of One," and "This Old Man," teach children the number names and give them beginning experiences in matching numbers to objects, especially if props are used to act out the song. Preschool children will not often engage in such counting activities and games on their own, so the teacher must be alert to opportunities and exploit them.

Some kindergarten children, particularly toward the end of the year, may be on the brink of rational counting. Consequently, plenty of counting experiences are in order. As they learn to read numbers, it is a good idea to plan activities that match the numbers to objects. This may be done with either commercial or homemade materials. For example, using two sets of large, unlined index cards, you can write or glue large numbers on one set and then have children match them with the second set that pictures groups of objects. Laminate all the cards for longer life. The groups on the picture cards can be of two types: groups in which all the members are the same object, size, and color and groups in which members have less relationship to each other. The second type might picture several children of varying appearance or a cluster of different toys or even objects that have no relationship to each other at all. This second type of grouping forces the children to start classifying groups based solely on their numbers rather than on physical attributes.

We observed one teacher who started story problem solving while children were learning to count. Each child was given a number (the highest to which he or she could count reliably) and made up a story with that number as the answer. Stories at the beginning of the year were very simple: "A boy took 1, 2, 3 candies, so he had 3." They progressed to quite elaborate, if computationally easy: "A girl had 2 books, and she got 2 more, so she had 4. And then she gave 1 away and had 3." Almost every child used fingers or object props all year and most answers involved counting out loud.

Primary children feel comfortable counting. Consequently, when they begin learning to add and subtract they tend to use counting techniques. Teachers need to remember, however, that a concrete operational child still needs concrete objects to understand counting or any other skill. Keeping this in mind, teachers should provide primary children with plenty of informal counting experiences related to objects and events in the school day. Oral games can be played that help the children realize that each succeeding number represents one more than the preceding number. For example, you might count to 25 with a group of children, stopping now and then to say something such as, "We just got to 12. What number came before it? Is 12 more or less than 11? What number comes after 12? Is it more or less than 12?"

Primary children learn other counting strategies as well: skip counting by 2s, 5s, and 10s, and counting backward. Providing them with plenty of opportunities to practice these skills builds a base for understanding subtraction and multiplication (NCTM, 2000).

Addition and Subtraction

As children have informal opportunities to add and subtract, they invent their own systems of computation. Teachers should respect, support, and encourage these systems and not impose adult-sanctioned traditional methods, at least through the second grade

(NCTM, 2000). The teacher's role, instead is to listen to children's methods of arriving at answers and encourage other youngsters to do the same. In this way, more roads to success are added. As well, research has shown that children who are given extensive opportunities over a longer period of time to invent their own computational strategies are eventually more successful in learning the standard algorithms than are children who were given the formal methods from the beginning (NCTM, 2000).

One second-grade teacher we observed started each day with a circle time that included a time line problem meaningful to the children. For example, he would ask, "How many days until the spring concert?" Students then told their answers and used the timeline to explain their computations. The variety of options for counting, adding, subtracting, and self-correction among peers was astounding.

As Colvin (1987) and Kamii and colleague (1985) learned in their studies of first graders, children find addition easier to understand than subtraction. In Colvin's classes, both processes were introduced at the same time, after pretests had shown that both processes would be new to all the children. Both were introduced with the same amount of care, using the same methodology, and an equal amount of time was spent studying each. Perhaps one reason that addition is easier is that it more closely resembles the positive direction in which children normally count. This suggests that teachers would do well to include informal activities that provide practice in counting backwards.

Preschool and kindergarten children can be given opportunities to join sets and count the objects in the newly created set. However, there should be no pressure to memorize the problems or answers (NCTM, 2000). The same materials that are used for classification—commercially purchased items or objects picked up on nature walks—can be adapted for making and joining sets. Or children may be ready to start with just one set and count on from there to tell how many more they need to reach a specific number. One game suggests giving children a few fish crackers, which they then place on a blue sheet of paper (ocean) (Maffei & Buckley, 1980, p. 147). You will have chosen a total number, 5, for example, that will be the same for all the children. The number of fish you first give to each child can be fewer than or equal to this total. Ask each child to tell you how many more fish will be needed to make five, then give the child that many, even if the answer is wrong. Brief questioning can focus on how the child came to ask for that number. The child then should count the total and discover, with little assistance from you, any need to recount. Once five fish are in each child's ocean, suggest various movements and ask questions that promote further thinking: "One fish swims on the top of the ocean while the others swim at the bottom. How many are swimming at the bottom? Send a fish to the top to keep the first one company. Now how many are at the top? All the fish except one swim to the bottom and a monster fish (the child) comes along and gobbles it up. Now how many are left?" Continue in this vein until all the fish are eaten.

Because primary children have more difficulty with subtraction, some theorists and researchers argue that it should not be introduced formally in the first grade. Instead, children should first feel comfortable with addition, taking time to understand it rather than being pushed into memorizing tables of sums (Kamii & DeClark,

1985). Primary children should be permitted to use manipulative materials in ways that are meaningful to them rather than being pushed into pencil-and-paper exercises or teacher-directed, manipulative activities.

One phase that young children go through is called *counting all*. They are first given six objects to count and then five objects to add on. Their approach is to start their count all over again with the very first object and count all the way through to the 11th object. Many educators try to "cure" children of this time-intensive practice, but others argue that this is just one example of the way children develop their logicomathematical understanding, and they should be allowed to outgrow the practice on their own. Defending this second view, Kamii argued:

> If children are left alone to add numbers on their own, they *will* figure out a way that is appropriate for them. If they do not figure out a way, this means that addition is too hard for them and ought not to be imposed on them. If they count-all, most first graders will sooner or later give this up, just as toddlers give up crawling when they become able to walk. (Kamii & DeClark, 1985, p. 69)

For many primary teachers, the challenge is to make sure that their children are given time and opportunity to really understand addition and subtraction as opposed to meeting an imposed set of deadlines for memorization of facts or place-value procedures. One way to achieve this goal, even in the most rigidly prescribed situations, is to avoid numerous practice sheets and multitudes of problems. The Japanese approach with young children, which has helped earn Japanese children the world's highest math scores, is to focus on one or two problems during a single learning session. Children are encouraged to think of as many ways as possible to solve a problem and to share those ways with one another and with the teacher. Such intensive problem solving and social interaction have proven far superior to the usual U.S. practice of assigning large numbers of algorithmic practice problems in which children try hard to reach teacher-approved answers.

Children in the primary grades are interested in and should be permitted much interaction with their peers. Thus, they should be given more group games and fewer independent worksheets. Games played with dice or cards can be invented or purchased. Various tossing games using available classroom materials provide experience in addition. For example, you might use a wastebasket and playground ball and count one or two points for every basket. Or an infant's ring-toss game can be adapted for a similar score-keeping game.

Measuring

Measurement deals with the extent, dimensions, or capacity of things. Most measurements in the adult world take place according to standardized units such as feet and yards, centimeters and meters, and pints and quarts. Before children can participate in and understand standardized measurements, they must be able to conserve in the Piagetian sense. If nonconserving children are shown two strips of paper of equal length, they may easily use their observational ability to state that the strips are,

In the preoperational years, youngsters begin to learn such mathematical concepts as measurement through active physical interaction with a variety of materials.

indeed, equal—but only if they are laid side by side. If one of the strips is moved laterally, these children may then argue that it has become longer than the other one. Similarly, if presented with a short, wide pitcher of water, they will believe its quantity increases when poured into a tall, narrow pitcher. Children who cannot mentally conserve size or amount from one position to the next are not ready to use standard measurements, which are based on logic.

Preschool and kindergarten children, however, can engage in nonstandard measurement activities. Furthermore, it is appropriate to have yardsticks, plastic quart jugs, measuring cups, and measuring spoons present in the classroom where they can be used in many ways and identified by their proper names. Some informal measurement activities might include:

- Using the entire length of a yardstick or broom handle to measure a wall, to compare lengths of different sections of the room, or to decide on the size of a garden.

- Using a measuring (or other) cup to see how many times it must be filled with water or sand to completely fill a quart, liter, or gallon jug.

- Using balance scales to compare the weights of rocks and sticks, buttons and magnets, or anything else of a small size. Determining how many of one item equal the weight of those of another provides additional practice in counting.

- Using long strips of paper to measure children's height. Write the name of the child on each one, and lay it out next to the others on a line. Taking just a few at a time, they can be ordered according to height. Toward the end of kindergarten, a large class project can be to seriate the entire class using these strips.

Primary children are ready for more formal measurement using standard rulers, weights, and containers. Formal measurement activities should be introduced in simplified form, and such materials will be readily available as part of classroom equipment. At the same time, nonstandard measuring activities should not be totally abandoned and can be relied on for approximations and for times when the informal approach may provide a better feel for and understanding of an object.

As the NCTM (2000) pointed out, "If children's initial measurement explorations use a variety of units, nonstandard as well as standard, they will develop understanding about the nature of units and the need for standard units" (p. 129). As an example, the teacher might have children measure their height first using string and then a yardstick. An experience such as this for children who are ready to understand demonstrates the superiority of standardized measurement.

Geometry

Geometry is the study of shapes, both flat and three dimensional, and their relationships in space. Geometry enters infants' lives from birth as they attempt to make sense of the shapes in their environment: crib bars, stuffed animals, mother's breast and face, the door to the bedroom. Geometric shapes become some of the first intentional scribbles made in young children's drawings, and they delight in their awareness of the shapes around them.

Such natural interest deserves encouragement and informal teaching intervention. In the 1950s, two Dutch educators developed a theory of *vocal development* in geometric understanding. The van Hiele theory has gained acceptance in the United States in recent years and applies to children from the early years through high school. An important tenet of the theory is that children do not grow through the stages automatically but with teacher assistance will do so competently (Teppo, 1991). What children are exposed to in the early years sets the stage for learning in geometry throughout their entire school experience. Through the primary grades, children are at the earliest, visual, stage in which they explore their environment to learn to identify the shapes within it. Activities such as describing, modeling, drawing, and classifying help them develop a spatial sense.

Preschool and kindergarten children can learn much from playing with blocks. They can:

- Compare and seriate shapes. Start with single shapes and have children compare two pieces according to size. Later, more pieces can be added until several items of one shape can be seriated.
- Classify and name shapes. Provide two shapes at first then, after much practice, add a third and fourth. Make large loops of yarn on the floor or provide boxes

From hands-on manipulative experiences in the preschool years to more derivative activities in the primary grades, geometry learning is enhanced by teacher-provided activities.

to place the blocks in. A good game to play for naming is Pass the Block. Children sit in a circle and, as music plays, they pass blocks in one direction. When the music stops, each child names the shape he or she holds.

- Trace and feel shapes. Children trace around a block with pencil, then color it in if desired. With a little practice, they can superimpose different shapes on one paper, coloring in some of the sections. Blocks can also be used as items in a "mystery bag." Two or three familiar shapes are placed in a bag and children take turns reaching in, feeling a block, and identifying its shape.

Plane figures can be explored through movement activities. Lay colored tape on the floor in geometric shapes large enough for children to walk on. Ask the children to jump, walk, crawl, and so on across specific shapes. They might count the number of children who can fit in one triangle or the number of steps it takes to walk the perimeter of a square.

Kindergarten and primary children continue to learn best from working with manipulatives and may find the illustrations in math textbooks confusing. Some materials that are appropriate are tiles, pattern blocks, attribute blocks, geoblocks, geometric solids, colored cubes, and tangrams. Computer games in which geometric shapes appear from different angles help children overcome their misunderstandings of book illustrations, which may show a shape from only one or two viewpoints. Some appropriate activities are:

- Building structures with various types of blocks to enhance spatial visualization.
- Folding and cutting activities such as origami or snowflake making.
- Exploring the indoor and outdoor environments to identify shapes and angles made by people and nature.
- Reading maps.
- Making graphs.
- Playing tic-tac-toe, Battleship, and other games that use grid systems.

All day long there are opportunities for children to increase their awareness of mathematics in the world around them. Mathematical phenomena may not always be so obvious as those of language, however. Thus, the teacher must take extra care to include mathematical learning whenever natural learning situations arise. Often this means recognizing opportunities to incorporate mathematics into other areas of the curriculum. The final section of this chapter provides suggestions for doing this.

MATH ACTIVITIES ACROSS THE CURRICULUM

Whether your usual curriculum is integrated or separated according to subject disciplines, it is possible to incorporate mathematics learning in many ways. The ideas that follow should be considered springboards to others of your own. Try adapting them to different classroom situations and curricular topics. The activities are divided according to subject disciplines and, within each section, from the simplest to the most difficult. Of course, you should consider the needs of individual children when determining the appropriateness of each activity.

As a beginning organizer, a curriculum web as shown in Fig. 3.1 is helpful. Also, Table 3.2 summarizes math activities for curriculum integration.

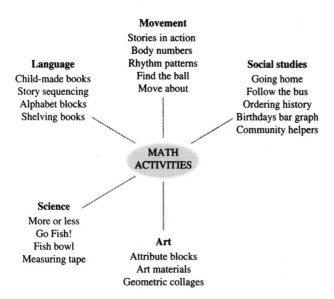

Movement
Stories in action
Body numbers
Rhythm patterns
Find the ball
Move about

Language
Child-made books
Story sequencing
Alphabet blocks
Shelving books

Social studies
Going home
Follow the bus
Ordering history
Birthdays bar graph
Community helpers

MATH ACTIVITIES

Science
More or less
Go Fish!
Fish bowl
Measuring tape

Art
Attribute blocks
Art materials
Geometric collages

FIG. 3.1.   A planning web for mathematics activities.

TABLE 3.2

Integrating Mathematics: Activities

Activity	Level*	Curriculum
Alphabet Blocks	P	Language
Art Materials	T, P	Art
Attribute Blocks	T, P	Art
Birthdays Bar Graphs	P, Py	Soc. Studies
Body Numbers	P, PY	Movement
Child-made Books	Py	Language
Community Helpers	P, Py	Soc. Studies
Find the Ball	P	Movement
Fishbowl	P	Science
Follow the Bus	Py	Soc. Studies
Geometric Collages	P, Py	Art
Go Fish!	P, Py	Science
Going Home	Py	Soc. Studies
Measuring Tape	P, Py	Science
More or Less	P, Py	Science
Move About	P	Movement
Ordering History	Py	Soc. Studies
Rhythm Patterns	P, Py	Movement
Shelving Books	T, P	Language
Stories in Action	P, Py	Language
Story Sequencing	P, Py	Language

*T = Toddler; P = Preschool; Py = Primary.

Language

1. **Shelving Books.** Two-year-olds are especially fond of making everything straight—and just as fond of making everything a mess. Three-year-olds love to dust and scrub and sometimes like to make everything straight. Let preschoolers help you keep the library corner clean and straight, and they will gain the added benefit of self-confidence, knowing you respect them enough to tackle an adult project.

   Turn the activity into a math experience by putting all the *tall* or *large* or *big* books on one shelf and all the *short* or *small* or *little* books on another. (Choose which vocabulary they will learn. If they know some of the words, introduce the others.) First, scrub, rinse, and dry each shelf. Then dust each book carefully and individually, repeatedly using the vocabulary of comparison.

2. **Alphabet Blocks.** This will work best outdoors or in an open space. Draw a line that children can stand behind. Each child takes a turn throwing an alphabet block over the line. The letter that turns up on top of the block is matched to other blocks that have turned up similarly before it. If it is the first time the letter has appeared, a new set is started. You should identify the letters' names, but children should not be required to memorize them.

   This is essentially a language activity, but it requires classification, a math-related skill. Counting can be added to the activity at the end of the game as the children count how many blocks there are of each letter.

3. **Story Sequencing.** Commercial flannelboard figures are available for well-known stories. They can also be handmade. Typically, there is one figure for each of the main characters and perhaps some props that move the plot along. If the collection does not include props, they will need to be made for this activity. As you read or tell the story, characters are placed (by you or children) in an appropriate arrangement for each stage of the story. Vocabulary should focus on what happened *first*, *second*, *third*, and so on. Later, children can do the activity independently. As you pass by and observe, use the ordinal numbers informally with the children.

4. **Child-Made Books.** When children write their own stories and make books from them, they can count the pages, being sure to count the backs, too, if they have been written or drawn on. Children can then count the number of words per page or the total number of words in the book. Discussion can focus on whose book is *biggest*, *smallest*, *longest*, or *shortest*. Children will have to debate the merits of counting pages versus number of words to determine size.

Science

5. **More or Less.** Throughout the year, children enjoy collecting items from nature: sticks, pebbles, shells, dirt samples, and more. These items can be counted and compared in different ways. Large rocks can be counted and their

numbers compared with small pebbles, yellow shells with pink ones, large sticks with small ones. If children are just beginning to count, make smaller subsets of larger collections. If they are beginning to read numbers, place a card or tag with the counted total next to each set. When the counting is completed, discuss which set has the most and which the fewest.

This is a good time to emphasize the difference between *much* and *many*, *less* and *fewer*. *Much* and *less* refer to mass quantities. *Many* and *fewer* refer to items that can be counted. Many adults confuse these descriptive words, so it should not be surprising if the children do.

6. **Go Fish!**   This is a popular children's game that provides plenty of opportunity to practice classification. Pictures can be glued onto 3-by-5-inch index cards and chosen according to categories currently under study. One example: classes of animals.

To play the game, each child is dealt five or six cards. In turn, each child asks the next on the left for a class: "Give me a mammal." If the second child has a mammal, she must give the card to the one requesting it. If she does not, she says, "Go fish!" and the child must take a card from the discard pile. Turns move to the left and the first child to lay down sets of four until his hand is empty is the winner.

7. **Fishbowl.**   This activity can be done when the fishbowl is new, then repeated and expanded on whenever the water needs changing. The teacher decides how much water the fishbowl needs and makes a dark line at that level. Children then use any pitcher to fill the bowl with water and count the number of pitchers required to get to the marked level. If the pitcher is a standard liquid measuring cup, the related vocabulary should be used. When the water needs changing, it can be poured back into the cup for disposal with a recount taking place.

8. **Measuring Tape.**   Any yarn can be used for a measuring tape, but it stretches and occasionally breaks. Bias seam tape provides a sturdy alternative. Try measuring class pets in ways that are appropriate for their type and size. Turtles can be measured from one end of the shell to the other. Small snakes can be held reasonably straight for a (very) quick measure. Rabbits can be measured around the middle. Attach the tape to the wall with the date the measurement was done. If the animal is a fast-growing infant, measure it again in a week or two. Other animals can be measured monthly. Place the second tape near the first and compare lengths. Children can discuss the animal's growth progress or lack of it. From this they learn about the difference between juvenile growth and mature stability as well as about the difference in growth rates for different animals.

Social Studies

9. **Community Helpers.**   Using index cards, make a set of pictures of various community workers, preferably those found in the children's own community. Make a matching set of cards with each worker's tools or hats or other articles

of identifiable clothing. As children match the appropriate artifact to its worker, they engage in classification.

10. **Birthdays Bar Graph.** On a large sheet of construction paper, list the months along the bottom. Each child draws a birthday cake on a small piece of construction paper. As children say their date of birth, they glue their cake above the appropriate month. The class then analyzes which month has the most birthdays and which has the fewest. Children can also look for months that have the same number of birthdays and which ones have none at all.

11. **Ordering History.** As children begin to learn about events that happened in the past, it helps to give them a concrete method of sequencing. Whether it is a news story they have seen on TV or heard about from their parents and older siblings, or the legendary history of the first Thanksgiving, creating a series of pictures provides the needed physical connection. As the children arrange pictures in the order that events occurred, use ordinal numbers informally: "What do you think happened first?" "Yes, that was what happened fourth. . . ."

12. **Follow the Bus.** Using a blown-up commercial map of your town or section of the city, identify the compass directions and print them on each side of the map. With a small toy school bus, children follow the patterns on the grid to go "north two blocks, then west one block" or "south one block, then east three blocks." If your town's roads are too complex for young children to make sense of, create an easily read grid yourself, and perhaps work with the children to create a town to go on it.

13. **Going Home.** Using the blown-up commercial map suggested in activity 12, have children place small rectangles where their homes are. Or, if you are creating a town on your handmade grid, children can choose where to place their homes. Use a piece of yarn to show how far it is from school to each home "as the crow flies." Each piece of yarn should be cut to size, after which children lay them next to each other along a line to determine who lives farthest from school and who lives closest to it.

Art

14. **Attribute Blocks.** Children make designs of their choice using a mixture of shapes and colors with commercially made plastic attribute blocks. When they are finished, children can sort the pieces by color into zippered clear plastic bags. If they are able, further sorting can take place according to shape. Bags can then be stored on a section of shelf with a matching symbol (red triangle, green circle, yellow square, etc.).

15. **Art Materials.** Take all the art materials—paint jars, fingerpaint containers, crayon boxes, paintbrushes—out for a good cleaning. (Preschool children enjoy the process more than the result. You can do this activity whether the materials actually need cleaning or not.) Put children in smocks and let them participate. When finished, discuss which sets should go in which place and organize accord-

ing to usage. If children are still interested in working, they can further organize within sets according to color of paint or size of paintbrushes, and so on.

16. **Geometric Collages.**   Have on hand a good supply of geometric construction paper shapes in different colors and sizes. Children can make collages on their own as you informally discuss the names of the shapes and comparative sizes. Or children can be directed to find pieces according to the shape names and colors you suggest. These are then made into collages or other pictures of their choice.

Movement

17. **Move About.**   Children repeat and continue patterns, such as two jumps, one clap, turn around; one step in, one jump, one step out, clap above the head.

18. **Find the Ball.**   In a group effort, the children lay out all the class playground balls in a row according to their size. Then each child identifies "his" or "her" ball as you describe it according to its attributes: "Yours is the largest ball"; "Yours is the ball in the middle"; "Yours is the second smallest ball." Balls can then be taken to the playground for playtime.

19. **Rhythm Patterns.**   The children sit on the floor in a circle. You clap a rhythm pattern, which the children imitate. Then the sequence is repeated with everyone counting, in rhythm, the number of claps.

20. **Body Numbers.**   Children use any or all of their bodies to make the shape of the number you call out. This can be done with fingers and arms while children sit at their desks. Or it can be done using the entire body in a larger area. Children should not be corrected if their shapes are hard to read.

21. **Stories in Action.**   Children are divided into groups sized according to the "number of the day," for example, 5. As you tell a story problem, the children figure out ways to act it out and discover the answer. Create stories that provide children with opportunities for creative movement. *Example*: Five little caterpillars are sitting in their cocoons waiting for the warm spring. Suddenly, two of them push out of their cocoons, wiggle their new butterfly wings, and fly away to the nearest rosebush. How many caterpillars are left in the cocoons? Now, these three caterpillars push out of their cocoons and wiggle their wings and fly to the rosebush to see their friends. How many butterflies are on the rosebush? How many caterpillars are left in their cocoons? How many cocoons did your group leave behind? (If needed, the butterflies can fly back to their cocoons to engage in one-to-one correspondence.)

EXTENDING YOUR LEARNING

1. Observe a preschool class for at least 1 hour. Make notes of every natural mathematics learning that takes place. Discuss your observations with members of your class.

2. Compare kindergarten and primary mathematics textbooks from several companies. How do they differ in the order and timeliness in which different topics and skills are introduced? Which ones promote the idea of informal, everyday mathematics, and which promote structured, teacher-led lessons? Which ones offer ideas for using interesting manipulative materials and which provide accompanying worksheets? Which books would you choose and why?

3. Invent a board game either for kindergarten and first grade or for second and third grades. Include in it at least two of the concepts discussed in this chapter. Try it out with other members of your class before you try it with children.

4. Give one or two of the Piagetian conservation tasks to a 3-year-old, a 5-year-old, and a 7-year-old. Two to try: (1) Create two rows of eight or nine pennies each and ask the child which row has more. Then spread out one row to fill more space and ask the same question again. (2) Make two equal balls of clay. Roll one of them into a long cylinder and ask the child which is bigger now. Compare the answers the children give and discuss the experience with others in your class who have also tried the tasks.

5. Try any two of the activities in this chapter's final section. Practice them first with other students in your class, then with children of the appropriate developmental level. To make this activity especially useful, create lesson plans for each activity before you try it out. Use the format provided in chapter 1.

VOCABULARY

Bottom-Up Method.   An approach to teaching mathematical concepts by providing children with the tools to figure things out for themselves then, with help, to generalize.

Informal Experiences.   Mathematical learning experiences that arise from everyday life and are built upon by the teacher in a nonprescriptive fashion.

Logicomathematical Knowledge.   Knowledge that goes beyond basic awareness of the physical to the perception of relationships and the creation of connections.

Naturalistic Experiences.   Mathematical learning experiences that arise from everyday life and contain little or no teacher intervention.

Physical Knowledge.   Related to the real world.

Social Knowledge.   Knowledge that is determined by societal or cultural design.

Structured Experiences.   Mathematical learning experiences that are planned in advance by the teacher and delivered systematically.

Top-Down Method.   An approach to teaching mathematical concepts through teacher directed experiences.

INTERNET RESOURCES

Web sites provide much useful information for educators and we list some here that pertain to the topics covered in this chapter. The addresses of Web sites can also change, however, and new ones are continually added. Thus, this list should be considered as a first step in your acquisition of a larger and ever-changing collection.

National Council of Teachers of Mathematics
www.nctm.org

PBS Mathline
http://pbs. org/teachersource/mathline/overview.shtm

References

Bandura, A. (1963). *Social learning and personality development*. New York: Holt, Rinehart & Winston.

Baroody, A. (1987). *Children's mathematical thinking*. New York: Teachers College Press.

Baroody, A., & Standifer, D. (1993). Addition and subtraction in the primary grades. In R. Jensen (Ed.), *Research ideas for the classroom: Early childhood mathematics*. New York: Macmillan.

Boyd, W. (1914). *From Locke to Montessori*. London: Harrap.

Charlesworth, R. (1997). Mathematics in the developmentally appropriate integrated curriculum. In C. Hart, D. Burts, & R. Charlesworth (Eds.), *Integrated curriculum and developmentally appropriate practice* (pp. 51–73). Albany, NY: State University of New York Press.

Charlesworth, R., & Lind, K. (1999). *Math and science for young children* (2nd ed.). Albany, NY: Delmar.

Colvin, S. (1987). *Introducing addition and subtraction symbols to first graders*. Unpublished doctoral dissertation.

Comenius, J. (1896). *School of infancy*. Boston: Heath. (Original work published 1633)

Dougherty, B., & Scott, L. (1993). Curriculum: A vision for early childhood mathematics. In R. Jensen (Ed.), *Research ideas for the classroom: Early childhood mathematics*. New York: Macmillan.

Ginsburg, H., & Baron, H. (1993). Cognition: Young children's construction of mathematics. In R. Jensen (Ed.), *Research ideas for the classroom: Early childhood mathematics*. New York: Macmillan.

Kamii, C., & DeClark, G. (1985). *Young children reinvent arithmetic*. New York: Teachers College Press.

Kamii, C. & Joseph, L. (1989). *Young children continue to reinvent arithmetic—2nd grade: Implications of Piaget's theory*. New York: Teachers College Press.

Kline, K. (1999). Helping at home. *Teaching Children Mathematics, 5*(8), 456–460.

Locke, J. (1964). *John Locke on education*. New York: Teachers College Press.

Maffei, A., & Buckley, P. (1980). *Teaching preschool math*. New York: Human Sciences Press.

National Council of Teachers of Mathematics. (1998). *1998–99 NCTM member handbook*. Reston, VA: National Council of Teachers of Mathematics. Author.

National Council of Teachers of Mathematics. (2000). *Principles and standards for school mathematics*. Reston, VA: National Council of Teachers of Mathematics. Author.

Piaget, J. (1975). *To understand is to invent*. New York: Viking. (Original work published 1948)

Piaget, J., & Inhelder, B. (1969). *The psychology of the child*. New York: Basic Books.

Read, K., & Patterson, J. (1980). *The nursery school and kindergarten*. New York: Holt, Rinehart, and Winston.

Teppo, A. (1991). Van Hiele levels of geometric thought revisited. *Mathematics Teacher, 84*(3), 210–221.

SCIENCE: CURIOSITY ABOUT THEIR WORLD

In countless ways, science is at work everywhere and at all times in this beautifully ordered, yet full of surprises, world. It's there for the looking . . . try to see the way children do: Our world is a huge hands-on museum, a well-stocked laboratory, a fascinating never-ending field trip.

Maryann Ziemer

▼ *Chapter Objectives*

After reading this chapter, you should be able to:

- ▼ Plan science experiences in relation to children's physical, social and moral, emotional, and cognitive development.
- ▼ Deyelop science curricula that reflect the needs of individual children.
- ▼ Begin to plan units of science study that integrate other subject areas.

As you think about and apply chapter content on your own, you should be able to:

- ▼ Find ways to enhance children's science learning by building on their curiosity.
- ▼ Model curiosity yourself as a teacher and a learner.

S cience is often the subject that is left for the end of the day should there be a bit of time left, or even ignored by teachers altogether. Yet, for young children, it is often the subject about which they have the most curiosity, excitement, and thirst for learning. What happens between those early years and adulthood that turns children off to the "huge hands-on museum" and "never-ending field trip" that is their planet and their universe? Could it be years of learning science through lifeless textbooks and rote memory tests? Underfunded laboratories staffed by teachers lacking in the knowledge and creativity to find the materials they need in the natural world or their own kitchens? Perhaps the attitude of some high school and college teachers that only very intelligent students or those of a particular gender are capable of understanding science?

Whatever the answers to these questions might be, beginning this minute, let us consider them irrelevant. Young children are fascinated by science, and if we take our careers as their teachers seriously and responsibly, we will foster and engage their curiosity about the world while keeping our own curiosity finely tuned and active.

By definition, science refers to knowledge that is gained systematically through observation, study, and experimentation. When applied to the natural world, it includes physics, chemistry, and biology as well as their derivatives and branches such as astronomy, geology, oceanography, ecology, botany, and zoology. Because the content of these sciences is physical, approachable, and interwoven with young children's lives, science is not only fascinating to them but an appropriate part of their curriculum.

Environmental studies, which incorporate both natural and social sciences, provide interest for young children because the focus is on their own lives. The following classroom description of such studies in action demonstrates how several learnings can take place at one time by using an activity centers approach. The teacher, before this experience, spent a year in England observing early education and its inclusion of the outdoors as a natural setting for learning, then brought many of the new ideas back to her own school.

FIRST GRADERS MEET THEIR ENVIRONMENT

Kathleen's first graders have spent many weeks studying the environment of the immediate area around their school, the adjacent fields and forests and the beach areas of their coastal island. Now they are learning about the ways in which the Native Americans of earlier times interacted with the same environment. Their studies have included the Native Americans' closeness to nature as well as the impact of their behavior on the environment. For example, Kathleen's children understand the positive effects of living without modern construction and facilities and the negative impact of burning all vegetation on the island to make it easier to catch deer.

Today, the children are working indoors at environmentally oriented centers. Although they may move about as they wish, everyone is expected to spend at least some time at each of the centers before the morning is finished. At one center, the children are making native-style dyes from found materials: marigold petals, green leaves, various mosses, hollyhock seeds, berries, a green tomato. One child observes the changing colors as he stirs his mixture and announces, "I'm making rainbow soup!" Another child gets down to the serious business of labeling the dye she has made from blackberries. Kathleen helps her sound out blackberries *but doesn't correct the spelling imperfections.*

Young children are fascinated by the world around them. Their natural curiosity can and should provide teachers with the impetus for much science learning.

At a second center, children are making fruit leather from applesauce and blackberries. When the work is done, the sheets of fruit are placed in the classroom dehydrator, which the children choose to call "the sun," understanding that this method is a modern concession to convenience and speed. Before this experience, the children had studied evaporation and the need to keep food edible, when there is no refrigeration, by drying it.

At a third center, a large salmon is temporarily in use for an art project. A dark dye is spread over one side of the fish and the children then make prints on large sheets of paper. They are aware that there will be a follow-up activity to dissect the salmon to learn how its body is constructed to maximize its chances for survival.

The fourth and final center requires the children to pound bark strips into smaller pieces for weaving. This is done with heavy rocks. Sharper stones are used to bring out softer fibers for other uses such as kindling, pillow stuffing, and fine weaving. The children have collected the bark themselves and can identify the types of trees from which the various pieces come.

The entire classroom has been redesigned to resemble a longhouse, including an impressive entryway from the interior hall and a stone-ringed "fire" for large-group meetings. When center time is finished, the children gather together around the fire to hear Kathleen read the story they have written cooperatively about their visit to a local reproduction of an early longhouse. Kathleen has laminated their individual stories and illustrations and bound them into a Big Book, which will now be kept as part of the class library. Several children were sick when the book was made, and she reassures them that since the book is bound with rings, they will be able to add their contributions in the near future. The entire class seems satisfied with their book, listening attentively to what each child has written and trying to guess or remember who drew which picture. It is apparent to the observer that what the children learned in the museum reproduction about the Native American environment has been reinforced by the activities at school.

On the surface, the morning activities in Kathleen's classroom seem to be an interesting collection of social studies activities. After all, the children are studying the historic life ways of Native Americans. Yet the center's focus is on the scientific aspects of local inhabitants' lives: learning successful ways to make dyes and from which materials, applying what they have learned about dehydration to make fruit leather, discussing the salmon's characteristics while creating prints and then dissecting it, and becoming intimately familiar with different kinds of bark. All these activities are practical ways to become acquainted with the physical, biological, and chemical properties of the local environment.

Through these activities the children are exposed to writing, reading, art, and social studies. Also, by labeling dyes, making salmon rubbings, weaving bark strips, and listening to the stories they wrote, they learn more about early Native American life. Because much of their learning happens in this integrated way, Kathleen's first graders are largely unaware of which academic subject they are studying. Instead, they see what they're doing as part of the larger study they are making of their island environment.

Because they have an intense interest in the environment and in preserving it, the children are not intimidated by activities that require scientific processes or that might be labeled chemistry, physics, or biology. In fact, they are inspired by what Kathleen sometimes labels "difficult tasks." These are activities that, by definition, require extra thought from the children. Most important in this attitude toward scientific learning is Kathleen's own interest and confidence in what she is doing. She is aware that children can be turned on to science only if the teacher first sets an example.

Kathleen's view of early childhood science—hands-on exploration integrated into a curricular theme and encouraged by teacher enthusiasm—is, in some ways modern but also reminiscent of much earlier philosophies. In the following section, we see how science education for young children has been altered to suit varying attitudes over time.

PERSPECTIVES ON HISTORY AND THEORY

From the beginning of schooling in the United States until today, religion and morality have been linked with children's science learning. Near the end of the 18th century, nature books were imported from England with the hope that children would learn about and love God's creation. Today, as we have learned more about this planet's beginnings, parents and education groups from different religious and philosophical views have struggled to ensure that those views are represented in school science curricula.

Additionally, there has been a long-standing controversy regarding age-appropriate science content and the best methods for teaching it. To understand the different views, we can return again to Locke and Rousseau. The Lockean view holds that there is a discrete body of knowledge about the world that children should learn efficiently and enjoyably. This view leads to a model of science education that focuses on choosing which science concepts children are ready to learn, then teaching those concepts in meaningful ways. Rousseau's view, on the other hand, is more permissive, suggesting that children should be allowed to roam free among nature's wonders, questioning the meaning of their surroundings as their interests move them. Only as children express interest should the adult intervene and then in a facilitative rather than an instructive way.

From the turn of the 20th century until the mid-1950s, derivatives of these two views of childhood science were both prevalent and, thus, in conflict with each other. One, structured and knowledge-based, saw a child as an intellectual learner; the other, based on nature study, played to children's interests, emotional development, and imagination. In 1957, when the Soviet Union began the space race by launching the earth's first artificial satellite, science educators took a closer look at the U.S. failure to be first in space and decided that the science curriculum needed revision. The next 20 years produced a number of federally funded science programs that included curricula designed to begin in kindergarten. Eventually, however, concern over civil rights and a back-to-basics curriculum, which didn't include science, dried up federal dollars. Science became devalued at all levels.

In recent years, interest has arisen again as it becomes increasingly apparent that the future of the world is being driven by science and technology at the same time that U.S. students' scientific knowledge has been compared unfavorably with that of students in most other industrialized countries. In 1990, Donna Jean Carter, then president of the Association for Supervision and Curriculum Development (ASCD), stated:

> Our science-deficient curriculums are effectively disqualifying the United States from contributing to the worldwide search for scientific and technological solutions and further reducing our economic power. In fact, with the increasing quality-of-life issues facing us today, such as environmental pollution and world hunger, to stay the course is to act as a lamb being led to slaughter. (p. v)

During the late 1980s and early 1990s, Carter's concerns were reflected across the U.S. science education community with resulting reform documents applicable to K–12 education: *National Science Education Standards* from the National Research Council in 1996; *Benchmarks for Science Literacy* from the American Association for the Advancement of Science in 1993; and *Science for All Americans* from the American Association for the Advancement of Science in 1989. These reform documents "espouse the idea that active, hands-on, conceptual learning provides meaningful and relevant learning experiences" and reinforce the observation that "all students, especially those in underrepresented groups, need to learn scientific skills such as observation and analysis at a very young age" (Lind, 1999, pp. 73–74).

As part of this reform, Project 2061 (named for the year that Halley's Comet will next return) was born. Six teams of elementary educators were assigned the task of revising science curriculum for the primary grades while holding to the following assumptions:

- The goal of teaching is to help all children develop scientific literacy.
- What children learn is fundamentally related to how they learn it.

- All children can learn to think scientifically. (Wishon, Crabtree, & Jones, 1998, p. 256)

By the mid-1990s, the publication of brain research indicating the important influence of the environment to learning from infancy onward; the wide adoption of Piaget's constructivist theory by science educators and their increasing acceptance of the concept of developmentally appropriate practice; and the 1994 call from The Carnegie Task Force on Meeting the Needs of Young Children to prepare children for learning in advance of entering school all led to the 1998 Forum on Early Childhood Science, Mathematics, and Technology Education (Nelson, 1999).

The forum brought together early childhood specialists and representatives from the National Science Foundation to "discuss how, when, and even if we should teach science, mathematics, and technology to pre-kindergarten children" (Nelson, 1999, p. v). As a result of the meeting, a series of papers was commissioned in which the following ideas emerged:

- Young children are capable of learning more than has been thought; since not enough is known yet about child development it can not be said for sure what experiences are appropriate for every child.
- Math and science are rarely found in early education.
- Teachers and caregivers of young children are frequently undereducated in math, science, and technology and, thus, not prepared to teach them. (p. vi)

These were not surprising ideas to the forum organizers who were responding in part to their sense that they were coming a bit late to the preschool discussion, that "the literacy people got there first. In other words, there is a common perception that the language arts play a predominant role in early childhood education, to the exclusion of mathematics and science" (Johnson, 1999, p. 16).

It is time, forum participants realized, to correct this deficit. Science and math can be taught in developmentally appropriate ways to even very young children. To do this successfully, science in particular must drop its tradition of teacher-centered, teacher-authority presentation of information to youngsters in favor of the constructivist approach that most early educators have come to accept.

A Theory of Early Science Learning for Today

In chapter 3 we discussed the Piagetian view of knowledge, as proposed by Constance Kamii and Rita DeVries, that there are three qualitatively different types of knowledge. The Kamii-DeVries framework can be applied to science learning as well. To review, social knowledge is that which is arbitrarily decided on by society and includes the naming of objects and ideas. When children learn animal classifications or memorize the names of garden flowers they acquire social knowledge. If memorizing names is the extent of children's learning, however, their knowledge is at a very shallow level. Physical knowledge is that gained by interacting with objects.

As children act on the objects or observe them, they gain a better understanding of their attributes. If this learning doesn't lead to further connections or meaning, however, again their knowledge remains shallow. Logicomathematical knowledge is that which makes connections and relationships among items of social and physical knowledge. For example, a child may observe that a bright, shiny stone rolls easily down the driveway. Seeing that a dingy gray stone doesn't roll as easily, she may conclude that ease of rolling is connected to color. Playing with yet another stone, however, shows her that some dingy gray stones are capable of easy rolling. The child begins to understand that it is the shape of the stone that affects the rolling. According to Piagetian theory, the child constructs this knowledge internally. Such construction is in contrast to externally imposed physical and social knowledge.

Social and physical knowledge are not unimportant, nor are the three types of knowledge mutually exclusive. Children need the social knowledge that tells them what things are named; and it is from acting on physical objects that they construct a logicomathematical framework. But it is self-constructed logicomathematical knowledge that provides truly internal understanding.

Teachers of early childhood science sometimes confuse physical knowledge with logicomathematical learning. They believe that giving children plenty of hands-on experiences will be sufficient, that they will just "learn by doing." According to Piagetian constructivist theory, the critical logicomathematical element is then lacking. ASCD science writers Loucks-Horsley, Kapitan, Carlson, Kuerbis, Clark, Nelle, Sachse, and Walton (1990) argued that simple, hands-on science makes

> no attempt to help [children] derive meaning from their experiences. They are either left on their own, or they are told what they should have observed or learned. Constructivist science is based on the notion that we learn best when we are able to construct our own knowledge. Helping children do this from real-life experiences is good science teaching. (p. 49)

It is important to remember that in constructivist theory, it is the active learning that takes place in thought that determines what is really learned, not just the hands-on activities that lead (or may not lead) to expanded understanding.

Science educators Christine Chaillé and Lory Britain (1997) agreed:

> The hands-on nature of activities is an important part of a constructivist curriculum, but in and of itself this does not make an activity a constructivist one. This is because the constructivist sees the essential activity as what goes on in the child's head, not in his or her hands. (p. 19)

The following section provides some ways in which teachers can help children progress from physical and social to logicomathematical knowledge.

Applying Constructivist Theory in the Classroom

Young children construct their own learning only when they are left free to experiment and manipulate on their own, with guidance and encouragement provided by a teacher when appropriate. Thus, formal instruction is a poor choice of method for most preschool and primary youngsters. Instead, children should be permitted to *be* scientists. That is, they should be allowed to observe, classify, hypothesize, predict, experiment, compute, and communicate the results of their findings. This type of early learning is sometimes called *sciencing*.

When children encounter the environment on their own terms, and thus engage in sciencing, they can be guided toward a number of the processes or thinking skills that adult scientists use. Children, of course, will use these processes at a level appropriate to their age and development.

Observation may be the most important process for young children. It has been described as "the fundamental building block for all of the other processes and thus must be stressed in every way possible throughout *all* of the various activities carried out in sciencing" (Neuman, cited in Smith, 1981, p. 8). Such an important skill is much more than simply a short viewing session. When young children observe, all their senses participate as they touch, smell, listen, taste, and watch. A baking experiment, for example, allows children to feel the dough's texture, smell the dough as it changes from raw to cooked, listen to the sound of the dough as they punch it down or stir it around, taste the final product, and watch each step as it happens.

Classification was addressed in the chapter on mathematics, and it is important in science as well. As children group and regroup objects according to their self-created classification schemes, they construct relationships between and among the objects. Some classifications that children might make as part of science experiences could be edible and nonedible plants or parts of plants, sea- and land-based animals, and frozen and liquid forms of water.

Prediction can be nonsensical or magical without some teacher direction. With teacher direction, young children can move toward knowledgeable logic. One school ran a contest for all children from kindergarten through 12th grade. The object was for each class to guess how many pieces of bubble gum were in a large glass container on the librarian's desk. The class with the closest estimate would win the bubble gum. The first graders, who had been practicing logical prediction in their science experiences, came in second, right behind the 11th graders. (The 11th graders generously shared their prize with the younger children.)

Prediction is guided by such questions as, "What do you think will happen if we...?" At first, children are not concerned about the accuracy of their predictions, particularly in the preschool years. With practice, however, they can reflect on the logic of their predictions and become more accurate, as the first graders demonstrated.

Experimentation provides children with an opportunity to predict, operate on, and observe changes. Chaillé and Britain (1997) suggest three basic questions to generate early childhood experimentation. The first, "How can I make it move?" leads to experiments in physics. The child who rolled stones of different colors and shapes down the driveway was asking this physics question.

"How can I make it change?" leads to chemistry experimentation. Children at an easel who have been given permission to mix paint colors ask this question of themselves each time they try to create a new shade.

"How does it fit, or how do I fit?" leads to experiments in biology. It also leads to the questions, "Who am I in relation to the rest of the world?" and "How do my actions affect my world?" Chaillé and Britain viewed these questions as important in helping children toward social perspective taking, in which children see the effects of their actions and subsequently develop sensitivity, empathy, and appreciation for the natural world. A biological experiment of this sort might be to deprive individual plants of water or sunlight or soil and then chart the results.

Communication takes place both during and after a science experience. Children talk informally about what they are doing, often to no one in particular. "I'm mixing the water in now," or "This stuff is turning green," or "Why won't it move anymore?" may be internal thoughts that need to be verbalized but aren't meant as conversation starters. You can talk informally, too, but should have a purpose in doing so. "I wonder what will happen if we put just one more block on top?" or "Is there some way we could make that a lighter pink?" are questions that foster thinking as well as continued communication.

At the end of a science experience, children can communicate what happened by dictating the events and results or by writing reports on their own. If primary children are working independently or in small groups at a center, it may be helpful to provide worksheets with a simple guiding structure. The sentence starters below are examples that can be changed according to the experience provided:

- The question we asked was. . . .
- First we. . . .
- Then we. . . .
- We observed that. . . .

One approach to sciencing that is particularly appropriate to children in the primary grades has been recommended by Canadian early childhood specialist Selma Wasserman (1988). She referred to it as *play-debrief-replay*. Wasserman suggested that, in addition to the scientific processes just discussed, children need to learn "what all scientists must know in order to be successful: how to fail and keep trying" (p. 230). Her 3-step sciencing process is designed to give children the skills and courage for such risk taking.

1. In the first *play* stage of the sciencing experience, the teacher prepares the children and the experience in such a way that scientific inquiry may lead to increased scientific understandings. Wasserman equated this stage with scientific investigation in which children "manipulate experimental variables; generate hypotheses; conduct tests; observe, gather, classify and record data; examine assumptions and evaluate findings" (p. 230). In this stage, the teacher avoids telling the children what to do but does facilitate their inquiries.

2. In the *debriefing*, the teacher helps the children reflect on their experience and extract meaning from it. The teacher uses reflective questioning to help children relate their findings to science concepts, extract new scientific principles, reconsider the conclusions they came to, and lay the groundwork for the next stage.

3. When children *replay*, they may repeat the first experience to see if they can replicate their results, they may alter an experiment based on their reevaluation during the debriefing, or they even may use the first experience as inspiration for a related but new experience.

This 3-step sciencing process is much like the activities of real scientists in actual laboratories, and Wasserman argues that this is the most effective way for children to gain their own best scientific understanding.

PERSPECTIVES ON DEVELOPMENT

Cognitive, social and moral, emotional, and physical development all pertain to the learning of science in the early years and are the focus of this next section.

Cognitive Development

Scientists employ mathematics in much of what they do. Astronomers, for example, use mathematical calculations to learn about the universe, including those parts they cannot see. Geologists use math to pinpoint the locations of earthquakes, geographers to calculate surface areas, and chemists to predict the rate of chemical reactions. Even in the primary grades, connections between science and math can be made. Children can learn about these connections by sciencing rather than by simply studying science as a subject.

The primary division in cognitive maturity is between preoperations and concrete operations. Children at both stages require concrete objects for effective learning, but it is in the second stage that logicomathematical learning develops. Before this learning takes place, the world only makes sense to children based on their egocentric view of it. Because some scientific learning does not evolve at the concrete operational level until late elementary school, children need preoperationally oriented learning experiences well into the primary grades.

In chapter 3, several aspects of development were discussed that relate to science learning. These developmental changes are those observed by Piaget in his studies of children.

Seriation requires children to place objects in a logical order (e.g., from largest to smallest). Preoperational children can find the smallest and largest objects but have difficulty grading things by size. Ordering objects found on a nature walk or on the playground can be an instructive activity for young children.

Classification has already been discussed, both as a scientific process and as a mathematics skill. Because young children can focus on just one attribute at a time, complex classification is beyond those students in the preoperations stage.

Conservation is another mathematics and science skill that only emerges with concrete operations. As children work with clay, mud, or sand, they don't realize that the quantity remains the same although the shape may change. Or, as they pour water from one container to another, they believe that the quantity changes with the shape of the container. Their understanding of science experiences with materials such as water and clay is affected by their ability, or inability, to conserve.

Children's perception of time can affect their experiences with science. Young children's understanding of the passage of time is limited. This will make it difficult for them to comprehend the time needed for an experiment, particularly one that takes place over several days or weeks. You can use simple charts and graphs to help them keep track of time as well as any physical changes. Longer periods of time also present a challenge as children try to understand the distances between our times and those of the dinosaurs or other extinct animals.

Other developmental issues center on the fact that science education involves the study of natural phenomena and young children have not yet learned to respond logically to those they observe. Until children are in late elementary school, for instance, many have trouble determining whether objects are alive or not. For young children, a deciding factor is whether an object moves or not. Thus, a car or train may seem as alive as a tree or a horse.

The concept of organisms changing over time is also difficult to grasp. Plants whose appearance changes as they grow are confusing to children, particularly if they must try to understand that a seed grows into a full-fledged plant, which then grows more seeds, which then turn into new plants. The caterpillar-to-butterfly sequence is totally beyond younger children's comprehension and should not be studied intensely until a later time, despite the attractiveness of this springtime wonder.

Piaget's (1932/1965) studies of children's understanding of cause-and-effect relationships led him to identify three basic characteristics that dominate their explanations of causality. The first of these is *animism*, or the belief that inanimate objects make decisions about the ways they act. For example, children may believe that the sun and moon take scheduled turns being asleep and awake, or that the sun shines because it wants them to be happy and warm. The second characteristic is *artificialism*, the belief that everything that exists has been built by humans, or by God in a human fashion. Referring again to the sun, a child might explain that God created the sun so we would be happy when we play outside. The third characteristic, magic, is used to explain cause-and-effect relationships that are too difficult to explain logically.

Social and Affective Development

The way young children feel about science is determined, to a great extent, by the attitude of their teacher. Social learning theory explains such development of children's attitudes in terms of adult modeling. Unfortunately, many teachers remember their own science learning as confusing, tedious, or difficult. They are often under pressure to accomplish so much other teaching that such a negative-seeming subject is easily deleted. Few have had opportunities or training to think scientifically or to engage in meaningful experiments (Nelson, 1999), and conversations in the teachers' lounge and elsewhere serve to reinforce the lack of interest or confidence that teachers have in teaching science. When teachers communicate their negative attitudes and lack of confidence about science, children respond by becoming negative themselves. This creates an unfortunate cycle in which, generation after generation, science learning is increasingly neglected.

If you feel undereducated in science or lack confidence, you can break the cycle by reading (many children's books are a good place to start), taking courses and workshops, and making an effort to demonstrate a more positive attitude. It is not necessary for you to portray yourself as extremely knowledgeable about science. If children raise questions that you are unable to answer, you can express enthusiasm for exploring the answer together. Modeling scientific curiosity is an important step in helping children keep their own natural curiosity as they grow older.

For children, as for adults, there is much to science that has a moral dimension. As children gain perspective-taking skills, they start to wonder and worry about the feelings of animals and plants. Their worries may well be compounded if they retain such early views as animism and artificialism. For example, children might believe that plants will suffer pain if they are deprived of water or sunlight. Teachers need to help children sort out their understandings as experiments are undertaken.

Teachers can also direct children's developing perspective-taking skills and moral concerns related to science. Some of today's issues can be adapted to children's levels of understanding. For example, concern for the environment can be applied to the environment in the school. Young children can lead drives to expand recycling activities, join in litter patrols, and care for the grounds. Their concern for animal welfare can be translated into responsible care for classroom pets.

Science usually does have a moral dimension to it. As children become aware of issues and are encouraged to act on their concerns, they increase their understanding of the importance of participating in science in a responsible way.

Physical Development

An awareness of the body and its senses is a vital part of early science study. The child's own body might be considered the ultimate in concrete learning materials, provoking curiosity and questioning. Such activities as brushing teeth, taking naps, and bathing not only promote health but teach children respect for their bodies. Teaching young children the names of body parts should be accompanied by activities that demonstrate what the body parts can do. If there is a line on the floor where the class gathers, it can be used for this purpose. Children can be asked to touch a knee or a finger to the line or perhaps one hand and the nose. Playing the Hokey Pokey is always popular with children and helps them understand body parts even when they aren't yet able to keep up with the instructions.

DIVERSITY AMONG CHILDREN

Children's understandings about science must be determined by their cognitive maturity as well as by their culturally based understandings of the world. This is particularly true toward the end of kindergarten and in the primary grades when children achieve concrete operational understandings at varying rates. Additionally, different children achieve different understandings at different times. Two first-grade girls, for example, loved to classify everything they could find outdoors and had no trouble sorting leaves and bark according to their appropriate tree names. For one girl, this level of sorting was as far as she could go. Meanwhile, her friend spent considerable time trying new ways to separate the treasures they had found—by color or size or degrees of perceived beauty. The first girl always watched for a while or wandered off, eventually returning to insist, "Now, put everything back where it's supposed to be!"

Activities such as this one make it possible to reach children at different levels. When the girls classified their nature objects, they chose the activity freely. The second girl increased her understanding of classification because the teacher came by to ask, "Can you find other ways to group the things you found?" and gave her a new idea. The first girl heard the same question but, being unready to respond, continued to engage in classification at her own level. Soon, however, she might be ready to understand more. At such time, she could learn from observing her friend and perhaps recall the teacher's encouragement. If her teacher were alert, a return visit with skillful questioning and commenting would provide further encouragement.

In science as in mathematics, girls and boys eventually come to perform differently and have different interests. Here it is the boys who succeed and the girls who fall behind. Yet investigators have not found any biological (genetic or anatomical) or intellectual causes for this difference. Something else seems to be at work. As Barbara Taylor (1993) pointed out, "Attitudes that discourage girls from science participation include teachers not expecting girls to excel in science, families encouraging boys and discouraging girls from taking science classes, and differences in teachers' treatment of girls and boys" (p. 8). Even science textbooks tend to show more boys than girls in their illustrations, as if to send the message that boys should pursue scientific interests and girls should not. Early childhood teachers have a special responsibility to encourage girls as well as boys to engage in and enjoy science—before the textbooks and society can convince the girls that they are not capable.

Curriculum Considerations for Children with Special Needs

Children with special needs are as likely as their typically developing peers to be curious about the world in which they live. They might be less skilled at asking questions, manipulating objects, recording information, or interpreting data, and they are sometimes hesitant to try things out because of a history of failing or fear of not knowing the "right" answers. Children with disabilities may know more than their peers about their bodies and how they work, because as they learn about themselves they learn about individual differences in biological makeup and often provide the best age-appropriate explanations of their own disabilities and delays. Good teaching, creative approaches to curriculum design, and sensitive teachers can instill confidence in experimentation, encourage curiosity, and guide exploration for all young children.

Sensory Impairments

The importance of observation in science was emphasized earlier in this chapter, and often children who do not see or hear well are especially good observers with their other senses. For example, a child who doesn't see can be asked to contribute more specific information about smell and touch than sighted peers, providing unusual

Encouraging young girls, as well as boys, to engage in sciencing may have positive implications for enjoyment of and competence in science later on.

classification schemes such as categorizing leaves by their texture rather than shape or size. Likewise, children who can't hear well sometimes can concentrate their attention intensely on objects without being distracted by the verbal comments of their peers. Teachers should encourage opportunities for children with sensory impairments to share their unique perspectives rather than assuming that they will be less astute observers than their peers. Children with vision and hearing impairments may be able to tell others in the class about eyes and ears and how these organs function and even explain the origins of their disabilities.

Cognitive Impairments

Children with cognitive impairments may take longer to formulate questions or continue to ask, "Why?" when others have moved on to more specific queries. They also may need reminders to connect one day's learning with the next day's lesson. A good strategy is to have peers answer the general questions, which allows the teacher to evaluate the peers' learning as well as encouraging partnerships and natural helpers among the children. Children with cognitive delays may continue to use preoperational thinking when their peers have moved on to concrete operations and benefit from extended experiences with concrete objects combined with supplemental direct instruction on concepts. Teachers can help immensely by labeling examples and nonexamples of concepts during hands-on lessons, or having peers do so. For instance, pointing out examples of *dark* and *not dark*, before introducing the polar opposite concept *light*.

Physical Impairments

Children with physical impairments such as cerebral palsy or juvenile arthritis may not be able to handle and manipulate objects with the coordinated actions necessary to carry out early experiments in physics and chemistry. Holding and releasing, pouring and stirring, poking and pushing, writing and drawing, may all be difficult. These children can participate, however, in generating questions and hypotheses and work with partners who can carry out actions for them. A child with poor coordination in her hands can take turns telling a peer what to try with mixing paints, for example. Children quickly establish a smooth routine for taking such turns in scientific pursuits, especially if an adult coaches them on the process for the first few trials. Computer programs can also simulate many science experiments, allowing children to use a single motion with a finger, joy stick, or head pointer, to carry out any number of actions.

Cultural Considerations

Children whose cultural backgrounds differ from those of their teachers may not share expected values about the scientific method or may have entirely different concepts about how the world works. Some cultures have no concepts of and no words in the language to represent internal organs, germs, the nervous system, or any of the basic biological knowledge we expect young children to learn in the science curriculum. Their understanding of the world is based in spiritual rather than factual and scientific knowledge. Children from subsistence cultures may have an advanced functional understanding of the plant world, seasonal variations, and weather patterns, but relatively little knowledge or interest in classification exercises. Families who have immigrated to escape war and persecution may have long histories of discouraging curiosity in children because of the associated dangers of exposure to injury, separation, and death.

Giftedness

The sciences offer children who are cognitively gifted a multitude of opportunities for intellectual growth. Although other children in a center or class might find that observation and classification offer just the right amount of challenge, gifted children might be ready for controlled experiments or simple reading research. Or, perhaps the rest of the class is content to try floating and sinking a variety of objects and talk about what they found, whereas the more advanced children are ready to record their findings on graphs and test new hypotheses. All children should be provided with opportunities to explore scientific concepts, but teachers should observe carefully to learn which ones are ready to engage in somewhat more advanced scientific processes.

FOCUS ON SCIENCE: THE DISCIPLINES

Science learning is available everywhere. Writers, educators, and scientists themselves have much to say about the pervasive nature of potential science curriculum:
Sometimes commentary draws on the wonders of childhood:

One of the glories of childhood is that children are natural seekers, finders, observers, keepers, and collectors. Their waking hours are spent searching, examining, investigating, and wondering, awestruck by the richly diverse nature of things around them. (Wishon, Crabtree, & Jones, 1998, p. 254)

Many seek to promote a science curriculum based on their positive experiences working with young children. Barbara Taylor (1993), whose career has included many of these experiences, said:

It is amazing to see how much time and interest can be involved in events that are seemingly common, and even boring, to older children or adults, such as using magnets to attract paper clips, being mesmerized by water, building up and knocking down blocks, or pouring rice between containers while listening to its crisp sound and watching its jumping action. . . . Science is all around us. We cannot escape it. And it is the magnificence of science that urges us to always move forward while we examine and use the opportunities around us. (p. v)

Taking the world-encompassing subject that is science and organizing it into a teachable framework is the first task of creating the curriculum. There are different approaches from which you can choose. One is to organize the curriculum according to the scientific concepts appropriate to each age: how plants get their food, where animals live, where rain comes from (Good, 1977). Another is to cluster lessons according to children's typical interests, such as the properties of things: color, shape, texture, magnetic properties; ecology and environment; walking in the woods, building a terrarium; or the patterns and relationships within properties: tastes, sounds, colors (Arnold, 1980). A related approach is to choose topics of interest and plan appropriate activities: air, animals, the body, color, ecology, food, machines, plants, water, weather, and so on (Taylor, 1993). It is also possible to organize the curriculum as adults do, grouping science study according to physics, chemistry, and biology experiences (Chaillé & Britain, 1997) or simply between the natural and physical sciences. Finally, an integrated approach (Schiller & Townsend, 1985) surveys the entire early childhood curriculum and environment and plugs in science activities and learning where they fit naturally. Any or all of these approaches can be used effectively, but this curriculum section and the following illustrative unit focus on the final two approaches. In this way, the integrity of each of the sciences remains clear while children's natural learning across the curriculum is given its due.

Physical Sciences

The physical sciences deal with inanimate matter or energy and include physics, chemistry, geology, meteorology, and astronomy. Many physical science topics are appropriate for young children, but it is always necessary to take into account the children's developmental levels. A lesson on air, for example, may be too advanced for younger students because the idea of unseen gases may be too abstract. Most experts agree that the study of electricity is more understandable if saved for the upper elementary grades, although simple experiments remain popular with many early childhood educators.

Whatever decisions you make about your physical science curriculum, be sure that you base them on close observation of the children you teach.

Physics deals with the properties, processes, changes, and interactions of matter and energy. Chaillé and Britain (1997) have found that moving objects by pushing, sliding, rolling, tilting, and throwing provides a comprehensible way for young children to learn about physical properties. They suggest four criteria that maximize children's experiences:

1. Children must be able to produce the movement by their own actions, allowing them to make the connection between what they do and how objects respond.

2. Children must be able to vary their actions; otherwise, they will be unable to affect the outcome of the activity significantly. For example, if children are rolling balls down an incline, be sure the incline can be adjusted, so that the children can experiment satisfactorily with different slopes.

3. The reaction of the object must be observable, or else children will make no cause-and-effect connection between their actions and the resulting reactions. For example, if children are rolling objects down a long tube, be sure the tube is made of clear plastic so that the objects in motion can be visible.

4. The reactions of the objects must be immediate so that children can make a cognitive connection between their actions and the results. This is especially important for preoperational children.

Many physics experiences are available throughout the day, simply by focusing children's attention on the physical properties of whatever activity they are engaged in. Other experiences require a plan for science learning accompanied by specialized materials. Some physics activities you might consider are:

• Point out that the playground swing is a pendulum and the slide an inclined plane. Have the class observe them in motion, then experiment with other pendulums and planes. Suggest that children vary the steepness of a wooden board while rolling toy cars down it. Have children determine if steepness alters the velocity of the cars. Attach identical heavy weights to strings of several lengths. Have the children experiment to see if the length of the string affects the length of the swing.

• Collect simple musical instruments from many cultures. Place them in a corner where children can experiment with them. Encourage children to use the instruments in different ways to achieve different types of sounds. Provide materials for homemade instruments, which can be compared for types of sounds: empty oatmeal boxes, other sturdy boxes, rubber bands, beans of various sizes for shaking instruments, and glasses filled with water at varying levels.

• As children learn about sounds, they can become aware that movement is necessary to make sounds. Have the class close their eyes while one child at a time makes a movement or does something with an object. Children then take turns trying to guess what object was moved to make noise.

- Have the class make paper airplanes of various sizes and shapes. Send several into the air at once, then try to determine why some fly farther and higher than others. Try to replicate the design of the most successful. Older children can measure distances, chart results, and revise designs to achieve the greatest success.

- Ask for donations of old appliances that children can pull apart and try to rebuild. Items with gears and levers are particularly prized.

Chemistry deals with the composition and properties of substances and the reactions that take place when substances are produced or changed into other substances. Since chemical changes often seem mysterious, children frequently believe that it is magic that makes them happen. An important goal for early chemistry experiences, then, is to help children grow beyond a magic orientation. Activities that relate to everyday experiences and materials are preferred over those that may be exciting and flashy but simply reinforce children's confusion. Some chemistry experiences and experiments, such as the following, encourage the transition to logical reasoning:

- Use rolls of toilet paper and basins of water, combining the two in various ways, then observing the results. Introduce the activity and then follow children's instructions as they try predicting what will happen when different combinations are tried. The paper and water can be placed at an activity center for free use. Some possible experiments: submerge clumps of paper made from large sections of the toilet paper; submerge single sheets; put an entire roll in the water, then squeeze; add food coloring to the water, and either observe its movement or stir in the dye and observe what happens to the paper (adapted from Chaillé & Britain, 1997).

- Have children experiment with various types of liquids and containers, observing that the liquids take the shape of the containers into which they are poured. Freeze some of the liquids, first having the class predict if they will take the shapes of their containers. Place the frozen shapes in containers of liquid, then watch them melt and take on the containers' shapes.

- Have children mix paints and observe changes that take place. Some paints may be thicker than others; some may have lumps in them; colors will change in different ways; and all take on the shapes of their containers.

- Make butter from whipping cream, using junior-size baby food jars. During group time, fill several jars about one third full of cream, handing them to individual children. Begin by asking children to predict what will happen when the cream is shaken. Each child shakes a jar 10 times as everyone counts, then the jars are passed to other children until everyone has had at least one turn to shake. As the cream changes form, have the children observe the differences and repredict what will happen. Eat the butter on crackers and compare its flavor to that of the commercial variety.

Biological Sciences

Biology, which includes botany and zoology, is concerned with the origin, history, physical characteristics, life processes, and habits of plants and animals. The effective early childhood setting contains both plants and animals that children interact with as a natural part of their day. These interactions are often less experimental than activities in other areas of science. In early childhood biology, the focus should be on observation of and participation with animals and plants. Your role becomes less facilitative of planned experimentation and more encouraging of a sense of wonder and appreciation of the natural world. Appropriate experiences include:

- Obtain one or two crickets from their habitat or from a fish bait shop. Place them in a jar with a ventilated cover. Add 1 to 2 inches of sand or soil and a dry leaf of crumpled paper towel. Keep the crickets for a few days only, providing a fresh bit of lettuce, apple, carrot, or celery every day. Children can observe and describe the crickets—body parts, number of legs, and so on. Discuss how a cricket moves and what it sounds like when it chirps. Demonstrate how a cricket acts as a natural thermometer. You can use it to figure out the current temperature by counting the number of chirps per 15 seconds and adding 40 (Fahrenheit) or by dividing the number of chirps in one minute by 7 and adding 4 (Celsius) (Kramer, 1989).

- Keep a gerbil, hamster, white mouse, guinea pig, or rabbit in the classroom. If you keep a rabbit, you may want to take it out of its cage from time to time. (Check first with all parents to be sure that no one is allergic to animal hair.) Have children observe the animal and describe its characteristics and behaviors. Older children can keep a record of behavior over the period of a day, and several days can be compared. Weigh the animal once a week on a balance or scale and record. A graph can be made to show any changes.

- Capture a spider in its habitat and put it in a large jar with a screened lid. On the bottom of the jar place about 2 inches of moist soil and add a stick or two for a perch and for web building. If you keep the spider more than a few days, provide it with a weekly meal such as a fly, cricket, or other spider. The meal should be alive and smaller than the spider. Have the class observe and describe the spider's parts, how it moves, and how it catches its prey. If the spider makes a web, observe its shape, how it is attached to the sticks, and how the spider interacts with it once it is built.

- Obtain one wide-mouthed glass jar for each child. For each jar, wet a paper towel and place it around the inside wall of the jar. Direct the children to wet several dried lima beans and place them between the towel and the wall of the jar. Fill in the empty space with soil. Children should keep the interior of the jar continually moist and observe daily changes as soon as the beans begin to sprout. They can keep a journal to record the beans' growth and measurements taken of their increasing height. Beans later can be transplanted to the class garden.

- Grow parsley or other herbs. (Parsley is usually the most reliable.) Cut clusters for the children to taste raw and to cook in various projects. Hang some clusters in a cool, dry, and relatively dust-free place. Have the children observe the change from green to greenish gray and from tender to crisp. Let them try the dried parsley and compare its taste and texture with fresh. As a class project, cook soup in two pots, one with fresh and one with dried parsley. Compare the two.

Because science is everywhere and at all times, because young children have a natural affinity for it, and because the most effective science program is one that is integrated into the total curriculum, it is important to incorporate it into children's learning throughout the school day. Some of the ideas already presented, such as those that involve painting or cooking, obviously have crossover value. Here are some other suggestions for integrating science into the curriculum.

- *In the block corner.* Children learn about gravity, simple machines, and inclined planes through their natural play. Posing appropriate questions ("I wonder what would happen if . . .") can lead to extended experimentation.

- *In the housekeeping corner.* Kitchen materials can include measuring cups and spoons, along with beans, flour, and rice. Focus your questions on classification (e.g., color, size, shape) and what would happen if the different items were mixed with water.

- *In the library corner.* Collect books that relate to current classroom science experiences, particularly those concerned with the plants and animals found in the classroom and the local geographical region.

- *As a part of social studies.* Expand on "What would happen if we . . ." science questions by asking similar questions concerning environmental change. Such questions can be starters for research or essays or simply topics for class discussion. *Examples*: "What would happen if all the cows became extinct?" "What would happen if the rain stopped falling?" "What would happen if all the water became polluted?"

- *As a part of movement.* Use movement experiences to observe and experiment with physics understandings. For example, throw different objects in the air and observe what happens to them. Discuss why they didn't continue flying away. Children can experiment throwing a ball or beanbag in different ways, using their bodies to fight gravity. Help the children notice how using more of their body and more movement creates more force (Gilbert, 1977).

These are just a few suggestions for incorporating science into other areas of the curriculum. You can find additional examples in the last section of this chapter.

Technology

John sits in front of the computer, a bit unsure of himself. He has turned the machine on, inserted a disc, and watched a menu appear on the screen. But now, there is a long list of choices from which to select. John mumbles to himself, "It's Winnie the Pooh *I want." He slowly moves the mouse through the list, then exclaims, "Oh!" and clicks on the right words. But now there are three subprograms to choose from. John looks thoughtful, then resolutely clicks his mouse on what turns out to be the right choice. Looking pleased, he begins singing off-key in accompaniment to the preschooler-oriented game in front of him. John is 3 years old. He is not yet literate.*

In this integrated activity, the class studied the body (science) before making the cut-outs (art) of fairy tale characters (literature). Soon, they will measure the body parts and compare them with other children's cut-outs (math).

Scenes such as this one have become increasingly common throughout technologically oriented societies worldwide. They have also become increasingly accepted by early childhood educators who once did whatever they could to keep this allegedly uncrete technology away from younger children in favor of a totally hands-on approach to learning. Karen Klein, a developer of software for young children (Krogh, 1994), recalled those times and a speech she made on the topic in the early 1980s:

> I still have a copy of that speech. It was all about the cautions, worries, and dangers of sitting little children in front of a computer: moving away from concrete, hands-on experiences; robbing kids of valuable time just as if they were in front of a TV; isolating kids from social interaction; decreased language development; and focus on a learning medium that would put girls at a disadvantage. (p. 249)

Then Klein observed what other researchers over the years were observing as well: that children increase in language development and problem-solving abilities if the computers are placed close to each other or if they share machines with one another; that children interact with characters on a screen in the same imaginative ways they

Earlier opposition to computer use for young children has been replaced by acceptance as software improves and the benefits to learning become more apparent.

do with dolls and blocks; that there are children who have trouble working with and putting hands-on materials together who have no difficulties with the computer versions, just as there are children who work best in reverse. Thus, over the years, Klein has been one of a growing number of software developers educated in the most current theories of early childhood development and education who apply their knowledge to the creation of developmentally appropriate commercial materials. Of course, if no one is around to turn on the machine, insert the disc, and choose from lengthy menus, then motivated 3-year-olds like John have to fend for themselves.

Douglas Clement (1999), a contributor to the Forum on Early Childhood Science, Mathematics, and Technology Education and a researcher in his own right, reviewing the research related to young children and computer-related technology concluded that:

- As adaptive hardware and software become increasingly available, even children with physical and emotional disabilities can use computers with ease.

- Computers do not isolate children but actually serve as catalysts for socializing.

- There is more spontaneous helping among children using computers than in other activities.

- Boys tend to take greater risks in reaching their goals, but girls are more concerned with accuracy, and computer experiences can be developed with consideration for this observation.

- Drill-and-practice software develops rote skills, but discovery-based software promotes conceptual skills.
- Open-ended projects lead to discoveries, but free explorations without any goals promote little learning;
- The greatest gains in intelligence, verbal skills, problem solving, conceptual skills, long-term memory, and manual dexterity are made by children who are provided with a combination of computer and noncomputer activities rather than just one or the other.

We would add that specific cognitive skills involved in the very earliest computer learning use cause and effect, if–then thinking, reading and discriminating icons, memorizing procedural sequences, and making and testing hypotheses. The interaction between young children and computers has emerged as an inevitability for our times. It is good to learn that contrary to what early education experts had predicted, the interaction can be a healthy one.

CURIOSITY: CRITICAL TO SCIENCE LEARNING AND BEYOND

Curiosity—eagerness to learn and know—is natural to young children, but it needs fostering. Enthusiastic and supportive adults who are themselves curious provide the most encouragement. Uninterested adults who squelch curiosity as creating too much mess, noise, or inconvenience contribute to the deadening of children's desire to learn.

Curiosity, while applicable to any area of learning, is most frequently tied to science, perhaps because it is essential to experimentation, observation of change, and the sense of wonder that underlie true science learning. George Raper and John Stringer (1987) said that early science learning

> is not merely teaching children a mass of scientific knowledge or content for its own sake, but it is concerned with stimulating the development of a curious and questioning attitude so that children can begin to understand more fully their natural and man-made environments; to begin to appreciate a variety of problems; and to develop a framework for their solution. (p. 1)

And, suggesting that those who work with youngsters have a special privilege and responsibility, Paul Chesler said:

> Many of the joys of working with children come straight out of their curiosity. A child's fascination with running water, whether it is a stream, the rain pouring down a spout, or the spray of a drinking fountain, should be a reminder to each of us that what we take for granted in our home or school is capable of supplying many hours of scientific investigation for a young child. (Tomich, 1996, p. 28)

Barbara Taylor (1993), writing about young children's science learning, said:

> Adults who interact with young children need to be constantly aware of ways to enliven the curiosity of children. It should be done with truth and excitement, based on the present environment, and with a positive attitude. This will help young children in their observation, invention, exploration, and discovery of the world and people around them. (p. 58)

Children who are curious about science tend to ask questions that begin with *why*. When children ask such questions, they are interested in reasons and explanations, and this attitude leads naturally to investigation. "This interest is similar to that demonstrated by any scientist, in that it leads to a cohesive body of knowledge. In other words, children think as scientists do—or scientists' thinking is much like that of young children—since both are interested in 'why' " (Raper & Stringer, 1987, p. 27).

Teachers can encourage *why* questions and other questions of scientific interest through an appropriate approach. Taylor (1993) reported research suggesting that children ask more questions when they are in smaller groups than when they are in larger groups; one-on-one relationships between adult and child foster even more questions; and children ask more questions when things are interesting and toys and materials are rotated. Teachers should also be aware that children express their curiosity in different ways. Some children touch, others verbalize, still others explore intensely, and some just examine objects quietly and independently.

Curious children always seem to have questions waiting to be asked, but teachers can promote curiosity in others by asking questions themselves. These questions should be phrased so that they lead to exploratory thinking. The key is to ask divergent rather than convergent questions. *Divergent questions* are those that are open-ended and lead to independent thinking; *convergent questions* seek a single or right answer. There are times, of course, when a convergent question is appropriate, because there really is a right answer, and it is important to know right now. For the purposes of fostering curiosity, however, divergent questions should be asked whenever possible. Some examples and comparisons are:

Convergent: Can you name the colors in these bottles of paint?

Divergent: What will happen if you mix some of these colors together?

Convergent: Can you divide these leaves into green and brown piles?

Divergent: What are some ways you can divide these leaves?

Convergent: How many legs does the spider have? How about the fly?

Divergent: What do you think might happen if we put the fly in the jar with the spider?

Children demonstrate curiosity when they ask questions and follow them up with exploration. Teachers foster curiosity when they ask open-ended questions and encourage children to follow through on their investigations. Although curiosity is basic to good science learning, it applies to all areas of the curriculum as well. When children wonder whether a new book will be good and try reading it to find out, when they wonder whether they really are taller than their friends and ask to be measured to be sure, or when they wonder what will happen if they place just one more block on an already tall tower, they have carried their curiosity across the curriculum.

The integrated science unit that completes this chapter makes use of children's curiosity, in this case about life in the sea. It is based on a unit that was created by a kindergarten teacher and taught over a period of about 2 months. Figure 4.1 demonstrates how the activities fit together across the curriculum.

A SCIENCE THEME: GETTING TO KNOW MARINE LIFE

In recent decades, the importance of the world's oceans as they pertain to the health of the planet as a whole has been the topic of much commentary in articles of opinion and research, conferences large and small, and entire books. Mari Lou, a kindergarten teacher, after reading widely on the topic, was struck by the importance of bringing this sense of urgency to children at an early age. Their generation, after all, would be the one that must take action before it is too late. Thus, she decided to provide her class with a knowledge of and appreciation for marine life. She spent weeks collecting books and other materials and creating activities appropriate for her 5- and 6-year-old children. Although she lives within driving distance of the Pacific Ocean and has had a longtime interest in reading about marine life, Mari Lou found it important to do some extra informational reading so that she would feel comfortable answering children's questions. Committed to an integrated approach to curriculum, Mari Lou planned the unit's activities so that they would include reading, writing, singing, and mathematics. When the unit was complete, it contained more than 50 activities, games, songs and fingerplays, and resource books. With Mari Lou's permission, a number of the activities have been adapted for this text.

Note how the activities relate to earlier suggestions from this chapter. For example, because this unit is essentially devoted to biology, there is a focus on observation and appreciation rather than on experimentation. The knowledge children gain from this unit is social (animal names and body parts), physical (much hands-on exploration), and logicomathematical (hypothesizing, decision making, and free explo-

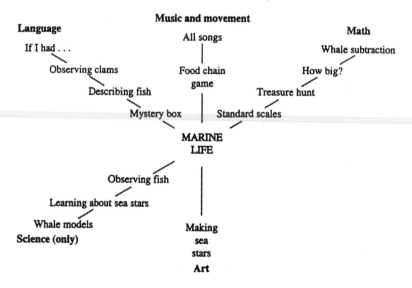

FIG. 4.1.   Curriculum web—marine life.

ration). Furthermore, children are given opportunities to observe and hypothesize or predict before they are given information. When experiences happen in this order, children's curiosity is fostered and enhanced.

SCIENCE ACTIVITIES ACROSS THE CURRICULUM

General Marine Life

1. **The Mystery Box.**   This is a good activity for starting the unit. In a fairly large box, hide a sea star (starfish), a whale model, and a small dish of sand. Children take turns asking the teacher questions that will lead them to identify each object. The questions must be phrased so that the teacher can answer yes or no. Once all three items are identified, the children try to determine what they have in common. Their place of origin can then be identified as the topic for upcoming study.

2. **Sand and Scales.**   Children work in pairs or groups of three. Each group has a tub of sand and a simple balance scale as well as an assortment of materials that will fit easily on the scale (scissors, a Lincoln Log, a Lego block, a beanbag, etc.). A tablespoon of sand is placed on one side of the balance. Each of the other items is weighed after the children predict if it will be heavier or lighter than the tablespoon of sand. Children record their findings on a chart with two columns headed *Heavier* and *Lighter*. To do this, they place each item on its correct side. If they choose, children can draw a picture of the item on its proper side so that the chart can be saved.

3. **Treasure Hunt.**   In the sand table, or in small tubs of sand, the teacher hides small, marine-related items (shells, rocks, etc.). The children hunt for the items, then classify them in groups of their choice. The teacher asks informal questions such as, "Which do you have the most of?" "The least?" "Can you group your objects any other way?"

4. **Food Chain Tag.**   For this activity you will need a large bag of popped popcorn, one plastic bag for each child, and approximately 13 lengths of green yarn, 8 lengths of black yarn, and 6 lengths of red yarn (all long enough to tie around children's waists)

   Tie a strand of yarn around each child's waist, identifying the green as plankton, black as clams, and red as crabs. Bags represent the animals' mouths. Children form a large circle and the teacher spreads popcorn inside it.

   The teacher gives a *go* signal, and the plankton start scooping popcorn into their plastic bag mouths. Each clam then tags any plankton that has food in its mouth. Tagged plankton must pour their popcorn into the clams' bags, then sit outside the circle while the clams continue feeding.

   Each crab may then tag any clam and take its popcorn. Tagged clams must sit outside the circle while the crabs continue feeding.

   The entire game takes just a few minutes, with mostly crabs left in the circle. Discuss the following questions with the children: Why are all the crabs left?

What would happen if there were no predators for the crabs? What happens to the clams if the plankton all die? Will this matter for the crabs?

Fish

5. **Observing Fish.**   Use three or four whole fish, preferably of different types. In small groups, children observe the fish by carefully touching and by using magnifying glasses. If a microscope is available, scales can be observed more closely. Children compare the fish with each other and hypothesize what different body parts are for.

   Before, during, and after this activity, children should have opportunities to observe the fish in a classroom aquarium. In combination with teacher questioning and children's hypotheses, some teacher explanation will identify the names and uses of the gills, fins, scales, and so on. One fish can then be dissected for further understanding of its body parts and their functions.

6. **Describing Fish.**   In small groups, or as a whole class, children brainstorm their descriptions of fish. This should be done after there have been plenty of opportunities for observation, as in activity 5. The descriptions can be dictated to the teacher who writes them on a chart, or children can choose their own favorites for their personal journals. Illustrations can follow.

Crustaceans

7. **Crab Observations.**   The children observe two crabs: one live and one cooked. The latter provides an opportunity for close investigation of its eight legs and two pincers as well as the mouth, eyes, and underside. The former provides a demonstration of the use of each. Observation and activities can be modeled after those in activities 5 and 6.

Sea Stars (Starfish)

8. **Learning About Sea Stars (commonly called starfish).**   This activity works best if you have access to the sea and can collect at least one or two samples of real sea stars, keeping them safe in a pail of seawater. Otherwise, use the books listed in the Resources section that follows this section, or others available to you, for pictures of various types as well as descriptions of how they live.

   Children observe the slow movements of the sea stars and gently touch them. They can count the legs on the live sea stars (a minimum of 5) and those in the pictures. They may be challenged to learn the names of several varieties: crown of thorns, web sea star, sunflower, blood sea star, brittle sea star.

9. **Making Sea Stars.**   Make models of favorite varieties of sea stars using baker's clay. Color can be added during the mixing.

   Recipe for baker's clay:

4 cups flour

1 cup salt

1½ cups water

Mix well and knead for about 5 minutes. After molding, bake at 350° for about 1 hour.

Mollusks

10. **Observing Clams.**   For this activity, you will need access to live clams. In a large, plastic dishpan, place about a dozen live clams in seawater. (You should have enough that children can observe in pairs.) Children touch and observe the clams, noting their feet and necks and the way they use them. Use magnifying glasses for a closer look.

    Later, give each child a drawing of a cross section of a clam (from the books in the Resources section or other available sources). Identify the clam's parts and label each one. Children may want to color or paint the clams to match the real ones they have observed.

11. **If I Had.**   Read the class informational material on the octopus, found in the books listed in the Resources section, or from a book such as *My Pet Fish* by Coleman (1998). Children then dictate sentences or stories to finish the starter, "If I had gills like a fish, I'd. . . ." Children can illustrate their answers.

Sea Mammals

12. **How Big?**   Cut several 30-foot pieces of sturdy tape or yarn. Thirty feet is the approximate length of an Orca (killer) whale, and children can use this as a basic measurement for comparison with other whales and familiar objects. Outdoors, lay the tape on the ground and measure how many children, lying down end to end, equal one Orca whale. Place two tapes together, lengthwise, to equal a sperm whale and count children again. Lay three tapes together to equal the largest marine mammal, the blue whale, and again count children.

    Compare whale sizes with objects around the school, such as buses, classroom wall, and playground equipment.

13. **Whale Models.**   Whale models can be purchased through school equipment catalogs and at educational supply stores. Models can be used to:

    • Learn the names and characteristics of the different species.
    • Learn how each kind eats and lives.
    • Classify according to baleen or toothed.
    • Order according to size.
    • Refer to for drawing or clay modeling.

14. **Whale Subtraction.**   For this activity you will need a collection of goldfish crackers and a small piece of blue paper for each child. On each paper place a given number of crackers, perhaps five or six. Recite the following poem:

> Out in the middle of the deep, blue sea
>
> Five (or six) little fish swam merrily.
>
> Along comes a whale as hungry as can be.
>
> . . . Gulp!

The children eat one fish, then tell how many they have left. The poem is repeated until all fish are gone. This game can be repeated with different numbers of fish, subtracting more than one at a time. Children should also remember which kinds of whales have teeth and eat fish.

15. **Songs.**   When Mari Lou taught this unit, she made use of traditional tunes such as "There's a Hole in the Bottom of the Sea." In addition, she created some of her own songs to familiar melodies. One purpose in writing them was to reinforce the children's learning, such as the fact that crabs have *pincers*, not pinchers. Any of these songs can be altered to meet the needs of a particular class. Also, children should be encouraged to create their own songs.

> Three Silver Fish
> (sung to "Three Blind Mice")
> Three silver fish, three silver fish
> See how they swim, see how they swim
> Their fins go left, their fins go right
> Their gills breathe in, their gills breathe out
> Did you ever see such a beautiful sight
> As three silver fish?

> Crabs Are Walking
> (sung to "Frere Jacques")
> Crabs are walking, crabs are walking
> On the rocks, on the rocks
> Watch out for their pincers
> Watch out for their pincers
> Pinch, pinch, pinch
> Pinch, pinch, pinch

> Do You Know?
> (sung to "Do You Know the Muffin Man?")
> Do you know the largest mammal
> Largest mammal, largest mammal?

Do you know the largest mammal
That swims in the salty sea?

Yes, it is the huge blue whale,
Huge blue whale, huge blue whale
Yes, it is the huge blue whale
That swims in the salty sea.

It's as big as three school buses
Three school buses, three school buses.
It's as big as three school buses
And swims in the salty sea.

Do It!
(sung to "If You're Happy and You Know It"; this song is a good choice for
extended ideas from the children)

If you're a clam and you know it
Stick out your neck
If you're a clam and you know it
Stick out your neck.
If you're a clam and you know it,
Then your neck will surely show it.
If you're a clam and you know it
Stick out your neck.

If you're a crab and you know it
Pinch your pincers.
If you're a crab and you know it
Pinch your pincers.
If you're a crab and you know it,
Then your pincers will surely show it.
If you're a crab and you know it,
Pinch your pincers.

If you're a shark and you know it
Show your teeth.
If you're a shark and you know it
Show your teeth.
If you're a shark and you know it
Then your teeth will surely show it.
If you're a shark and you know it
Show your teeth.

Resources for Teaching Science

The following examples of books and kits offer information and ideas for teaching
about sea life.

1. *If You Were a Fish*, by S. J. Calder. New York: Silver Press, 1989.
2. *Investigating Science—Sea Life*, by Barbara Laver. Huntington Beach, CA: 1987.
3. *Manatees*, by F. Staub. Minneapolis: Lerner Publications, 1998.
4. *My Pet Fish*, by L. Coleman. Minneapolis: Lerner Publications, 1998.
5. *Seal Surfer*, by M. Foreman. San Diego: Harcourt Brace, 1996.
6. *Super Seashells and Other Sea Life*. This kit provides shells and activity and information cards. Dominguez Hills, CA: Educational Insights.

EXTENDING YOUR LEARNING

1. Choose a field of science you would like to know more about. Ask a children's librarian to show you all the books available on the topic. Read them, and consider ways you could share them with young children. If there are experiments, try them yourself. Expand your knowledge by checking out books from the adult section. When you feel comfortable with your knowledge and your ability to engage in the experiments, try some of them with children. When done, analyze the experience. Were the experiments too easy? Too hard? Did they encourage independent thinking? Were you able to ask questions that fostered thinking?

2. Choose something in your natural environment about which you are curious. Ask questions about it that will lead you to learn something new. Research the answers to your questions.

3. Try adapting the Marine Life unit to suit your own teaching needs. You can make use of the activities and their principles while changing some specifics. Some suggestions and ideas to think about:

   - You'll need to alter reading and writing activities depending on the age and skill level of students.
   - You can substitute different animals for study, perhaps comparing animals from different bodies of water.
   - Be sure to allow room for firsthand exploration. This is especially important to keep in mind if it is necessary to substitute pictures for some of the real objects.
   - Don't hesitate to teach biological terms, including names of body parts, even to very young children.

4. Wherever you are working or caring for young children, take time out to note what they are curious about. Make a list of absolutely everything. Do you see trends that could lead to further investigation? Follow their interests and create a miniunit. It might be a hypothetical one or one on which you actually follow through.

5. Enroll in a science course that will fill in gaps in your knowledge. It could be sponsored by a college or university, last an entire term, and require major effort, if you have the time. Otherwise, look for a short course, workshop, or field trip sponsored by an environmental organization, a district education office, or the like.

6. Go back to the science activities at the end of the chapter. Choose one and write a lesson plan using the outline in chapter 1. Be specific about your learning objectives.

7. Use national, state, or district science standards for a specific grade level to generate objectives for science lessons and activities. Design procedures for assessing what children know before you begin teaching and for evaluating learning at the end.

VOCABULARY

Animism.   The belief that inanimate objects make decisions.

Artificialism.   The belief that everything that exists has been built by humans, or by God in a human fashion.

Classification.   The grouping of objects or ideas according to their possession of like characteristics.

Convergent Questions.   Questions that lead toward a single correct answer.

Divergent Questions.   Questions that are open-ended, with no single correct answer.

Play-Debrief-Replay.   A structured method of learning through play in which children explore a topic freely, then reflect on what they have learned, and finally learn through additional play based on their increased understanding and knowledge.

Prediction.   To say or estimate in advance of factual proof, what one believes to be fact.

INTERNET RESOURCES

Web sites provide much useful information for educators and we list some here that pertain to the topics covered in this chapter. The addresses of Web sites can also change, however, and new ones are continually added. Thus, this list should be considered as a first step in your acquisition of a larger and ever-changing collection.

Eisenhower National Clearinghouse for Science and Mathematics Education
   www.enc.org/classroom/index.htm

ERIC CSMEE (Clearinghouse for Science, Mathematics, and Environmental Education)
www.ericse.org

National Science Education Standards
www.nap.edu/readingroom/books/nses/html

References

Arnold, L. (1980). *Preparing young children for science*. New York: Schocken.

Carter, D. (1990). Forward. In S. Loucks-Horsley, R. Kapitan, M. Carlson, P. Kuerbis, R. Clark, G. Nelle, T. Sachse, & E. Walton (Eds.), *Elementary school science for the '90s*. Alexandria, VA: Association for Supervision and Curriculum Development.

Chaillé, C., & Britain, L. (1991). *The young child as scientist*. New York: HarperCollins.

Chaille, C., & Britain, L. (1997). *The young child as scientist: A constructivist approach to early childhood science education* (2nd ed.). New York: Longman.

Clement, D. (Ed.). (1999). Young children and technology. In *Dialogue on early childhood science, mathematics, and technology education*. Washington, DC: American Association for the Advancement of Science.

Gilbert, A. (1977). *Teaching the three r's through movement experiences*. Minneapolis: Burgess Publishing.

Goldhaber, J. (1994). If we call it science, *then* can we let the children play? *Childhood Education, 71*(1), 24–27.

Good, R. (1977). *How children learn science*. New York: Macmillan.

Guha, S., & Doran, R. (1999). Playful activities for young children. *Science and Children, 37*(2), 36–40.

Johnson, J. (1999). The forum on early childhood science, mathematics, and technology education. In D. Clement (Ed.), *Dialogue on early childhood science, mathematics, and technology education*. Washington, DC: American Association for the Advancement of Science.

Kramer, D. (1989). *Animals in the classroom*. Menlo Park, CA: Addison-Wesley.

Krogh, S. (1994). *Educating young children: Infancy to grade three*. New York: McGraw-Hill.

Lind, K. (1999). Science in early childhood: Developing and acquiring fundamental concepts and skills. In D. Clement (Ed.), *Dialogue on early childhood science, mathematics, and technology education*. Washington, DC: American Association for the Advancement of Science.

Loucks-Horsley, S., Kapitan, R., Carlson, M., Kuerbis, P., Clark, R., Nelle, G., Sachse, T., & Walton, E. (1990). *Elementary school science for the '90s*. Alexandria, VA: Association for Supervision and Curriculum Development.

Manganus, V., Rottkamp, K., & Koch, J. (1999). Science is about not knowing, but trying to find out. *Science and Children, 36*(5), 38–40.

Nelson, G. (1999). Preface. In D. Clement (Ed.), *Dialogue on early childhood science, mathematics, and technology education*. Washington, DC: American Association for the Advancement of Science.

Piaget, J. (1965). *The moral judgment of the child*. New York: Free Press. (Original work published 1932)

Raper, G., & Stringer, J. (1987). *Encouraging primary science*. London: Cassell.

Schiller, P., & Townsend, J. (1985). Science all day long: An integrated approach. *Science and Children, 23*(2), 34–36.

Smith, R. (1981). Early childhood science education. A Piagetian perspective. *Young Children, 36*(2), 3–11.

Sterling, H. (1999). Teaching with Dewey on my shoulder. *Science and Children, 37*(3), 22–25.

Taylor, B. (1993). *Science everywhere: Opportunities for very young children*. Orlando, FL: Harcourt Brace Jovanovich.

Taylor, B. (1999). *A child goes forth: A curriculum guide for preschool children* (9th ed.). Upper Saddle River, NJ: Merrill.

Tomich, K. (1996). Hundreds of ladybugs, thousands of ladybugs, millions and billions and trillions of ladybugs—and a couple of roaches. *Young Children, 51*(4), 28–30.

Wasserman, S. (1988). Teaching strategies. Play-debrief-play: An instructional method for science. *Childhood Education, 64*(4), 230–231.

Wishon, P., Crabtree, K., & Jones, M. (1998). *Curriculum for the primary years: An integrative approach*. Upper Saddle River, NJ: Merrill.

5

SOCIAL STUDIES: LEARNING
TO LIVE TOGETHER

*Men don't know how to live together as men because they have not learned
to live together as children.*

Sylvia Ashton-Warner (1908–1984)

▼ *Chapter Objectives*

When you finish reading this chapter, you should be able to:

- ▼ Plan social studies activities in relation to children's physical, social and moral, and cognitive development.
- ▼ Plan social studies activities taking into account the needs of individual children.
- ▼ Plan a social studies theme unit that integrates other curriculum areas.

As you think about and apply chapter content on your own, you should be able to:

- ▼ Observe and analyze your own behavior and attitudes toward children to encourage a more democratic experience.
- ▼ Consider and practice conflict resolution approaches that will work well with children and with your teaching peers.

T he social sciences include a wide array of disciplines: history, geography, economics, anthropology, social psychology, political science, and civics—all of them concerned with the structure of societies and the ways in which humans live together. When the social sciences are presented to elementary and high school students, they typically are referred to as the social studies, and topics such as current events and values education may be added.

Choosing the correct terminology for learning about society at the early childhood level is problematic. Toddlers have only a foggy understanding that their daily interactions constitute a social situation; preschoolers are just beginning to learn that relationships may go better with rules and courteous behavior; for kindergartners, a primary concept to learn in their first year of school is that their classroom constitutes a minisociety. Thus, for the earliest years, neither *social sciences* nor *social studies* is an appropriate term, for children are actually living what they learn, not studying it. In elementary school, primary grade children may be taught that they are learning social studies. However, the most effective methodology for teaching this curriculum has turned out to be letting young children discover, invent, and research on their own. In other words, they learn best by being social scientists, not social studiers. Nevertheless, longstanding tradition dictates the use of *social studies* as the appropriate term for all grades through high school. So, we encourage and admire the ability of young children to live their social learning and to research and learn in ways that approach adult scientific methodology, but we bow to tradition in our discussion here. Social studies it is.

The focus for any one of the social studies is, as we have said, the ways in which human beings relate to each other. World history is full of evidence that humans frequently do a bad job of relating to one another. Indeed, history books frequently have been organized according to the buildup and resolution of wars. Current world history is no exception; as peace breaks out in one section of the world, conflict emerges in another.

Perhaps it is too idealistic to hope that helping young children relate well to one another can change the world. On the other hand, it is known that there is a clear connection between children's social successes and failures and their behaviors as adults. Children in the infant room, preschool, and primary grades are learning social behaviors and attitudes that will carry them through many years to come. It may be argued, then, that the most critical social studies learning for young children pertains to human relationships. This is not simply a matter of imposing discipline or managing your classroom effectively so that children get along well with each other. It is making the social studies real and vital to the life of the classroom. Avoidance of war can be taught from a very early age, first in relationships, then at the local level, then with comparisons to events in the wider world.

The vignette that provides the theme for this chapter is a very personal one. Here, one of your authors shares with you her yearlong struggle to create a kindergarten environment based on democratic values and peaceful conflict resolution.

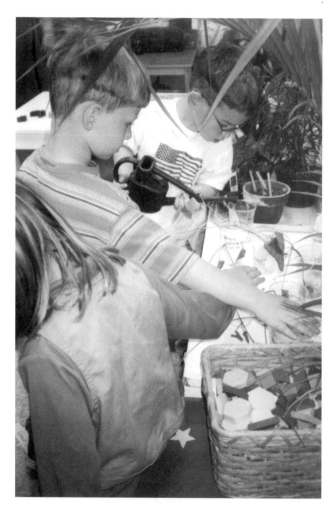

Classroom activities that require cooperation provide informal opportunities for learning to live together successfully.

SUZANNE'S HANDS-ON SOCIAL STUDIES IN THE KINDERGARTEN

The year did not begin well, which was somewhat of a surprise to me. The previous June I had sent 23 children off to first grade thinking that, at last, I had discovered the secrets of superlative teaching and managing. Now, September had arrived and 25 unmanageable, cranky, impudent, and combative children informed me daily that the coming year would be no picnic and that the previous one had succeeded because the children, not I, had been outstanding.

Most of the conflict situations occurred during free play, either within the classroom or outside, although teacher-led group discussions could be treacherous, too. Something had to be done.

Just before the winter holidays I pored over the children's records and files and discovered that 13 of the children were younger siblings. As I thought about the children's behavior, this seemingly trivial detail began to make sense. For half the class, accustomed as they were to struggles with older brothers and sisters, it seemed necessary to fight their way into everything they did. And once successful, they became defensive, whining, and accusatory. They didn't know yet that in their classroom they could be cooperative and generous and still come out ahead.

In deciding how to deal with the problem, I concluded that I would continue my usual role as a facilitating guide but that my facilitation would take a different direction. Over the next few months I tried several ideas with varying degrees of success.

Because it was impossible to hold large-group discussions, I divided the class into two or three smaller groups and then dropped in on them as seemed necessary. The small-group meetings were kept to no more than 10 minutes, although they had sometimes run 30 to 45 minutes the previous year. Even with smaller groups and shorter time spans, however, discussions often provoked fights. Nevertheless, we gradually learned to discuss the pros and cons of controversial issues, to vote, and to live relatively graciously with the will of the majority. This was a hands-on lesson in civics and political science that wasn't entirely successful because, at the end of the year, it was still necessary to meet in small groups in order to keep harmony.

Another effort might be termed hands-on sociology. Despite my best efforts at mixing and matching, free play always found the girls in the housekeeping corner and the boys with the blocks. This situation provided an appropriate opportunity to help the children think through why they made the choices they did. One morning, I gathered my courage, put everyone in a single large group, and asked why they played where they did. The boys said they didn't have much interest in the doll corner but didn't know why. The girls declared that they would really like to play with blocks but that the boys wouldn't let them. The boys maintained total innocence and made a great show of inviting the girls in, but, as it turned out, their playing styles were just too different. The boys wanted to construct intricate buildings, whereas the girls preferred to slap a few blocks together and bring in the dolls. The class was called together in a large group once again, solutions were discussed, and a vote was taken. For the next few weeks there were "girl days" and "boy days," with the opposite sex not allowed within 10 feet (necessary to avoid verbal squabbles) of the block corner. After a while, the girls lost interest and went back to the doll corner permanently. Although this wasn't what I had hoped for, there at least had been a period of time when the children considered a social situation, discussed it, and made group decisions.

During the year, I devised a variety of social studies activities in an effort to make the class more cooperative. When we played store with real money (a study of economics), the children were forced to cooperate, because every store was required to have two clerks and two customers buying together. When we mapped the inside of the building (geography), the children learned to cooperate, because the project was done in small groups. When we posted pictures of our parents as children (history), the children were paired, and each of them had to talk about their partner's family rather than their own.

Although that school year was the most difficult one in my memory, progress was certainly made. It was a year when everything we did related in some way to the social studies, in which the primary focus was on conflict resolution.

Each year that you teach will be different, because the children you teach will be different. Because their collective and individual needs will vary from year to year, your approach to social studies teaching must be flexible. One year you might choose, as Suzanne did, to focus on cooperation in virtually every social studies activity, whereas this might be unnecessary with another class. Whatever direction your decision making takes, it will be more successful if it reflects a sound understanding of the way children develop and learn.

PERSPECTIVES ON HISTORY AND THEORY

Comenius, whose writings helped to take education out of the Middle Ages and into the Renaissance, provided the foundation for modern-day social studies, even though that term was not used in his time. However, his contention that children first learn about time and space as these concepts relate to their own lives has as much importance now for the study of history and geography as it did then. Thus, young children learn about their own experience (yesterday, last week, and today) before exploring the rest of the world. Likewise, they begin by mapping their desk, their room, and their school before they create maps of larger spaces.

Basing social studies on students' real-life experiences was again put forward at the beginning of this century by Maria Montessori and John Dewey. Montessori believed that children as young as age 3 should be permitted the freedom to create their own little "societies in embryo." The last years of her life were spent in exile in order to avoid the fascist control of her schools by the dictator Mussolini. It became her belief that if children were trusted with self-government from a very early age and if they were given guidance in the creation of a democratic society, they would be less likely as adults to accept the philosophies and control of a Mussolini or a Hitler.

Dewey's laboratory school at the University of Chicago was a living experiment in the social studies. He believed that children couldn't be taught *about* democratic processes; they had to experience them firsthand.

As a teacher, you will find that it takes both courage and experience to provide children with the right balance of independence and adult guidance needed to create a democratic atmosphere. If Dewey was right, however, the long-term results may be well worth the effort.

Dewey's philosophy of education was enormously influential in the early years of this century. In both social studies and other areas of the curriculum, he emphasized educating to the needs and interests of the child rather than to artificially created "disciplines." In 1916, he recommended integrating the various social sciences into a single field, social studies (Seefeldt, 1997). The purpose was to create in the elementary school an activity-oriented curriculum in which relevant concepts from all the social sciences could be used simultaneously to explore something of inherent interest to the children.

In the following years, Dewey's philosophy influenced developers of early childhood and elementary social studies programs. In the 1930s, Lucy Sprague Mitchell created the "Here and Now" curriculum as a movement away from dry, rote memorization of academic knowledge and toward learning based on children's firsthand experiences, interests, and needs. "Anything that was given to children that was secondhand, before children had an opportunity to experience it for themselves, was considered dangerous to Lucy Sprague Mitchell" (Seefeldt, 1997, p. 3). She, too, argued for a social studies program that began with the home and extended outward, making specific suggestions for each grade:

Kindergarten: Home and Neighborhood

1st Grade: Community and Its Helpers

2nd Grade: United States

3rd Grade: People in Other Lands

A similar expanding-communities approach was proposed by Paul Hanna during the same era. Its underlying philosophy was that "we live in a series of communities, each of which is contained in larger communities" (Schuncke, 1988, p. 28). Hanna's suggested topics were:

Kindergarten: The Child

1st Grade: Family and School Communities

2nd Grade: Neighborhood Community

3rd Grade: The Child's Communities: City, Metropolis, Country

Despite these promising moves away from rote learning, subsequent decades of social studies learning took a negative turn. The Dewey–Mitchell-Hanna approach was often interpreted as nondirective learning through which children, left to their own devices, would *only* learn about what was near and dear to them. As might be expected, not much learning took place. The eventual backlash from this misapplication of Dewey's theories threatened to return children to learning singular social sciences through dull, lifeless memorization of facts. Today, we realize that children need directed learning along with freedom to explore and that they need information about faraway places as well as those nearby. Much of this new understanding can be attributed to the work of Jean Piaget and Jerome Bruner. Bruner, taking his cue from Piaget's views of development, said that social studies instruction for children should include

- A match between new knowledge and prior knowledge.
- Activities designed to explore social studies data.
- Activities designed to use information, not just memorize it. (Maxim, 1987)

To summarize what we have learned from a long history of teaching social studies, young children are most attracted to learning that reflects their own lives. Such learning is most meaningful to them and provides a natural starting place that can be used to expand their learning outward. Teaching techniques should be activity oriented and should avoid rote learning that is meaningless in terms of the child's own experience.

PERSPECTIVES ON DEVELOPMENT

As one might expect, the social studies offer numerous avenues to fostering children's social growth. A good number of cognitive and emotional skills are involved as well. As you certainly recognize by this point, youngsters of varying ages, backgrounds, and temperaments learn and understand at differing levels and through different methods. The following explanations of development related to social studies learning can offer useful guidelines for making curricular choices. Keep in mind the concept of the zone of proximal development, that the choices you make should move children from what they already know to the new knowledge and attitudes they are just ready to grasp.

Cognitive Development

Space and time concepts are elements of cognitive development that are integral to the social studies. Each should be taken into account when planning the content of your lessons and appropriate teaching methods.

Geography, for example, is a social science that requires mapping skills, which, in turn, are based on well-developed concepts of space. Children do not develop these skills and their underlying concepts until the upper elementary years or beyond. Consequently, adult-style mapmaking is inappropriate in the early childhood years. Children first must be able to orient themselves in space, a process that begins at birth and that teachers can nurture through appropriate activities. For example, a geography curriculum designed to help children orient themselves in space can be based on movement exploration (Seefeldt, 1997). Elements of this program can include:

- *Body awareness.* Its shape in space, how it moves and rests.
- *Force and time.* "Limp, energetic, light, fluid, staccato, slow, or quick."
- *Space.* Where the body is in relationship to the environment; its path through space; high, middle, low positions.
- *Locomotion.* Moving through space at different levels.
- *Weight.* Managing body weight in motion and in relationship to others.
- *Isolations.* Managing various movements of individual body parts.
- *Repetitions.* Getting to know a movement better by repeating it. (p. 218)

These elements may not directly relate to the adult definition of geography, but they do provide children with a better orientation to space, which is a prerequisite for adult geography.

Although research has not yet shown us any developmental sequence for interpreting and making maps, children as young as 3 years old have demonstrated that they understand what one is. Keeping in mind children's need to play and experiment in a hands-on way, we suggest that 3- and 4-year-olds can learn related concepts with games such as Candy Land or Chutes and Ladders; 5-year-olds can follow basic line maps while on a walking field trip and make their own classroom maps; and primary children can begin working with adult-style maps and globes (Seefeldt, 1997).

Concepts of time are closely related to the study of history. Although toddlers begin to develop a sense of time, particularly as it relates to their own daily schedules, they are notorious for their reticence in learning the concept *later*. Children are about 5 years old before they begin to develop an adult sense of time. The sequence of learning for most children seems to be the concept of day, followed by week, month, and year, and finally short time periods such as minutes and hours. Not until they are about age 7 can they tell time in the conventional sense or be sure what a year is. It is usually at about age 8 that children can look at the future apart from their everyday lives (Bauer, 1979). Reflecting on these steps in development, one can see why the formal study of history doesn't usually begin until the fourth grade, although

As children learn about yesterday, today, and tomorrow they begin to understand time and history.

even preschoolers can learn to appreciate their own histories. The following suggestions provide children with a better understanding of the passage of time and prepare them for the later study of history.

- Use daily routines to help orient children to the repeated passage of time. For the youngest children, this means helping them understand that outdoor play comes after naptime and that parents come back following their nap. Teachers can help older children recall that different activities occur on designated days of the week and help write up complex weekly schedules for all to remember.
- For children who cannot yet tell time, position play clocks or old, unused clocks next to the room's real one. These can be set to the times when specific events occur. Children should also be given opportunity to play freely with the clocks; you can informally help them compare times with the real clock or learn what the various configurations are called.

- Adopt a nearby tree that changes with the seasons. Draw pictures of its different cycles and keep them in an album or attach them to the appropriate months on the class calendar.

- Study the children's own histories, collecting pictures of them from infancy to the present.

- Use pictures to depict the sequence of daily events, to give a sense of time sequence—before and after, first and last—without requiring the ability to tell time.

Social and Affective Development

The 20th century gave us three quite different theoretical ways to understand social and emotional development in the early years, each of which offers valuable insights into social studies learning. These are discussed here in the following order: a psychological view in the Freudian tradition, a social learning approach that rejects stage development in favor of environmental influences, and a constructivist theory that gives children's own efforts more credence than do other views.

In Erik Erikson's (1963) psychoanalytic theory of development, there are three stages at which you can expect to observe early social studies learning: stage 2, autonomy versus shame and doubt; stage 3, initiative versus guilt; and stage 4, industry versus inferiority. For children at stage 2 struggling between autonomy and shame and doubt, the time is right to set the stage for social studies learning. You can encourage the kinds of autonomous decision making that will be needed later when studying democracy. Helping children develop a sense of themselves as self-directed actors provides a foundation for later discussions about their social identity. Informal interventions produce seemingly casual questions such as, "Which do you think you'd like to do now, play with Legos or try a new puzzle?"

Initiative, attack, and conquest, all elements of stage 3, suggest that it is now appropriate for teachers to introduce short-term projects. Social studies themes now make sense, particularly if they match children's interests. A 4½-year-old once asked his teacher, "When are we going to do fire engines in here?" an idea that hadn't yet crossed her mind. Because the rest of the class responded to his idea with a hearty, "Yeah, when?!" they soon embarked on a study of firefighters and their equipment.

Elementary age children, well rooted in the worker–producer role of stage 4, are ready for thematic units that can be as long and involved as their interests permit. One second-grade class began a simple query into the history of their classroom (the building had once been a very large house) and ended up spending 6 months on an extended project complete with reports to the PTA. Possible feelings of inferiority, the negative aspect of this stage, can be headed off by providing encouragement rather than being negative or judgmental.

The social learning view of child development, which argues against stages, is most closely associated with Albert Bandura (1963, 1969). Bandura and his followers argued that Erikson's trust, mistrust, autonomy, shame, doubt, and so on are slippery for the adult observer to define. Teachers and counselors might observe the same child's behavior and assign different psychological explanations to it depending on their own philosophy or educational background. Furthermore, Bandura argued that children don't all go through universally predictable stages; there is too much influence from such variables as family, biology, and culture. Thus, if teachers want children to learn about such concepts as democracy, conflict resolution, and justice, they must themselves behave democratically toward others, resolve conflicts peacefully, and treat others, particularly their own classes, in ways that are just.

Young children are often unaware of such modeling unless the adults around them explicitly discuss it. For example, two teachers who team-taught in a class of 4- and 5-year-olds once staged an argument to show the children how friendly resolutions can come about. At the end, one of the teachers turned to some nearby children and said, "I'm so glad that Ms. Early and I can disagree and still be friends." Ms. Early then said, "The best part is that we didn't have to hurt each other." The children seemed stunned that teachers might actually argue but relieved that it ended so well. The teachers were rewarded in coming days when they heard their actual words repeated in doll corner arguments.

The third theory of social development is most closely associated with Jean Piaget's theory of cognitive development. His early observations of children led him to conclude that cognitive and social and moral development are actually intertwined. That is, children's cognitive development can proceed without equal social and moral development, but social and moral development is impossible without sufficient cognitive development to help them reason about their actions. Although Piaget observed children develop through stages, he did not think they were influenced by inner conflicts as did Erikson but rather by interactions with the environment. Before beginning elementary school, children progress through a *heteronomous* or authority oriented *stage*. Once in the primary grades, they begin a transition toward more autonomy in their thinking.

To a great extent, Piaget's research was based on his observation of children's evolving understanding of rules and justice. Rules, of course, are related to laws, an important element in our society and thus an important part of social studies learning. In the earliest heteronomous stage, children relate to rules as the rules relate to their self-interest. Furthermore, children frequently obey simply because the adults are bigger or have more power, not understanding the knowledge and responsibility that go with these attributes. At this stage, you can have children help create some of the classroom rules, focusing on the idea that rules are important for their own benefit, for their safety, and for the good of their very own class.

Primary grade children in the transitional stage are fascinated, even obsessed, by rules. Because they often believe that rules are unchangeable and made only by higher authorities, it is even more important at this stage to have children join in their creation. By second and third grade, children can learn both that rules may at times be unjust and that children themselves can participate in changing them.

It is usually during the early elementary years that children begin to recognize the needs of others, to take first steps at putting themselves in others' shoes. It is surprising to many adults when a primary child takes the initiative in starting a class- or schoolwide drive to assist an underprivileged group that is currently in the news. Yet this is the stage when children are first discovering such needs and can relate to them. Their new interest can spur them on to action, particularly if teachers and parents are supportive. It is also important to help young children understand, however, that sending one bundle of food or clothing will not cure all the suffering. Many young children become confused and disillusioned when the media continue to focus on a problem that they have worked to cure.

It is interesting to point out here that since the 1970s, some women researchers and moral philosophers led by Carol Gilligan (1982) have challenged both Erikson's and Piaget's theories of social development, pointing out that their research reflected a view that was totally male, equating boys' development with human development. Piaget's concept of justice, Gilligan said, underlies male ideas of morality; the concept of caring is the basis for female morality. This is one argument that caregivers and teachers of young children can easily deal with. Both justice and caring should be emphasized as youngsters learn about their social world. The unit on conflict resolution that concludes this chapter focuses on both.

DIVERSITY AMONG CHILDREN

The social studies provide a natural opportunity for creating curriculum that takes into account the diversity found in your classroom and community. As you plan for this teaching, another opportunity presents itself to examine your own understanding of social studies issues. For example, learning about other cultures is an important part of social studies curriculum; so is learning about democracy. Combine these two, and you may discover discrepancies in your views when compared with others'. The students at one university were working hard at understanding one another's cultures as they interacted in various organizations. At times, however, their taken-for-granted perceptions hindered their understanding of one another. On one occasion, two student organizations working together needed to make a major decision and, to the students in one of the groups, the democratic process was taking longer than they thought it should. The impatient students were from an all-White organization, and they were heard by a teacher complaining about the others, all Native Americans. "Why can't they get their act together?" one student said. "We know we can't make a perfect decision and get everybody to agree, but we have to decide *something*." This comment was followed by increasingly derogatory remarks about people from the other culture and their inability to make decisions or get anything done. Two days later, the Native Americans returned from discussing the issues among themselves and announced that they had come to a unified position. They were in total agreement with one another, but they had found it necessary to modify some of the original expectations of the two-group project. The White students were a bit taken aback. They were surprised not only by the other students' total unity but by the positive nature of the modifications.

The misunderstandings between the groups arose from their different views of the democratic process. For the students in the all-White organization, the rule of the majority was an underlying value of democracy. The idea that everyone in the group should agree was outside their expectations. The students in the Native American organization superimposed their traditional value of gaining consensus on group issues onto their understanding of the democratic process. Although the first group's method may have achieved a quicker decision, the second's was more thorough and ultimately more satisfying to everyone.

As you contemplate teaching your children about different cultures and about the values of democracy, it will be important for you to keep in mind your own definitions and perceptions. Then you must take the time to question those definitions and perceptions to be sure they are shared with your children and their families. Otherwise, you may find yourself in a difficult situation such as the university students faced.

Curriculum Considerations for Children with Special Needs

The social studies provide a perfect context for addressing issues of diversity in the classroom, with an emphasis on how children interact among themselves. Cultural diversity has been addressed earlier in the chapter; here we address children with identified developmental disabilities and delays. Issues of fairness and caring are paramount when discussing issues of inclusion for all children in classroom decision making. The children themselves are often the best sources of solutions to difficult questions that teachers in inclusive classrooms face daily. "How can we change the library corner so that Arliss, who uses a wheelchair, can fit in there?" "What should we do if Jeremiah can't use the playground equipment?" "What should we do when Jenny screams and hits?" "Do we all have to wait if Ben is going to be so slow?" Take note that the children who are the subject of the previous questions are not always those with identified disabilities.

Facing challenging issues together with a group of peers builds a sense of belonging and competence for children that can't be reproduced in any other setting. Children with and without disabilities develop and act on values in such settings, and feel empowered to participate in decisions about themselves and their peers.

Sensory Impairments

Children who can't see or hear well need additional sensory input to access the social studies curriculum. This might mean using modified materials, for example, topographical maps for those who are blind, or adapting instruction, such as letting children who can't hear well handle musical instruments for longer than most children. Social interactions throughout the school environment are enhanced when adults or peers take the time to describe nonverbal aspects of communication and explain what is happening to children with visual impairments. If a child uses sign language, it can be helpful for everyone in the class to learn important signs for feelings, so that children can communicate directly when they are happy, sad, angry, afraid, worried, or upset. Children who are deaf may consider themselves part of the deaf culture, and having an adult from the same culture visit the class is sometimes beneficial during the primary grades. Additional classroom discussions and decisions can be made about children's interactions with specialists. Recognizing Braille and American Sign Language as separate forms of verbal and written communication and making comparisons to English explicit also promotes understanding of similarities and differences among social groups within the classroom.

Cognitive Impairments

Young children with cognitive delays often exhibit social skill deficits, because there is such a strong cognitive component to negotiating the social landscape. The more subtle aspects of social interactions, such as reading facial expressions and voice tone or remembering the reactions of peers to particular words and actions, often escape children who need more concrete cues. Abstract concepts such as family, government, and values can also be difficult and may require supplemental instruction with many examples and nonexamples.

Cultural Considerations

If the children in your class come from diverse backgrounds, studies of their cultures provide the here-and-now immediacy appropriate to early childhood education. Such studies also contribute to the self-esteem of the children whose cultures are being studied and to the broadening cultural respect of the rest of the class. If your children are more monocultural, it is important to expand their horizons by bringing in cultural studies from other children within the school or from people in the larger community.

Combining studies of your children's cultures with your own growth in cultural understanding may take some effort, but the results can be extremely beneficial for everyone. Here are some suggestions for making your efforts positive:

- Talk to family members who represent the various cultures in your class. Discuss with them your plans to learn about other cultures and ask for suggested books, videos, and information on cultural events that would increase your knowledge.

- Invite family members to participate in the learning experiences of the class. Based on your initial discussions, invite those who are most enthusiastic and comfortable first. As the less enthusiastic observe what is happening in the class, they may become more comfortable about participating.

- Remember that the majority culture needs to be studied as well. When customs and beliefs are brought to the conscious level and examined, they are less likely to be taken for granted as the *right* or *real* way of doing things.

- As you collect materials for classroom activities, question their authenticity and their broad applicability against what you are learning about the culture. Do they represent just one class or group of people? Do they apply to the children in your class who come from that culture? Do they portray stereotyped views that may be colorful but have little to do with modern everyday life?

- If your children speak other languages, find ways to celebrate their ability. Make their knowledge a part of your study, giving the children opportunities to teach some of their language to the rest of the class. Label classroom objects and projects in different languages.

- Try taking nothing for granted about your own culture. This is a *very* difficult suggestion to carry out and should be a lifelong effort. As you communicate with the parents of your children, spend as much effort listening as you do in talking. If you sense that they are not interpreting your comments in the way you meant them, ask questions to see if their cultural definitions and perceptions are the same as yours. This will be important as you study other cultures and the majority culture as well. You might start by thinking about your own definition of democracy and of how that fits into the structure of your classroom. Do you come from a culture that shares the definition of either of the two groups of university students described earlier? Or is your own view slightly different? How will this affect what you want to communicate to your class? Do your students' parents share your views? If not, what have they communicated to their children, and how will this affect your teaching?

- Make sure materials reflect a diverse group of children and families in pictures and text so that all children see themselves reflected in the curriculum.

Taking into account the varying cultures in your classroom community when creating social studies learning is both an opportunity and a challenge. If you see these opportunities as a way to grow and learn, your experience, on the whole, should be positive.

Social and Affective Impairments

Because the social studies are based on human endeavor and associated concepts, any child who has a disability or delay in the area of social development is at risk for difficulties in mastering curriculum content. All young children are prone to emotional outbursts and social mistakes, so in the early years, it is difficult to tell who has a social skills deficit and who is just socially immature. Some children may receive intensive social skills instruction during the primary grades to prevent more serious behavior problems later on, and the regular classroom is the proving ground for those interventions.

Children with autism and other pervasive developmental disorders often have such severe social learning disabilities that their interactions will not conform in form or content to others in the group. These children often have strengths in particular areas of the curriculum, for example visual–spatial skills required for map making, on which teachers can capitalize for group participation. Typically developing young children are generally flexible and nonjudgemental and often learn alternate patterns of interaction easily, especially if a teacher models, guides, and gives specific suggestions when a situation calls for it.

Giftedness

Youngsters who are capable of high levels of social and moral reasoning are not necessarily at an advantage. The concept of fairness, for example, develops over an extended period. In kindergarten, most children outgrow an earlier view that fair

When youngsters engage in the social studies, there are opportunities for working on commit-tees, doing research in the community, and creating a variety of visual representations of what they have learned.

sharing means giving more and better goods to those who are bigger or stronger or prettier. The predominant kindergarten view is that there is but one definition of fair sharing: equal quantities for all. This generally is followed in the first grade by an emerging understanding that whereas equality is good in many instances, there might be others in which a "poor person" deserves a little extra to balance things out. If just one or two kindergartners attain this understanding while the rest of the class is still arguing for strict equality, friction, annoyance, or even anger can follow. Talking to such children individually about ways to deal with their concerns more graciously is an important teacher task.

FOCUS ON SOCIAL STUDIES: THE DISCIPLINES

In the broadest sense, human beings are involved in the social studies from birth. Learning to differentiate self from other and understand a caretaker's response to various types of crying provide the infant with a social education. Social studies continue to be learned in a natural way as the child grows older and enters preschool or kindergarten. The vignette from Suzanne's teaching experience contains many examples of social learning that occurred as part of the ordinary flow of classroom life. Yet such informal social lessons were only a part of the social studies agenda.

Recall that during that difficult year of teaching, she quite consciously developed social studies lessons and units built around the disciplines of political science, economics, sociology, and civics. The children were exposed to small-group lessons in how to discuss controversial issues, and they learned how to vote and to live by the will of the majority. They learned how to confront and to resolve (at least temporarily) a gender-based conflict concerning rights to the block corner. They also learned lessons in consumer economics and money matters in their simulated store, and they learned about space and mapping within the confines of their own school and classroom. Finally, they learned lessons in history and culture by studying the lives of their classmates' parents.

A well-rounded social studies curriculum requires such formal academic experiences to go with the equally important informal experiences in getting along well together. Inattention to the more formal teacher-planned activities was directly responsible, in decades past, for the demise of classrooms that followed the lead of Dewey and Mitchell. When they argued that children learn best from their real, personal experience, their intent was to overturn a long tradition of irrelevant rote learning. In their enthusiasm to banish meaningless rote learning, however, many teachers ignored children's need to learn something academic. The "back to basics" movement of recent years was, in large part, an attempt to restore to the social studies curriculum a more even balance between academic learning based on the social science disciplines and less formal lessons keyed to classroom social interactions.

The balance between formal and informal social studies lessons depends in part on the age and abilities of the children you teach. It is inappropriate and probably impossible to teach formal social studies to infants and toddlers. Gradually, however, more formal learning is possible, as long as it is balanced by sufficient play and teacher-planned learning relates to children's real lives. Within this more balanced context, young children can learn much from the formal social studies disciplines.

History

History is an account of the past: the telling, analyzing, and explaining of the human story up until today. Academic concepts related to history include time, continuity, change, conflict, and the past. As you know from our discussion of cognitive development, such concepts are difficult for young children to grasp, even for those who are in the early years of elementary school. Nevertheless, it is during the primary grades that children begin to grapple with these concepts, and teachers can assist them with activities that help make the concepts more clear.

Time

When young children begin to engage in daily routines, they begin to understand the passage of time. Knowing that the day always begins with a song and ends with a story helps them understand the length of a school day. Children in the primary grades can make time lines. These useful teaching devices are often relied on in the upper elementary grades to teach major events in history. In the primary grades, they can be divided by days, weeks, or months and focus on children's own personal histories. Typically, time lines are made in cooperative groups and are drawn on long sheets of butcher, or similar, paper divided appropriately. They can also be made individually using adding machine tape.

Continuity

Daily routines can be important for teaching continuity as well as time. If some routines are done continually over long periods of time, the continuity that is sometimes part of history is learned intuitively. As children begin to learn about holidays, their understanding of historical continuity becomes more explicit. The traditions associated with these special days are generally the focus of study, and guests from different generations can share the traditions that have been carried forward through time. For example, winter holidays from many places include lights in one way or another, representing continuity across cultures during dark winter months.

Change

Young children like to know that "now I can do it and before I couldn't." Helping them see change as personal progress gives children a positive outlook on a part of life and history that can be unsettling at times. One way to do this is to match preschoolers to their baby pictures. Primary children can study the history of their school or neighborhood, combining research into written records with oral history interviews.

The Past

Daily conversations that touch on yesterday, last week, or earlier this year help children to differentiate lengths of past time. During these informal discussions, it is your responsibility to help children focus on these varying time spans and to observe their understanding of them. One simple version of a time line can be a division between *today, a little while ago*, and *a long time ago*. Pictures of the way people dressed or different kinds of toys are examples of possible features for this time line.

Geography

Geography deals with the physical surface of the earth; the earth's division into political units; relationships of people to their physical environments; the use people make of the earth's resources; and cross-space comparisons of single interests such as industry, artistic development, or education. Geographical concepts include place, space, direction, location, region, physical and cultural change, population growth and distribution, maps, and environment.

Some of these concepts provide appropriate learning for early childhood classrooms. Often, two or more concepts interact within a more generalized geography learning experience. A good example of this is found in the concept of mapping. When children learn about maps, they must have some understanding of place, space, direction, location, and possibly region and environment. As you have read, young children develop such concepts over quite a few years. Thus, creating adult-style maps is developmentally inappropriate for most children through kindergarten and, for some, into the primary years. Mapping can be done appropriately, but it needs to be redefined to fit children's cognitive development.

Seefeldt (1997) suggests three ways of introducing maps to preschool and primary children:

1. *Survey the children.* Show your class a rather simple map of your city or town and ask if they know what it is. As you listen for answers, note which children seem completely baffled and which ones remark on the things they see. This will give you an idea of the extent of their knowledge and suggest ways to extend it.

2. *Use firsthand experiences.* To help make abstract map concepts more concrete, it is important to relate them to children's interests and needs. Using or making a map for a field trip or a walk around the neighborhood relates directly to their lives.

3. *Develop concepts.* Children cannot comprehend maps until they understand some basic concepts. These include representation, symbolization, perspective, and scale:

   • *Representation* means that children know that one thing represents something else. When they build cities with blocks, children understand that the blocks represent houses, stores, and so on. Three-dimensional objects such as blocks, boxes, dollhouses, and sticks are appropriate mapping materials in the preschool years. Paper shapes glued on larger sheets of paper may be introduced at some point during these years and carried through the primary grades. Lines on paper are generally appropriate from late kindergarten on.

     Symbolization is the concept that a symbol represents a real thing. At first, pictures of things children want to put on their maps may be best; later, they can use more abstract symbols. The use of colors in maps is important to explain to children. They readily understand that blue means water, but it can be helpful to take them outside to look at an actual road to see that its not really blue or red.

   • *Perspective* on a typical map is a bird's-eye view. Children can attain this by standing on their desk chairs, going to the top of a hill, or looking down from a tall building.

   • *Scale* is a difficult concept for young children and an absolute understanding should not be expected. Photos of the children and various objects can be used to demonstrate that the real things are larger than the representations.

Sociology

Sociology is the study of humans as they interact within groups: how people affect the groups to which they belong; how groups affect the people within them; the relationships between and among groups; and the ways in which groups are created and structured. Concepts related to sociology include groups, institutions, society, norms, individuals' roles, and socialization.

Children belong to groups and institutions. They bring to school the influence from their families and religious organizations. Within the school there are academic groupings, including the grade they are in and the social groups they create more informally.

An informal study of sociology can and should take place throughout the school year, and an awareness of group interactions can be part of other social studies projects. For example, as you involve parents in school activities, send notes home, or have conferences, you are bringing the concept of family informally into the school. More formally, children may study different configurations for family groups and their own places in them.

Anthropology

Anthropology is the study of cultures as they have developed over time, as they exist now, and in comparison with other cultures. The concept of culture includes so much—language, literature, art, music, law, religion—that anthropology is often viewed as an umbrella social science that covers all the others.

For young children, there are some useful, enjoyable, and appropriate learnings from anthropology. Having older children teach their favorite games to younger children, for example, not only demonstrates culture but shows how enculturation takes place. Songs and folktales from different parts of the United States or from around the world can be compared to those from the children's own culture. Holiday customs and traditions can be studied in the same way.

Economics

Human beings have needs and wants that must be satisfied by varying amounts of resources. The study of the patterns and systems by which people do this is the field of economics.

Young children have needs and wants, and for many, economics concepts are part of their lives as soon as they are big enough to sit up while being wheeled through the grocery store in a shopping cart. Sunal (1990) suggested the following concepts as being important and understandable for young children: wants and needs, scarcity, identifying resources, planning, ordering goals, goods and services, buyers and sellers, producers and consumers, money, and making choices.

Activities Sunal suggested include such things as having the class list needs and wants for the classroom and later checking items off as they are obtained; helping children recognize the factors of production by identifying items needed to complete classroom tasks; and visits to both service-oriented shops (repair shops, beauty shops) and places that sell goods (grocery stores, auto dealerships).

Political Science

The ways in which social units both large and small govern or manage themselves is the focus of political science. Concepts include political systems, political institutions, government, patriotism, public policy, power, authority, and social control.

Even very young children have some understanding of politics, particularly if they have heard of the president or other authority figures. They tend to view such people as positive, benevolent, and personal (Seefeldt, 1997), perhaps believing that they can call them on the telephone or talk to them via the television.

As children are given opportunities to create rules, make various classroom decisions, and generally participate in the running of their schooltime lives, they are creating their own systems of governance. In the primary grades, with some teacher guidance, it is appropriate for children to suggest consequences for those who disobey the rules. (Younger children, and even some primary children, have a hard time choosing consequences that appropriately fit the disobedience.)

Patriotism may be a controversial concept for you as a teacher. Parents and other citizens want to instill patriotic values in children from the earliest years, but the symbols usually associated with patriotism are too abstract for children to understand. A prime example is the flag to which children are asked, often daily, to pledge allegiance. Asked to define *pledge* or *allegiance*, young children may give personally creative but nonsensical answers. If you listen to them as they recite the pledge, you will hear a wide variety of interpretations, with familiar words substituted for the actual ones. Some teaching ideas you might find helpful:

- Explain the meaning of the stars and, perhaps, the stripes.
- Focus on a few key words to learn and define.
- Say the pledge less often so it remains special.
- Sing flag-related songs, recite poems, read stories.
- Have children create a flag for the classroom with symbols that have meaning to them.

Values Education

Even more potentially controversial than patriotism, values education is still an important part of children's social studies learning. Again, parents and other citizens want children to learn appropriate values in school. However, most of these people want the children to learn *their* values. In a diverse society such as ours, this means that there are numerous views on what is appropriate, including the view that values education is the responsibility of home and church alone.

In recent years, several approaches to values education have been developed for school use. Probably the longest standing and best known is values clarification, which provides children with a three-step process for developing a value: thoughtfully choosing a course of action, showing satisfaction with the choice by prizing it, then acting then on the prized choice (Raths, Harmin, & Simon, 1966). The teaching methods and materials associated with values clarification are most appropriate for older children, but other approaches can be applied in the early childhood classroom.

Generally, these approaches are based on Piagetian theory and subsequent work by Lawrence Kohlberg. First, they take into account the developmental levels of children as well as the observation that within one classroom children may be operating at a variety of levels. Second, they provide opportunities for children to create their own learning with guidance being offered by the teacher, as necessary. Another approach you might try is one that Suzanne and a colleague (Schuncke & Krogh, 1983) developed for kindergarten through primary grades. It has three steps:

1. *Warm-up.* Introduce the topic in a way that piques their interest. ("Have you ever wished you could use a wonderful toy that wasn't yours?" "Have you ever had a wonderful toy you didn't want to share?" Then read or tell a story in which the protagonist must make a value-laden decision. But stop before the decision is made. You can use a book that is designed for this purpose (such as Schuncke and Krogh's *Helping Children Choose*), or you can use any good story in which such a decision has to be made.

2. *Action period.* Ask the children to suggest courses of action for the protagonist. ("She should only share with her best friend." "She should only share with the girls." "She should share with everybody.") Until they have done this a few times, it may be that only one idea will surface. Accept it and don't push for more; as this step proceeds, children may think of more story endings.

Have children volunteer as story characters to role play each suggested ending, developing the plot so that they can see the consequences of the action that has been suggested. At first, it may be helpful, especially with younger children, for you to take one of the minor roles in order to move the action along.

3. *Debriefing.* At the end of each enactment, ask each of the characters how he or she feels about the way the story turned out. ("I'm a boy, and I didn't like it that she only shared with the girls. It wasn't fair." "I didn't mind sharing with everybody, but then I didn't get to play with my new toy very much. I should've just left it at home.")

After all the suggestions have been acted out, children may want to discuss the pros and cons of each. It is important, however, that no one feel pressured into accepting the ideas of others. If they do, they may just be following popular opinion and not growing individually. It's usually not a good idea to take a vote on the best answer. You may find that children will talk to you or each other on an individual basis later, thus providing an opportunity for them to construct their own values in a very Piagetian sense.

The various social science disciplines all contain concepts that are appropriate in some way for young children's learning. Much of the time, learning will be informal, as in Suzanne's experiences described at the beginning of this chapter. Other times it will be more formal, as in the suggestions just given. In either case, it is important not to make the mistake that occurred over so many decades when the focus was so strongly on the here and now that little or no learning took place. It is equally important that social studies teaching not be rigid and dry.

The social studies, because they have their basis in human endeavors, are naturally interesting to most children. For the same reason, and because they are so varied, the social studies can easily be integrated with one another and with all other areas of the curriculum. At the conclusion of this chapter are examples of how this can be done.

A SOCIAL STUDIES THEME: CONFLICT RESOLUTION

A study of conflict resolution can incorporate virtually all the social studies. For example, studying the Civil War involves the history of the experience; learning about the battlefields and their effect on the war's progress involves geography; learning how each side financed the war involves economics; comparing northern and southern governments uses political science; whereas studying the ways in which combatants interacted with one another and with civilians involves anthropology and sociology. Finally, the difficult decisions made by all participants can be studied as a part of values education.

Young children are not yet prepared either cognitively or affectively for formal study of this sort. With good reason, the expanding curriculum recommended by social studies researchers does not begin such studies until about the fourth grade. Nevertheless, children are exposed to the perplexing realities of major conflict from a very early age. Sometimes this happens as they watch the evening news on television or hear older people discussing a story from the newspaper or even read it themselves. Perhaps there are relatives in the military who are engaged in conflict. Certainly children's games are often built around warlike situations.

Depending on what is happening in our current history, children will react to major conflict with varying degrees of interest and fear. There are no firm answers about ways in which teachers can help children deal with these concerns. One place we can look for answers is in the recollections of people who lived through major conflict either as children or as the caregivers of children.

For example, Anna Freud and Dorothy Burlingham, in their 1943 book *War and Children*, described their experiences in World War II England, where they directed three wartime nurseries. Some of the difficulties children had in understanding the war around them arose from their stages of development. For example, one child reminisced, "Do you remember the first night here when we all were so noisy that the Germans dropped a bomb on our house?" As the authors concluded, "In Janet's mind the bomb was dropped as punishment because the children were too noisy" (p. 178).

Kati David (1989), a child survivor of World War II, grew up to interview others who had also lived through the experience as children. She discovered that the 100 survivors she interviewed all experienced the same reactions to their hardships despite very different circumstances. Physical hardships such as cold and hunger left them "relatively indifferent" (p. 14). The primary fear was of being separated from their parents; those who had experienced separation suffered far more. Bombings and air raids were not feared by most children, particularly when they were given extra attention and affection during the raids. Those who had been most fearful claimed that their feelings were transmitted to them from fearful adults. Only 3 of the 100 survivors were still bitter about having gone through the war, with most feeling that they were strengthened by the experience and more appreciative of life.

Even when children have no direct contact with war, they develop concepts about it from an early age. Today, in the United States, many or most children are exposed to conflict in some form on a regular basis during their many contacts with television.

Carol Seefeldt's (1997) review of research on children's perceptions of conflict provides a number of conclusions that are useful for teachers:

- Children begin forming ideas of political systems about age 3.
- By age 7 or 8 children understand war and peace fairly well.
- Girls are less likely than boys to be interested in war and war games.
- Six-year-olds demonstrate more hostility than children of other ages.
- Third and fourth graders are most likely to rate wars as glamorous.
- Older children condemn war more frequently than younger ones.
- Young children have difficulty separating real war from fantasy.
- Young children may believe they can cause someone to die if they get angry, or cause war by their misbehavior.

Dealing With Conflict

Children experience conflict both in the world at large (as they observe it on television or through their parents' eyes) and in their own worlds (as they learn to deal with difficult human relationships). Following are some examples of how you can help children relate their own conflicts to larger conflicts in the adult world.

Conflict Large and Small

Children not only observe adult conflict, they engage in conflict themselves. The similarities between the two are noteworthy. Here are a few major sources of conflict, with examples of how they have been played out at both levels:

- *Conflict over territory*

  —A major cause of World War II was Adolf Hitler's belief that Germany had a need to expand into territory belonging to other countries. The other countries, of course, were not in agreement.

  —Yolanda and Chet, focused only on their own game, decided on a long-distance race, thus expanding the space they needed. Zooming their trikes across the blacktop, they broke up a game of hopscotch. The hopscotch players were incensed.

- *Conflict over resources*

  —A reason given by Saddam Hussein for invading Kuwait in 1990 was that Kuwait was extending its oil lines under Iraq's territory.

  —Three groups of first graders were working on an art project that required scissors, glue, and tape. Scissors, however, were in short supply, and the children spent much time and energy trying to convince others that their own need was immediate and greater. Sometimes they hid the scissors under their own paper to have them available when needed.

- *Conflict over values*

—As abortions have become more common and easily available in the United States, citizens have disagreed with each other about the morality of legalized abortion. For some, a woman's right to determine her physical state and future circumstances is paramount; for others, the embryo's right to life is more important.

—Joelyn and Tish watched Ben take a few coins from Matt's desk. They whispered about what to do. Joelyn argued that they should inform Mrs. Davis right away, because stealing was wrong. Tish argued just as vehemently that tattling was wrong.

Teachers may not be in a position to alter world conflict, but they can affect the outcome of disagreements over similar issues at a more personal level. If Yolanda and Chet's teacher has taken the time to instill responsibility and respect for others, the two children will not only apologize but will help restore the hopscotch game to its original condition. The first-grade teacher could try two completely different solutions: only embark on activities when supplies are sufficient, or purposely have too few supplies and develop a system for sharing happily. In Mrs. Davis's case, it will be important to discuss tattling with the class, helping them know when it is important to share information with an adult and when children should work out problems on their own. This kind of discussion may need to continue off and on throughout the entire school year.

Learning to share resources is a lesson that not only begins in the early years but spans ages and nations.

De-escalating Conflict

Response to conflict may sometimes be aggressive ("an eye for an eye") or passive ("turn the other cheek"). But, as William Kreidler (1984) said, "The difficulty with these aggressive or passive alternatives is that they are not, after all, particularly effective ways of handling conflicts. They tend to be accompanied by physical or emotional hurt, humiliation, and suppressed anger. They also tend not to solve problems" (p. 13). Whether the combatants are toddlers, third graders, or even warring adults, another option—de-escalation techniques—can work more effectively. "De-escalation cools the conflict, keeping it from spreading and becoming more violent. At its best, conflict resolution is a de-escalation of a conflict that channels it along functional rather than dysfunctional lines" (p. 13).

When you want to help children de-escalate conflict, think of the following four points:

1. *Who is involved?* How many children are fighting? How mature (capable of reasoning) are they? How angry is everyone?

2. *Is the time right?* Is there time enough now to deal with this, or would it be better to do it later? Are the children still too angry to talk?

3. *What de-escalation technique would be most appropriate?* What is the real problem here? Have these particular children used this technique before? Do I need to help them learn the technique?

4. *Should the resolution be public or private?* Is this situation one that would be embarrassing or humiliating if other children witnessed the de-escalation time? Could the other children in the class help in the resolution? (Adapted from Kreidler, 1984, p. 17)

Helping children learn to de-escalate and resolve conflict in positive ways is a developmental process. When toddlers first discover that their relationships with their peers cannot always go their way, it is too soon to begin teaching the complex interactions involved in the de-escalation process. Instead, consistently applied interventions usually work best. Examples include:

- Divert the attention of each involved child to another activity of interest.
- Offer hugs and attention all around.
- Remove one or more children from the area.
- Remove the controversial toys or materials from the area.
- Sing or play music as a diversion and peacemaker.

As children grow old enough to talk and understand adult language, their ability to reason grows also. It is at this time that conflict resolution techniques can be introduced.

SOCIAL STUDIES ACTIVITIES ACROSS THE CURRICULUM

The following activities offer techniques that are appropriate for different ages and levels of development. The techniques may be used informally throughout the school year as a way of helping children experience the social studies firsthand, or you may pick and choose activities for a more formal lesson or unit that takes place over a defined period of time. This is particularly appropriate for children in the primary grades, especially if world conflict is much in the news. Table 5.1 suggests the levels at which each activity is most appropriate. However, you should feel free to adapt the activities to different ages. This is particularly true if you are teaching kindergarten, where activities suggested for preschool may be most appropriate at the beginning of the year and, toward the end of the year, some of the primary activities may be of more interest. This table also lists other curriculum areas into which that activity may be integrated. Some of the activities are adaptations from other sources, and these are given in abbreviated form. Full references are provided at the end of the chapter.

Activities at the beginning of this section are more appropriate for toddlers and very young children; those at the end are appropriate for primary children only. Most of the activities are suitable, with some adaptation, for all ages.

TABLE 5.1

Conflict Resolution: Activities

Activity	Level*	Curriculum	Adapted From
Classifying the News	P, Py	Math	
Cooperative Musical Chairs	P, Py	Music	
Dance It Out	P, Py	Movement	
Drawing on Peaceful Ideas	P, Py	Art	Kreidler
Early Etiquette	T, P	Movement	
Hello, I Like You	T, P	Movement	
How Do You Feel?	P, Py,	Movement Language	Kreidler
Is Everybody Happy?	P, Py		Kreidler
Jumping to Conclusions	Py	Movement	Kreidler
Ocean Friends	P	Movement	Sambhava and Luvmour
Open Ended Stories: Role Play and Puppets	Py	Language	Schuncke and Krogh
Open Ended Stories: Structured Discussion	Py	Language	Schuncke and Krogh
Peace Collage	P, Py	Art	
Peaceful Sounds	T, P, Py	Movement Music	
Picturing Peace	Py	Art	
Rewriting the News	P, Py	Language	
Silent Drawing	P, Py	Art	Sambhava and Luvmour
Talking in More Than Words	P, Py	Language	Kreidler
Toy Classification	P, Py	Math	Sambhava and Luvmour
War Play	P, Py		Carlsson-Paige and Levin
What If . . .	Py	Language	

*T = Toddler; P = Preschool; Py = Primary

1. **Early Etiquette.**   A major reason for the practice of good manners is that it shows thoughtfulness toward others. This alone can go far toward preventing potential conflict situations. Learning to say "please" and "thank you" is possible from the first appearance of speech. Respect for one another's property—even if possessed only for a few minutes—can be taught from toddlerhood on. From the very first day of school, children learn that they walk around, not through or over, each other's toys and projects. With young children, this teaching should include role play or a game of follow the leader, with you leading, or both. If you play the game, challenge the children to walk behind you without touching a single thing. Then take them on as complicated and difficult a walk as possible for their age.

   Any other aspect of etiquette can be taught in the same way: Define the desired behavior, take the time to introduce it, then make the point through a role-play or game situation. (It should be noted that etiquette is not simply culturally determined polite behavior. At its best, etiquette is an expression of thoughtfulness toward others.)

2. **Peaceful Sounds.**   Play snatches of different kinds of music as the children move to each piece. Include music that is extremely loud and thunderous and some that is quiet and peaceful. For very young children, just two choices are sufficient, whereas older children can concentrate on more. After they have danced, ask the children which music made them feel more peaceful. Play this music again as they move in peaceful ways.

   With older children, an amusing, but instructive, discussion can ensue if you ask them to imagine and act out what would happen if the peaceful music were played to accompany a battle.

3. **Hello, I Like You!**   Children sit in a circle with one child outside. This child pats another on the head and the two run in opposite directions around the circle. When they meet, they stop, shake hands, and say, "Hello, I like you!" The first player runs back and sits down, and the second player pats someone else on the head to continue the game. Keep the group small and be sure everyone gets a turn. As children mature, the game may be extended so that each child says, "Hello, I like you because . . ." and thinks up the rest of the sentence.

4. **Ocean Friends.**   Children imagine the room is filled with water. They swim around with beanbags held on their head with just one finger. If a bag is dropped, the player freezes. A nearby friend takes a deep breath and dives down to get the bag and replace it on the player's head. As children become more proficient, they can try moving without touching their beanbags.

5. **Dance It Out.**   Give the children a clearly explained conflict situation. Have them express through movement a peaceful resolution. A few volunteers can share their solutions by showing them to the rest. If there are many volunteers, children can pair up and show their ideas to their partners.

6. **War Play.**   Despite your best efforts, children may still engage in war play even if they must resort to secrecy and index fingers as weapons. Use this

opportunity to help children gain control over their impulses, understand others' points of view, distinguish between fantasy and reality, and better understand world news.

- Engage the children in thoughtful dialogue:
  "Can you use the gun so it catches people instead of kills them?"
  "After you catch the bad guys, how can you help them learn to be good?"
- Help children see a positive resolution to the game. "How can we make this war end peacefully/so everyone is happy/so everybody can be a good guy?"
- Teach the uses of a truce. Introduce a white flag to each side. When it is waved, all fighting stops and one side suggests a way the war can come to a close or has an opportunity to discuss the issues that they are fighting about.
- If the war game reflects current world issues, challenge the children to help the real foes resolve their conflicts by playing out different solutions.

7. **Toy Classification.**   Gather a collection of toys, both the school's and those children bring. Mark off two areas on the floor and label one *War Toys* and the other *Peace Toys*. Individual children place single toys in their correct classification. Once this is done, place a single toy in the other area and challenge children to suggest ways it could be used to fit there. Repeat with others. Children should begin to understand better how items that are not weapons can be used hurtfully if the attitude is wrong as well as how weapons can be redefined for peaceful interaction.

8. **Peace Collage.**   From magazines, children cut out pictures that remind them of peace and peaceful solutions to conflict. As these are glued on a large sheet of butcher paper, which is then hung for display, brief conversations can be held about the experience as it teaches them to work harmoniously, cooperatively, and peacefully.

9. **Silent Drawing.**   Two children share one paper and one marker or large crayon. They remain silent while cooperatively making a picture. Afterward, discuss the ways in which it was easy or difficult to communicate peacefully.

10. **Cooperative Musical Chairs.**   Play this like musical chairs, except that children are not removed when the chairs are. Instead, children must share the remaining chairs. Because there is no focus on competition, the game may be stopped at any point, particularly if there is concern about safety.

11. **How Do You Feel?**   Choose an emotion (e.g., anger, frustration, happiness, sadness) and an activity (walking, shaking hands, sweeping the floor, throwing a ball). Children act out one of these, then do the same activity with a different emotion. Discuss possible consequences for acting in these ways. (Walking angrily may lead to bumping into a pole; walking happily may lead to awareness that someone needs your help.)

12. **Talking in More Than Words.** Children role play both mean and peaceful ways to say different things. *Suggestions*:

> I don't want to play with you.
>
> We don't want you to play with us.
>
> That isn't fair.
>
> You just knocked my work over.
>
> That's my crayon you're using.

As a follow-up, discuss whether it is easier to act in a mean or peaceful way, what makes being peaceful difficult, and why it is worth the extra effort.

13. **Is Everybody Happy?** Present an interpersonal conflict situation to the children. Define the needs of both sides strongly enough that the solution is not one-sided or simple. For example, Brett and Meredith are building an airport in the block corner. They need one more block to finish the last side and are reaching for it just as Elena and Tim do, too. Elena and Tim need the block as a picnic bench in the doll corner. Ask, "Are Brett and Meredith happy?" "Elena and Tim?" "How could they solve their problem?" As suggestions are given, ask, "Would that make everyone happy?" When the answer is yes, explain that they have created a win–win situation because all sides win.

14. **Drawing on Peaceful Ideas.** Present a conflict situation as in activity 13. Children divide their paper in half (younger) or in fourths (older). Have the children draw one solution to the problem in each section. Children then write or dictate labels for each solution and, perhaps, stick a star on the solution they think is the best one. An informal discussion of why they placed the stars as they did will help children think through the reasons that some solutions may work better than others.

15. **Classifying the News.** Collect a fairly large group of news and magazine pictures that show people in conflict and in cooperative situations. Mix them together, and ask children to classify them as they see fit. Permit them to be free in their classifications. When they choose to classify the pictures into conflict and harmony, ask how they can tell which is which. Identify the body language and other aspects of the situations that convey what is happening.

16. **Rewriting the News.** This activity is appropriate when children bring up adult conflict that is appearing on the news. Or you may bring in a newspaper article to read to them. Have the children identify the combatants and clarify briefly why they are angry. Show on the globe or a map where the conflict is taking place if the issues are territorial. Children then list possible peaceful solutions to the problem. This should include discussion of the pros and cons of each solution from the point of view of each side.

17. **Open-Ended Stories: Role Play or Puppets.** Choose any story from your school collection or reading program in which there is interpersonal conflict.

Read it to the children, stopping at a point at which a decision must be made to resolve the conflict in some way. The children then suggest a short list of possible solutions and act out each one themselves or with puppets. Let each enactment go further in its plot than the original suggestion to see how the decision might play out in real life. At a good stopping point, ask each character how he or she feels about the way things have gone. Permitting, even encouraging, negative solutions will provide more understanding as children see and feel the results. It is very important to establish a rule that prohibits physical contact in the role play or even between puppets.

18. **Open-Ended Stories: Structured Discussion.**   Essentially, this is the same as activity 17, but less active. As each suggestion is made, list it on the chalkboard, leaving extra space between each one. Instead of acting out the solutions, ask the children how each character will feel. To the right of the solution, draw a face of each character with an appropriate feeling expressed. This need be no more than the standard smiley face with changes in the mouth's direction and a bit of hair on top to differentiate the characters. Volunteer children may draw in the appropriate mouth after you create the rest. Once each solution has been illustrated, observe the chalkboard to see which ideas generated the largest number of satisfied characters. Usually, the most peaceful, fair solution will have the most. Other times, a complex issue will yield no clearly "good" solution. This is also important for children to learn.

19. **Jumping to Conclusions.**   First, explain the meaning of *jumping to conclusions*. Then, show a picture or provide a brief description of a situation, and ask what is happening in the picture of the scenario. Some possibilities:

   This child is crying. Why?

   The man is angry at the boy. Why?

   The lady is laughing at the man in the truck. Why?

   The children suggest possible answers. As they do so, they should jump forward. Have two or three possible conclusions for each situation.

   Then discuss how jumping to conclusions can cause problems in human relationships and how it might affect conflict. Give children an opportunity to share times when someone drew an incorrect conclusion about themselves.

20. **What If?**   Children write stories and illustrations describing what would happen in various swords-into-plowshares situations. Some suggestions:

   What if tanks became tractors . . .

   What if grenades became chickens . . .

   What if arrows became pencils when they landed . . .

   What if bombs became balloons . . . (and what messages would you put inside them?)

21. **Picturing Peace.** Either individually or cooperatively, children draw a picture or diagram of the most peaceful world they can imagine. Or they can draw a picture from the current news, imagining the most peaceful possible solution.

22. **Social Skills Instruction.** Teach the steps of a specific skill directly through modeling and role play. This is especially useful if the entire class, or a small group of children, are struggling with a particular situation, such as joining in others' play. Have the children generate scenarios, identify steps for joining (approach, wait for a break, ask politely), then model and have the children role play their own scenarios.

EXTENDING YOUR LEARNING

1. Create a miniunit for a single age group, perhaps one with which you are working now or will in the near future. The suggestions that follow can be supplemented with other ideas you find helpful in chapter 5. Choose a social studies topic of interest to you or to the children with whom you are currently working. Identify the social sciences with which it most closely relates.

   - Define the learning goals of the unit.
   - Choose five or six activities that work toward your identified goals. Identify any other areas of the curriculum that integrate with social studies.
   - Try teaching at least one activity to your children or others who are available (even neighbor children will do).
   - Analyze what went well and what didn't. Adjust your activities accordingly.

2. Choose the social science with which you are least familiar. Visit a store or library to obtain any book in the field that is of interest to you. If you don't have time to read the entire book, try the first three and the final chapters. Then choose one interesting thing you learned from the book and create an activity that can teach that idea, concept, or fact to young children.

3. Begin a collection of social studies resources. Old *National Geographics* are often available at book sales for nominal cost and offer much visual information about the world. Easy-to-read maps of all kinds will be useful if you teach in the primary grades. Write to consulates and embassies for any educational materials they have to share. Check through bookstores and libraries for high-quality social studies literature.

4. Choose a culture or country from those that are represented in your region's schools and about which you know little. Do an in-depth study of this culture or country. Read its history and learn its geography. Read literature written by its best authors. See films, if they are available. Talk to people from the culture or country. As you learn more, ask yourself if your attitudes and, possibly, your stereotyped views of the culture or country have changed. Think, too, about the effect your new knowledge will have on your teaching, if any.

5. Use national, state, or district social studies standards for a specific grade level to generate objectives for social studies lessons and activities. Design procedures for assessing what children know before you begin teaching and for evaluating learning at the end.

6. Go back to the social studies activities at the end of the chapter. Choose one and write a lesson plan using the outline in chapter 1. Be specific about your learning objectives.

VOCABULARY

Autonomous. Having self-government; functioning independently without the control of others.

Heteronomous. Subject to another's laws or rules with little capability in self-government or independent control.

Perspective. The appearance of physical entities as determined by their relative distances and positions.

Representation. The understanding that one thing represents another.

Scale. The proportion that a map bears to the area it represents.

Symbolization. The concept that a symbol represents a real object or idea.

INTERNET RESOURCES

Web sites provide much useful information for educators and we list some here that pertain to the topics covered in this chapter. The addresses of Web sites can also change, however, and new ones are continually added. Thus, this list should be considered as a first step in your acquisition of a larger and ever-changing collection.

National Council for the Social Studies
www.ncss.org

PBS Social Studies Line
http://pbs.org/teachersource/what_new/social/thismonth_social.shtm

References

Bauer, D. (1979). As children see it. In K. Yamamoto (Ed.), *Children in time and space* (pp. 3–14). New York: Teachers College Press.

Bandura, A. (1963). *Social learning and personality development.* New York: Holt, Rinehart & Winston.

Bandura, A. (1969). The role of modeling processes in personality development. In D. Gelfand (Ed.), *Social learning in childhood* (pp. 185–195). Belmont, CA: Brooks/Cole.

Carlsson-Paige, N., & Levin, D. (1987). *The war play dilemma*. New York: Teachers College Press.

David, K. (1989). *A child's war: World War II through children's eyes*. New York: Four Walls Eight Windows.

Erikson, E. (1963). *Childhood and society*. New York: Norton.

Freud, A., & Burlingham, D. (1943). *War and children*. Westport, CT: Greenwood Press.

Gilligan, C. (1982). *In a different voice*. Cambridge, MA: Harvard University Press.

Kreidler, W. (1984). *Creative conflict resolution*. Glenview, IL: Scott, Foresman.

Maxim, G. (1987). *Social studies and the elementary school child*. Columbus, OH: Merrill.

Raths, L., Harmin, M., & Simon, S. (1966). *Values and teaching*. Columbus, OH: Merrill.

Sambhava, L., & Luvmour, J. (1990). *Everyone wins! Cooperative games and activities*. Philadelphia: New Society Publishers.

Schuncke, G. (1988). *Elementary social studies: Knowing, doing, caring*. New York: Macmillan.

Schuncke, G., & Krogh, S. (1983). *Helping children choose*. Glenview, IL: Scott, Foresman.

Seefeldt, C. (1997). *Social studies for the preschool–primary child*. Columbus, OH: Merrill.

Sunal, C. (1990). *Early childhood social studies*. Columbus, OH: Merrill.

6

THE EXPRESSIVE ARTS: CREATIVITY IN ACTION

Self . . . is at the very least a growing awareness of mind and body existing in a spatial and temporal continuum. It begins very early in life and can be facilitated through rich exposure and opportunity for artmaking.

Charles A. Bleiker

Of all the beautiful things in this world, there are few that surpass the images of music in childhood. Music emerges magically from children, as they search for and find ways to represent their world.

Patricia Shehan Campbell and Carol Scott-Kassner

▼ *Chapter Objectives*

When you finish reading this chapter, you should be able to:

▼ Make decisions about curricula in visual art, music, movement, and drama based on an understanding of child development.

▼ Begin infusing the curriculum as a whole with the arts curriculum.

▼ Explain the importance of creative experiences to the lives of young children.

As you think about and apply chapter content on your own, you should be able to:

▼ Identify your artistic strengths, and plan for carrying them with you into the classroom.

▼ Identify the artistic areas in which you are lacking, and consider ways to expand your knowledge.

Ⅰn the adult world, the expressive arts include drawing, painting, sculpture, architecture, music, literature, drama, and dance. Although they do not disdain utility entirely (some artistic products may be useful), their focus is on the aesthetic—on beauty and creativity. The arts add richness to life, lifting our thoughts and feelings beyond the mundane and commonplace events of our everyday lives. In the world of early childhood, the expressive arts are all this and more. They provide cognitive, social, emotional, and physical development opportunities in the education of the whole child.

Consider, for example, a group of 3-year-olds dancing spontaneously to music the teacher has provided as pleasant background during playtime. Perhaps one or two of the children have seen older siblings practicing their ballet steps. They imitate and teach the steps to each other, all the while inventing movements of their own. To this cognitive, social, and physical experience they add the emotion of joy that comes from the freedom, creativity, and beauty of the activity. In this one activity is demonstrated the richness that is added to life through an expressive art and the deeper influence that such an experience brings to the development of young children. Thus, this final chapter has a dual goal: to conclude our discussion of curriculum with those areas that provide a very pleasant "icing" to the "cake" and to argue that those same areas are an important part of the cake itself.

This chapter focuses on three topics: visual art, music, and movement and physical education. Movement as a general curricular area covers both creative expression and sports activities. The latter, for very young children, can almost be considered an art form, as we shall see, and is therefore included in this chapter, although not generally thought of as expressive art. Young children participate in music by singing, listening, moving, composing, and playing—even making their own—instruments. Finally, children's visual art includes drawing, painting of all kinds, various types of sculpture, and work with clay or similar materials.

Perhaps the expressive arts, more than any other curricular area, lend themselves to educating the whole child. Children's capabilities in arts-related experiences are influenced by their level of development, and conversely, the arts curricula contribute to all areas of youngsters' development.

PERSPECTIVES ON DEVELOPMENT

By now, it should be clear that it is as important to understand how young children grow and learn as it is to have a good grasp of content; a knowledge of both areas provides teachers with the grounding that is necessary for good teaching methodology. In this final chapter, the development of the whole child is considered again. The complexity of the discussion, however, is somewhat greater, because the arts cover a wide range of developing capabilities. Skills related to spatial understanding, for example, are important to movement activities at any age, are intimately intertwined with all visual arts experiences, and are applicable to music as children become old enough to read notation.

Researchers in each of the arts disciplines have observed children's developmental stages as they pertain to their specific area, and we consider each in turn. First, however, a short discussion regarding the more general domains of development is in order.

Cognitive Development

Infants, or older children who are developmentally delayed, require little cognition to respond to music with intuitive rhythmic movements or to hold a crayon as it makes colored marks on a flat surface. Cognitive development is required increasingly, however, for more thoughtful performance. Growing knowledge about the world around them provides the content for children's artistic creations. Concentration and focus are necessary for satisfying process and satisfactory products. Decisions must be made: Should I make this tree the usual green or would pink be prettier? Does this music ask for big movements or small?

As well, specific cognitive concepts apply to learning in the arts disciplines. Understanding of *spatial relationships* instructs children as they learn to draw an adult larger than a baby, dance across the floor without bumping into furniture or other children, or gauge the distance to the finish line in a relay race. (See chapter 5 for a description of the development of spatial understanding.) Language helps youngsters to provide sounds and words to their music and to explain their works of art or create accompanying stories. (See chapter 2 for more information on language development.) The concept of time is important to the development of rhythm, not only in dance-related movement but in sports-related activities as well. (See chapters 3 and 5 for more about time.) As children learn to classify they can place music into major or minor keys, rhythm into slow or fast tempo, colors into dark or light value, shapes into large or small items, and so on. (For more on classifying, see chapter 3.)

Traditionally, the arts have been thought of as an add-on to the academic curriculum from first grade or even kindergarten onward. Their value, it was thought, was in providing an aesthetic and pleasant release from the rigors of more important learning. Research in recent decades, however, has demonstrated that including the arts in education at any age can increase general academic and cognitive scores (A+ Schools, 1999). Emphasis on this connection by those hoping to make an argument for keeping the arts in budget-strapped schools has led to a concern by some that such emphasis may have buried a valuing of the arts on their own merits. This concern remains largely within the arts community however, and legislatures quite regularly aim to cut budgets back to the basics, not understanding or simply disregarding the strong ties of the arts to cognitive development.

Social and Affective Development

In many ways, the arts are very personal, providing creative experiences that develop intrapersonal, rather than interpersonal, abilities. A small child focuses on her own sheet of art paper or ball of clay, becoming aware of what others have only when she decides she needs some of it. Or, she may dance with 10 other children while thinking only of her own acted-out fantasy, conscious of others only as she needs to avoid hitting them. When children are very young, arts experiences become social only when teachers make them so: The art experience might turn social during the cooperative creation of a mural; the dance might be created in small partnerships. Since both solitary and social approaches are favored in centers and classrooms, it is important that caregivers and teachers are aware of related developmental stages.

Infants and young children have much to learn about themselves before they can look outward to the rest of the world, and their social and affective development reflects this need. Socially, children are heteronomous (other directed) until the primary grades, when they take their first steps toward autonomy. Thus, their social (and moral) decisions are based on what grown-ups and bigger children tell them to do or might think about them, not on what they might internally perceive as correct. Emotionally, youngsters spend their early years resolving issues related to trust of their caregivers and the beginnings of autonomy; taking the initiative and feeling guilty when it is inappropriate; and feelings of inadequacy when diligence and hard work fail. (See chapter 5 for a more in-depth description of these theoretical stages.) When children are provided experiences that permit them to express their emotional conflicts, rejoice in their victories, and expand their social awareness and interaction skills, their social and affective development is fostered and enhanced.

Physical Development

Each area of development undergoes great changes between infancy and the primary grades, but the physical domain's evolution is the most outwardly dramatic. Caregivers of babies and toddlers are accustomed to complimenting their charges on being able to sit up, feed themselves successfully with a spoon, or take their first steps. Those responsible for preschoolers share the joy of first tricycle rides, jumps on and off stairs, and marks on paper that appear to represent the real world. Kindergarten and primary teachers observe their children gaining such sports-related skills as throwing, catching, running, and balancing on a beam—all of these a far cry from the aimless wiggling of arms and toes just a few short years before.

Because the levels of physical development have not been considered in previous chapters, we describe them here in some depth. In addition, you can refer to chapters 2 through 5 in the book in this series entitled *Early Childhood Development and Its Variations*. Our discussion reflects the widely accepted views of Gabbard (1992) and Gallahue and Ozmun (1998). Their works draw on the results of their own and others' research.

Reflexive Movement Phase

Reflexes are involuntary movements made in reaction to a stimulus such as light or touch. Some reflexes will be useful throughout life: sneezing, blinking, yawning, and coughing, for example. Others disappear after about 6 months and reappear later as voluntary behaviors; examples include the swimming reflex, in which an infant held at the water's surface immediately makes swimming motions, and the stepping

In the fundamental movement phase, youngsters develop the strength and coordination that provide the foundation for later sports skills.

reflex, in which the infant makes stepping motions when held upright. The connections between disappearing reflexes such as these and their later voluntary counterparts remain unclear, although they may serve as "neuromotor testing devices . . . that will be used later with conscious control" (Gallahue & Ozmun, 1998, p. 81).

By the time infants are about 4 months old, voluntary movements overtake reflexes. At this point, children can use the information learned from the reflexive phase in new ways through more intentional behaviors.

Rudimentary Movement Phase

Rudimentary behaviors such as sitting and crawling are both basic and voluntary. These behaviors increase as an infant's nervous system matures, and their practice helps the infant establish postural and manual control as well as locomotion skills. The ability to engage in and control voluntary movements begins first with the head and neck, then moves downward to the legs. It also moves outward from the shoulders to the elbows and fingers. For example, infants generally can lift their heads and chests when they are 2 months old, sit up between 6 and 8 months, and stand alone by about 1 year.

Rudimentary behaviors include movements that are basic for survival and lifelong activity: moving the head and upper trunk, rolling over, sitting, crawling and creeping, standing, and walking. A youngster's demonstration of all these behaviors progresses in predictable sequences from primitive and immature to efficient and mature over different periods of time. For example, a baby can sit fairly well if given support at four-months, can sit alone at about 6 months, and can move alone from a prone position to a sitting position at around 8 months. Similarly, walking appears at about age 1, with the first steps being uncoordinated side-to-side movements. Fully mature, straight-ahead steps become normal by the time the child is 4 or 5 years old.

Fundamental Movement Phase

Fundamental or basic movements are general activities such as running, jumping, throwing, and catching, which form the basis for advanced, often sports-related, skills. At about age 2, children begin to acquire these basic movements, and by age 7, they are capable of efficient, coordinated, and controlled fundamental motor behaviors.

As we just mentioned, one such skill is running. Most children make an awkward try at running at about 18 months old, develop an elementary level of competency between ages 2 and 3, and achieve a mature running form and good speed at about age 5. Jumping is another skill that appears in a primitive form at about 18 months, when children often try jumping off a step or other high object. A real self-propelled leap is usually tried at about age 2, but good height and distance are achieved at about age 4 or 5. Although both running and jumping are sports activities that are engaged in and improved on through adulthood, young children only develop a simple, basic level of these skills. Yet this basic level of achievement is necessary for future sporting success.

What constitutes maturity in skills such as running and jumping are coordination and the skillful use of various body parts to achieve balance, height, distance, speed, and so on. This applies to a number of skills that emerge and develop during the early years. Hopping, for example, requires more rhythm, strength, and balance than two-footed jumping. Although some children accomplish this skill during the preschool years, others really can't hop comfortably until they are about age 6; girls tend to progress more easily than boys.

Galloping, sliding, and skipping require a lot of balance, which probably explains why most children don't attempt these skills until around age 4. Skipping is usually the last of the three to be mastered; again, girls usually are more skilled than boys.

Boys, however, shine in throwing skills. Overarm throwing appears in its most primitive form at 6 or 7 months, when babies can sit up on their own and try to propel an object to another place. Catching capabilities tend to appear after throwing. Catching is an activity that promotes a fear reaction in many children, causing them to turn their heads away from an oncoming ball, thus ensuring that they will drop it. With practice and increased confidence, most children lose this fear and can participate in two-handed catches in easy situations by the primary grades.

Bouncing and rolling a ball are two favorite activities for young children. At age 2, some children can perform a single two-handed catch and bounce; by age 5 or 6, children can dribble the ball as long as it doesn't move away from them. Intentional rolling is attempted between ages 2 and 4; by age 6 most children have mastered the skill.

Kicking and striking (batting) are two fundamental skills needed in later sports such as soccer, football, tennis, and baseball. Kicking skills begin to appear at about age 2 and, for most children, mature at age 5 or 6. Striking skills appear at about 3 years old and become efficient at 4 or 5.

Although girls more easily master skills such as skipping and hopping, boys are quicker to acquire catching and throwing skills.

We should point out that all these sports-related skills do not necessarily emerge naturally through maturation. The vast majority of children, Gallahue and Ozmun (1998) noted

> require opportunities for practice, encouragement, and instruction in an environment that fosters learning. Failure to offer such opportunities makes it virtually impossible for an individual to achieve the mature stage of a skill within this phase and will inhibit further application and development in the next phase. (p. 85)

If practice and instruction are not provided, mastery may never be achieved at any age. It is entirely possible that as an adult you shy away from trying some new sports or physical activities for this very reason.

Historically and traditionally, teachers have spent more time and effort encouraging the fundamental skill that relates most closely to schoolwork: manipulation. *Manipulation* has to do with the use of the hands and a mature, refined level may not be achieved until age 8, well after many schools expect such performance. Babies can make pincer movements at about 9 or 10 months, and they can hold crayons and markers in the fist at around 18 months, although experimentation with methods continues through preschool. A reasonably mature skill develops by age 7.

As with the large muscle skills, children gain coordination in writing and drawing from the inside part of the body outward. At first, they write or draw using the shoulder and arm and then add the elbow. They add the wrist, fingers, and thumb last.

Accompanying manipulative development are stages in drawing that begin with random scribbling (ages 1 to 2½). Children may watch the lines appearing on the paper, but they watch mostly out of curiosity, not intention. They then advance to controlled scribbling (ages 2½ to 3½), in which they look at the paper more often and seem to have some visual control over the marks. Scribbles are named later (ages 3½ to 4), usually after a drawing is finished and the child realizes that the picture looks like something. Intentional attempts at representation (ages 4 to 5) coincide with an improving ability to hold the drawing tool. As children gain real control of the implement, they move to a stage called preschematic drawing (ages 5 to 7). Baselines appear, and for the first time, figures with all their body parts stand on them. The final schematic stage (ages 7 to 9) accompanies children's thoroughly comfortable grasp of the tool. The baseline grows thicker, representation is based on realism, and there is less experimentation.

Sport-Related Movement Phase

During this phase, the fundamental movements that were established during the prior phase are refined, combined, and applied to new situations. Depending on the theorist, the phase is divided into two or three stages that cover the elementary years and all of adolescence. Teachers can expect to see the beginnings of the first stage during the primary years as children start using the fundamental movements they have just attained by applying them to games. Hopping is essential for hopscotch; running is used in races and ballgames; kicking is applied to soccer and kickball; striking, catching, and throwing are essential for softball; better balance is needed for gymnastics and bicycle riding; and walking is taken for granted in just about every activity of life.

Children make roughly equal progress in both their gross and fine motor capabilities. The sport-related improvements have their counterpart in activities requiring the use of hands and fingers. Writing, drawing, painting, clay modeling, carpentry, and other handicrafts are all tackled with more confidence and capability. Children are able to stay within the lines on a written page. They may be enthusiastic about learning both to print and to write in cursive letters. During these years, boys and girls are very nearly equal in their motor development.

As we have seen, the expressive arts are intimately related to all aspects of development. By definition, being expressive involves emotions and the body, both of which are enhanced by competent cognitive, interpersonal, and intrapersonal skills. Providing children with arts experiences fosters growth in all these areas while enriching their lives with greater exposure to music, visual art, and movement.

DIVERSITY AMONG CHILDREN

As you know, not every child fits into the standard mold of development, and not every child has the same cultural response to the school environment and curriculum. One of the positive attributes of the arts curriculum is that it naturally provides an appropriate means of expression for the widest possible diversity. Children can move in response to the same music whether they are in a wheelchair or are totally mobile. Or they can use the same art materials to create objects or pictures that portray their own or others' cultures. In your curriculum planning, you should take into account the similarities and differences among children. Then you will be able to decide if an expressive art activity provides enough freedom to serve various needs or if adjustments should be made so that everyone can participate to the fullest. Ask yourself the following questions:

- What are the intellectual needs of gifted young children that might affect their participation in visual art? Music? Movement?
- What are the characteristics of intellectually challenged children that might need to be taken into consideration when planning curriculum in each of the arts?
- What are some of the physical challenges that children might have that could influence curriculum plans for each of the arts?
- What are some possible social or emotional difficulties that should be taken into consideration when planning group and individual art activities?
- What are some cultural differences that might influence children's understanding of and participation in each of the arts?
- What are some cultural differences in your own community that might affect children's responses to the arts curriculum?

Child diversity covers many aspects of development and culture. As you write your responses to these questions, be sure to add your own observations.

Curriculum Considerations for Children with Special Needs

The expressive arts provide an important part of the curriculum for young children who have developmental delays and disabilities. Creative pursuits in the form of art, music, movement, or drama can insulate students who struggle with academics during the preschool and primary years, offering an arena for success, emotional release, and exploration of self. Creativity springs from one's inner state of being and requires no more than fundamental movement abilities and a willingness for expression.

Sensory Impairments

Children who have visual impairments are often interested in sculpture and work with clay, playdough, and similar materials. They are sensitive to differing textures of material and often recreate objects they have explored with their hands. The differences between visual and tactile knowledge of the world are often clearly depicted in their work. Vision is clearly no prerequisite for playing a musical instrument or singing, and there are a number of recording artists, particularly piano players, who are blind. Children who are deaf or have hearing impairments can appreciate rhythm through use of strong bass instruments and melody through light and laser displays. Visual cues for the beat and loudness of a song can be conveyed using hand signals, and a group of children "singing" in sign language is a wondrous sight to behold. We once saw a holiday pageant in which two deaf children and the sign language club signed as everyone else sang "Silent Night," and the entire class signed the middle verse in silence. It was lovely.

Cognitive Impairments

The world can be a frustrating and confusing place for youngsters who are slow to understand. Art, music, and movement can offer a welcome respite from always trying to make progress—catch up, keep up—for any child who is struggling to acquire academic or social skills. Painting and drawing lend themselves easily to self-expression, because colors, brush strokes, and use of space convey emotion directly without the necessity for complex thought processes. Children with autism, who often have strong visual–spatial skills, can excel at construction and have produced beautiful abstract and representational art with vivid colors and bold designs. Movement and dance are natural outlets that can channel excess activity into creative pursuits for children who are hyperactive. The repetition of songs and dances is beneficial for young children who need extra practice to remember, and even a small part in a primary grade drama production offers a multitude of opportunities for youngsters to work with peers, learn about sequencing and timing, develop language skills, and feel a sense of pride and accomplishment.

Physical Impairments

There are many artists with physical disabilities, including some who paint and draw with their mouths or feet, and singers who perform from wheelchairs or using crutches. Some of the voices we listen to each morning on the radio belong to people who broadcast from wheelchairs. People with physical disabilities often have intense life experiences that are depicted with intensity and beauty in art, music, or drama. Learning about such role models empowers young children to feel competent despite physical limitations and can encourage them to find their own forms of expression.

Chronic Illness, Abuse, and Trauma

The creative arts also can be therapeutic for children who have painful and frightening life experiences. For youngsters who are confined to beds at home or in the hospital, drawing, sculpting, painting, singing, and listening to music offer opportunities to express feelings and to create. The use of art forms to revisit and resolve the pains of abuse, war, accidents, violence, loss, grief, and illness has resulted in beautiful and touching pieces produced by children of all ages. The real beauty of creativity for some children is the opportunity to create something more positive than the reality of their daily lives and to express intense emotions in a socially acceptable way.

Giftedness

A child who shows an emerging talent in one or more of the arts or sports in the early years should be permitted to enjoy, explore, and experiment freely just as other young children do. The early recognition of such talent may be important to later success, but forcing extra practice, drawing too much attention to unusual skills, or insisting on performance for others can nip children's enthusiasm in the bud, turning love of an art or sport into dislike and refusal to participate. In addition, in considering the development of the whole child, we recognize that early emergence of one set of skills may not mean that complementary skills in another area develop at the same rate. For example, a child with a fierce throwing arm or eye for batting accurately may well be too young to understand the importance of team play or the reasons for following the rules of the game.

FOCUS ON THE EXPRESSIVE ARTS: DEVELOPMENTAL STAGES

Unless otherwise indicated, the stages given here come from the classic research of Rhoda Kellogg (1970), Viktor Lowenfeld and Lambert Brittain (1982), and Dennie Wolf and Martha Davis Perry (1988). The following sections discuss each of the expressive arts in turn.

Art

Infants and Toddlers

There are art educators who argue that the skill of drawing begins to develop when an infant, just weeks old, appreciates the virtual images made in the air by involuntary movements of hands and feet (Bleiker, 1999). Over the course of the infant's first year, in this view, observations of splashing puddles or bathtub water, banging of pots and pans, and so on offer continual opportunities to witness artistic processes and to learn to use art implements. "The world to the infant becomes both palette and paintbrush" (p. 49).

When observation turns to action at the end of the first year, process becomes everything. Simply holding a pencil, crayon, or brush is an interesting challenge, and the tools are treated like any other object or toy. For example, a marker might be wrapped in a piece of paper and called a hot dog just as easily as it might be used to make a mark on the paper. If children do attempt to draw, they watch with extreme interest, fascinated by the marks that appear on the paper. As children watch the marks being made, interesting geometric shapes may appear, but these are made by accident, not by design. Before their second birthdays, children are often able to record the correct number and general location of parts on a body. For example, they might make a slash mark for a head, another below it for the belly, and two at the bottom for feet.

Preschoolers and Early Kindergartners

During these years, children begin to control their scribbles and eventually give them names, although the labels are generally the result of postdrawing observation, not intention. Once children realize that their scribbles do resemble something, intention

For a toddler, the process of holding a colored marker and witnessing the impressions it makes is a fascinating experience.

becomes a factor, and they can engage in beginning attempts at representation. Earlier accidental geometry is replaced by each child's personal system for recording spatial information. Through all these developments, children's feelings may be as important to the drawing as any visualization. Even after attempts are made at representation, feelings may influence the results, as when a smaller but more powerful friend is portrayed as very large. Generally, objects in pictures are found facing forward and floating in space. At this age, children have no understanding of background or dimension.

Late Kindergartners and Primary Children

During the kindergarten year, most children's artwork takes on characteristics that make it more adultlike. Figures in drawings now stand on a baseline and may look at each other instead of at the viewer. A sky is drawn across the top of the page, and for the first time, human figures may be given clothing. With experience, children begin to perceive that it is possible to make objects look farther away by making them smaller or by placing them toward the top of the page. They also learn to overlap objects. With this maturation comes a reluctance to experiment with ways to portray everyday objects and people. Each child develops a system of representation and prefers to stick with it once it is comfortable.

Implications for Teaching

The uncoordinated movements of the infant may be viewed by some as preparation for work in visual art making, but it is difficult to define exactly when true art production actually begins. Before kindergarten age, children do not set out to have an aesthetic experience or to be expressive, and they certainly do not conform to any formalized artistic standards. Rather, they use art media as one way to interpret their world. As David Baker (1990), past-president of the National Art Education Association (NAEA) said:

> As their mark making becomes picture making, children literally create for themselves a way to mediate reality, to give meaning to the relationships they perceive in the world and the unique encounters they have with them, and to communicate in an abstract manner with what they understand and feel. . . . Picture-making and object-forming activities are increasingly understood to be the primary means with which preschool and primary school children prepare themselves to master the conceptual sets, beliefs, values, and behaviors that make them functional within their culture. (p. 22)

Before kindergarten, children do not engage in intentionally artistic expression but use art media to interpret their world.

Young children need daily opportunities to expand their creativity through a variety of art media.

In recent years, art educators have been as influenced by the developing positions of NAEYC as have others involved in early childhood education. Conversely, NAEYC position statements have provided confirmation of positions long held by art educators themselves. Some of these include the understanding that youngsters "need uninterrupted periods of time to become involved, investigate, select, and persist at" art activities; that the "teacher's role in child-chosen activity is to prepare the environment with stimulating, challenging activity choices and then to facilitate children's engagement"; and that "workbooks, worksheets, coloring books, and adult-made models of art products for children to copy are not appropriate for young children, especially those younger than six" (Schirrmacher, 1998, p. vii). Furthermore, young children should have daily opportunities for art experiences using "a variety of art media, such as markers, crayons, paints, and clay . . . for creative expression and representation of ideas and feelings" (Bredecamp & Copple, 1997, p. 132).

One art educator believes that "well-meaning teachers of children get confused about what art is" (Colbert, 1997, p. 211). To clarify the issue, she listed what art is *not*:

- Coloring or painting predrawn pictures, cutting and pasting predetermined patterns.
- Following the teacher's example to assemble and connect assorted materials such as a vinyl leaf glued to a refrigerator magnet.
- Copying a teacher's model by following step-by-step instructions.

• Shaving cream or pudding paintings and other tactile experiences.
• Craft projects that have steps so difficult the teacher does most of the work.

Specifics about suitable materials, activities, and teaching approaches are, as one would expect, somewhat different for each age:

• Toddlers should not be expected to produce finished artwork but should be permitted to explore and manipulate a variety of materials and tools. Because they are still learning what is and is not suitable for putting in the mouth, art projects should *never* include food as an art material. For the same reason, all materials should be nontoxic.
• Three-year-olds are beginning to have better control over their scribbles and enjoy naming what they produce, but representational products still should not be a goal of their teachers. When teachers demand of young children, "What is that?" they convey the sense that only representational art is to be valued. "Tell me about your drawing" is generally followed by enthusiastic description (sometimes made up as it goes along.) Fine motor skills can be enhanced by supplying and supervising the use of a variety of materials and tools; drilling children in their proper use and expecting good coordination can cause consternation and refusal to participate.
• Four- and 5-year-olds are gaining control over their use of materials and a related ability to plan and carry through their art projects. Daily opportunities for art experiences remain important, and the view that they should be part of a once-a-week special curriculum or based on predrawn patterns is inappropriate teaching practice.
• School-age children retain the need for more than the once-a-week experience. Teachers can incorporate art experiences into the curriculum as a whole. They should be careful not to substitute patterned "craft" activities for real art experiences, particularly where directions must be followed to yield identical products. (Schirrmacher, 1998; Bredecamp & Copple, 1997)

In general, teachers must walk a fine line between providing the skills and inspiration required for successful artistic experiences and imposing too much intervention, between allowing freedom and giving too much structure. For many teachers, the latter approaches—too much intervention and structure—are more attractive, despite the fact that they do not give children the opportunity to grow in self-expression. Reasons for choosing the path that generally is viewed as developmentally inappropriate (Bredecamp & Copple, 1997) might include the comfort of knowing that an activity and its outcomes are teacher controlled and thus expectable, neat, and tidy; a perceived lack of artistic capabilities of the teacher; minimal teacher training in providing support for the discovery process; and a widespread belief that creativity is a talent that people either have or don't have, thus arguing against providing open-ended experiences for children. Teachers often use the excuse that they need time to get other work done, so they give children coloring sheets and dittos to fill the time (Szyba, 1999).

A policy statement from the National Art Education Association provides some generalized guidance for teachers of young children with the statements that children should be:

- Given appropriate materials in a playful setting.
- Given sufficient time to really be involved in a project and to finish it.
- Encouraged to use their own images and ideas.
- Given help when they need it.
- Provided opportunities to work both alone and in groups. (Colbert & Taunton, 1992)

In the following sections, we see how these recommendations can be accomplished with materials and activities found in most early childhood sites.

Materials and Activities

A primary requirement in selecting materials and activities is that they are safe. Young children are fascinated by art-related materials and explore them to the fullest, often placing them in their mouths. For a few children, oral exploration lasts even into the primary grades. Thus, all materials should be checked for toxicity. This includes crayons (which are usually safe), markers, paints, and even the dye in colored papers. Materials used in collage or sculpture are often small, and tasting-stage children should be closely supervised. Additionally, children should not use scissors until they are able to keep them out of their mouths and handle them carefully. Sharp instruments of all kinds should be kept from children who are still awkward in their movements, unless close supervision is provided.

Once safety is established, choose materials for their high quality and aesthetic appeal. High quality does not necessarily mean high expense. Clay and fingerpaint, for instance, can be made from scratch, and expensive tempera paint can be extended by adding soap flakes. Novelty and frequent change are not necessary because children enjoy creating new and interesting experiences for themselves using familiar materials. You can bring variety to the familiar by providing paper in different shapes or by setting out crayons from the cool colors one day, warm colors the next.

In considering the materials suggested here, take into account their developmental appropriateness for the children with whom you work.

Painting. Almost all children love to paint, and teachers should provide opportunities daily, if at all possible, even through the primary grades. Easels provide room to use arms and hands freely, to step back and observe the developing picture, and to be away from the rest of the class for a while. Painting on a table or floor can also be enjoyable, usually allowing for more socialization and, perhaps, less drippy mess. Children can help prepare the paint, an activity that can be expanded to include experimental color mixing.

Probably the easiest way to keep the original color in each container is to provide a brush with each one. The clips holding paper on the easel should be easy enough to handle so that children can learn to remove the paper themselves. Sponges and access to a water source make it easy for children to wipe up all but the most major spills. As you plan your painting area, consider the steps that children will take to paint, clean up, and ready the area for the next painter. Make the steps clear to the children, and you will have to intervene only minimally.

For very young children, a joyful "painting" activity is to take buckets of water and broad brushes outdoors on a warm day. Everything in sight can be painted, from the building walls to playground equipment to the concrete sidewalks.

Fingerpaint offers children a sensory experience quite different from tempera paint. Some children are put off by the prospect of touching it and should not be pushed into the experience. One way to encourage these children is to suggest that they try dipping just one finger in the paint to make a few tiny marks on the paper. Over a period of time, most children will become willing to participate with enthusiasm. Traditionally, fingerpainting is done on a flat surface rather than on an easel, as this allows for more upper body control. Despite its name, fingerpainting can make use of palms, fists, elbows, and forearms. Relatively sophisticated pictures are possible with some experimentation.

Fingerpainting is usually done on glazed paper, which protects against leakage. Children could also paint directly on a tabletop, then carefully press paper onto the surface to make a print.

Other types of prints can be made with any interesting (and disposable) object. For instance, children in kindergarten can carve a potato half into an interesting shape for an original design. The potato half can then be dipped into a shallow container of thick paint and pressed onto paper. Notepaper or postcards can be made this way for gift giving. With the addition of laminating paper, placemats can also be made.

Drawing.   Crayons are staples of the early childhood setting. Larger sizes are usually recommended, although, given a choice, children generally reach for the smaller crayons. A combination collection with free choice of size and color is probably the best approach.

Even more popular than crayons are markers, which come in many interesting shapes. Veteran teacher Sydney Clemens (1991) suggested a homemade marker holder to keep them capped and fresh. Make a mound from clay. Place the caps from a collection of markers in the mound, burying them almost to their edges. When the clay has hardened, place the markers back in their caps. The markers can then be removed and replaced easily during drawing activities.

Chalk is another good drawing tool. It can be used on paper, chalkboard, and sidewalk. It is a good idea to have some chalk handy for spontaneous use outdoors. Children also enjoy having part of the class chalkboard reserved for their own use.

Construction.   Children love working in three dimensions. Construction is an art-related activity that changes depending on the materials at hand. This is the perfect opportunity to make use of found objects and assorted junk. Some of the many items that can be used in construction are scraps of wood, various styrofoam shapes, shells, buttons, feathers, paper scraps, yarn, fabric scraps, magazine pictures, box lids, leaves and twigs, and bits of ribbon. Construction activities can include:

• *Collage.* Use sturdy paper, alternating colors for variety. Squeeze white glue directly onto collage items, or put some glue in a small paper cup and have children dip collage pieces into it or smear the glue on the pieces with a popsicle stick. Any lightweight object is appropriate for collage. Vary the collection of objects frequently so that children's interest will remain high. Fabric scraps, bits of colored paper, uncooked macaroni or noodles, buttons, and various lengths of yarn are all easily obtained collage items.

• *Sculpture.* Objects that are too heavy for collage can be fitted together to make sculptures. Children can use white glue, tape, even string to form freestanding pieces. To make a sculpture transportable, you will need to provide some sort of base; scrap plywood is a good choice. More easily obtained and usually free are styrofoam meat trays; request them from your market's meat department.

Sculpture also can be done with clay and play dough. Older children enjoy clay that hardens when dry. Younger children, who primarily enjoy the process of squashing and modeling, prefer reusable clay that can be worked less formally. To keep interest high for older children, provide plastic knives and other tools for shaping.

• *Woodworking.* Kindergarten is a good time to introduce construction with wood. It is important to supply children with real tools, which are generally safer and more successful than toy versions. It is equally important to show children specific techniques for safe and successful construction, perhaps to supply goggles, and to create a list of rules. Scraps of wood may be brought from home or obtained either free or for a low price from a lumberyard. Children should sand the wood pieces before using them. (Some children may enjoy the sanding process as much as follow-up construction.) Two bins or boxes can be used to store sanded and unsanded wood. Confining woodworking to the outdoors keeps down noisy confusion in the classroom, but it only should be done there when children can be monitored closely.

Art Appreciation

Even infants and toddlers can begin to develop an aesthetic sense, and each succeeding year provides opportunities for children's growth in appreciation for and understanding of the beauty around them. Thus, making the center or classroom beautiful is a first step in helping children appreciate art. From the very beginning of life, sculpture that can be touched and art prints that show the work of accomplished artists can provide times of enjoyment. Plants and flowers, draped fabric, even carefully arranged objects from science classification activities also make the environment more attractive. Books with good artwork on their covers can be displayed and discussed during storytime.

It is important that all these objects of beauty be displayed at the children's eye level rather than the teacher's. Squat down to their level, and view the room as they do. Generally, items containing some degree of complexity should be readily observable; the upper reaches of the room can be reserved for large swatches of color or left blank.

Most teachers and parents like to see children's artwork posted, but younger children often do not share this view. Always ask children first if they would like to have their art products on display. If the experience has been a satisfying one, a child may well prefer to carry the results folded up in a pocket or hidden safely in a cubby, rather than put on public display.

Museum visits offer an opportunity for children to begin to understand and appreciate the adult concept of art. Although you may not live close to a major art museum, most towns have small museums or private galleries. These are actually preferable for young children. Children as young as 4 years old can enjoy interacting with a single painting, noting the brush techniques and later imitating them, learning to differentiate the subtle shadings in colors, and talking about the feelings the painting imparts—feelings that might be unique to them.

Music

Of the three expressive arts discussed in this chapter, music may be the least influenced by the stages of development that you reviewed earlier in the chapter. Some thinkers have argued that music deserves special recognition in terms of human development. In his 1983 book *Frames of Mind*, Howard Gardner argued that there are seven separate intelligences that we each possess, and he honored music by making it one of them. (The others are linguistic, logical–mathematical, spatial, bodily kinesthetic, interpersonal, intrapersonal, and the more recently added naturalist.) This concept carries with it the view that children's musical intelligence can be nourished or diminished depending on environmental influences, including those in child-care centers and schools. Research that took place in the 1960s and 1970s validates this point of view.

In the 1960s, Edwin Gordon tested students between the ages of 9 and 18 on their ability to recall the tonality and rhythm patterns presented to them in various musical selections (Feierabend, 1990). He found that the musicality of 9-year-olds remained quite stable over the following years, whether the children participated in band, choir, or music lessons or had no musical training at all. A decade later, Gordon developed a simplified version of the test to investigate the musicality of younger children. The rather surprising results have important implications for early childhood education.

Although scores stayed stable for children older than 9 years, younger children actually lost their ability to retain tonal and rhythmic patterns when they had no musically stimulating experiences. The greatest loss occurred between the ages of 5 and 6. Gordon did one more study to see what would happen if children in the primary grades were given musical experiences when they had had none before. He discovered that there could be some improvement until age 9 but that children's abilities were never quite so good as if they had had earlier experiences.

No studies have been done on children under age 5, but Gordon's tests coupled with Gardner's theory of multiple intelligences have led some to conclude that children

> are probably born with their own level of music intelligences that begin to atrophy unless supported by a musical environment. . . . In the upper grades, a teacher can teach more music literature or present more information about music, but in kindergarten the teacher can change the children's music intelligence for life. (Feierabend, 1990, p. 15)

The importance of musical experiences for young children is apparent. To make developmentally appropriate curriculum decisions, some understanding of capabilities at each age is important. The following overview is drawn from the work of many researchers over many years of observation (Jalongo & Collins, 1985; Bayless & Ramsey, 1991; Kenney, 1997.)

Birth to 6 Months

From birth, infants become more active when they hear lively music and calmer with lullabies. Babies not yet 1 week old have been observed discriminating between pitches and rhythm patterns. By the end of the first month, they can make melodic sounds that have rhythm to them, and a month later can actually echo sounds made by their mothers. These first months constitute a period of listening and responding to all the sounds around, musical and otherwise.

Six Months to 1 Year

Sometime during the first year, musical babbling occurs as a response to music in the environment. Attempts to join in the singing of mother or caregiver emerge by the eighth month. At about the same time, infants begin to distinguish between individual songs and show musical preferences. They might rock and sway or clap their hands to music they like; they may also look with displeasure when music they don't like is played. Enjoying the sounds made by hitting and kicking or shaking rattles is a part of this age.

One to 3 Years

Creativity emerges as toddlers memorize snatches of songs and incorporate them into their play. They even begin to create their own songs. Control of the singing voice grows as does an interest in controlling, rather than just enjoying, the sounds made by banging and shaking objects. This leads to much experimentation with sounds of all kinds. Toddlers also develop a feeling for themselves in space and learn to control their movements as they sway, rock, bounce, and twirl to melody and rhythm.

Three to 4 Years

During their fourth year, youngsters are able to listen attentively to music that they like and maintain a rhythm during movement. For many, music becomes an important way to express and communicate ideas and emotions, and creative drama is often combined with spontaneous singing. From now until about age 7, sound structures from the child's culture are mastered. Singing and circle games that include dancing with others are popular, although physical coordination is still difficult.

Four to 6 Years

As physical coordination grows, children are able to move in a variety of ways to different rhythms and melodies. Pitch and tonal control also improve, although getting through an entire song with musical accuracy is rare. Nevertheless, by 5 years

As children's physical coordination grows, they are able to respond in expanding ways to rhythms and melodies.

old, children can sing an average of 10 musical notes and can echo pitch patterns provided by the teacher. Also by age 5, youngsters have definite musical preferences, but these can be developed and altered by the adults around them. Interest in playing simple musical instruments is high, and improvisations can be long, complex, and rambling. If they haven't already learned a good collection of songs, children in this age group will tend not to sing spontaneously.

Primary Years

During the first school years, children become more accurate in matching pitches as they sing, although doing so in a group may be difficult. They become interested in learning to play musical instruments "correctly" while still retaining an interest in experimentation. Coupled with their emerging ability to read the written word, children can learn to read musical symbols for rhythm, pitch, and expression. Most children can move and clap with accurate rhythm, although if they do not have a background of dancing and movement, they may be reluctant to do so without teacher direction.

Implications for Teaching

The reported observations that young children lose interest in spontaneous singing and movement if these are not encouraged from an early age indicate the importance of a caregiver's and a teacher's role in giving youngsters these experiences. Curriculum guidelines and standards for younger children as provided by the Music Educators National Conference (MENC) include the following:

- Young children should be provided with many opportunities to explore sound through singing, moving, listening, and playing instruments
- Music literature should be of the highest quality and can include traditional children's songs, folk songs, classical music, and music from other cultures.
- Teaching methods should be based on play—child directed and teacher supported.
- Teachers should provide individual experiences and group time.
- Music experience should support the child's total development—physical, emotional, social, and cognitive.
- Teaching should include improvisation and composition as well as singing, playing instruments, and listening.
- Curriculum should emphasize relationships among the arts as well as among curricular areas outside the arts.
- Teachers should develop valid and appropriate assessments (related activities)—paper-and-pencil tests are inappropriate. (Kenney, 1997)

Based on our review of development, on work with children by the authors just mentioned, and on the MENC's guidelines, we make some general recommendations:

Infants.   Sing lullabies, and traditional children's and folk songs while interacting with or holding the baby. Games such as patty-cake and chanted nursery rhymes, especially when the infant is gently bounced on the knee, provide rhythm experiences. Provide infants with exposure to selected recorded music. As soon as they are old enough to control them, provide babies with safe toys that make musical sounds.

Toddlers.   Provide youngsters of this age with opportunities for improvised singing, and teach them some simple songs, making sure to include plenty of repetition for the sake of memory and imitation. Chant poems and nursery rhymes while bouncing or rocking a child. Provide opportunities for free movement while playing varying kinds of music, both slow and fast, louder and quieter. Let toddlers explore the uses of basic instruments and objects that make interesting sounds. Help their musical vocabulary grow by verbalizing what they are doing ("You made a very soft sound") and the instruments they explore ("That drum makes loud sounds, doesn't it?").

Preschoolers.   Continue to add to children's repertoires of songs; those with repetitive patterns are especially popular. Children like group games with songs attached (although they do not understand rules until around the end of kindergarten.) Use a recording or musical instrument to accompanying movement experiences in which children try out different forms of locomotion (walking, jumping, skating) in rhythm. Use singing to get children's attention, announce snacktime, describe what they are doing, and so on. Sing their names, and wait for them to sing yours back. Introduce a music center that contains a variety of instruments for experimentation.

Later Preschoolers and Kindergartners.   Continue to introduce songs with repetitive patterns, play group games that include music, provide musical movement experiences, communicate through singing, and create a music center for experimentation. With all these, more sophistication can be introduced. Repetitive patterns in songs can be more complex, a rule or two can be added to games, echoing of melody and rhythm can be longer or more challenging, the music center can contain a greater variety of instruments. In addition, adult-style musical instruments can be introduced by visiting musicians, with discarded or elderly versions of the same instruments added to the center. As children begin to learn about the written word and experiment with making letters, they can create their own notation systems for the music they create.

Primary Children.   Provide primary children with expanded singing experiences by teaching them rounds and traditional and folk songs, especially those with multiple verses. Also, let them improvise and create new lines to familiar songs or short songs of their own. Continue to give them experiences with musical instruments, showing them simple rhythmic or pitch patterns to accompany singing and dancing activities. Introduce standard notation and help them write down brief compositions. Play music of many kinds at varying times of the day, identifying the instruments by their sounds. Share pictures of the instruments or actual examples if possible. As well, identify the composers, and tell a bit about their lives.

Movement

> Four-year-old Benjamin ran through the autumn leaves, chasing the rubber ball that his mother had just thrown him. Suddenly, he became aware of the crunchy sound of the leaves and changed his gait to an exaggerated shuffle. "Sluff, sluff, sluff," he said in rhythm with each step. Forgetting the ball entirely, he began to imitate a leaf that had just begun to fall, still saying "Sluff, sluff, sluff," but changing the shuffle to a falling-down dance.
>
> Three-year-old Tomiko was on her first visit to an art museum. While her parents asked a guard for directions to the special exhibit they had come to see, Tomiko wandered a short distance away to have a better look at a statue of the Winged Mercury atop the entryway fountain. For a while she just stood, seemingly transfixed. Then, slowly and unself-consciously, she lifted her right arm and left leg in imitation of the statue's stance. She held the position as long as she could, discovered she was about to lose her balance, and recovered by inventing a little dance that permitted her to "fly" back to her parents.

In both of these illustrations of movement, the children began the episode with basic transportational movement—each one was just going from here to there. And in both cases, the movement became something else. Benjamin lost interest in chasing the ball and was caught up in the beauty of the leaves. Tomiko became so engrossed in the statue that her whole body joined in. As the children engaged in their experiences, in a sense they actually *became* the leaf or the statue. Such becoming, which requires conscious effort and the overcoming of embarrassment for most adults, is natural for young children. Because they are natural to children, because real mastery often is unattainable without adult intervention, and because they integrate well with all aspects of the curriculum, movement and dance are important to the early childhood center or classroom.

Implications for Teaching

What happens in the center or classroom, of course, must be developmentally appropriate. Three general approaches are recommended depending on *levels of skill attainment*. Children who are at the *initial stage* of learning a skill should be permitted much exploration time, with demonstration of correct performance only in extreme cases and typically with older children. As youngsters begin to gain more control over the skill in the *elementary stage*, teachers should continue to provide exploration opportunities, but this now can be combined with some adult instruction. Finally, as they are ready to approach *mastery stage*, children are ready for direct instruction, modeling, and even some beginning drills.

An example of this sequence is demonstrated in the ways in which children learn to catch various types and sizes of balls. An infant crawls after a moving ball, perhaps patting it, sucking on it, or briefly holding it before it slips away. A toddler enjoys a rudimentary sort of catching and rolling game as she interacts with an adult caregiver facing her from 1 or 2 feet away. For both the infant and the toddler, it is appropriate to provide the ball for free exploration, interact as the youngster seems to prefer, and totally avoid any sort of structured drill and practice. By preschool, the child catches the ball, clutching it to her body. If, at this point, an adult intervenes, she may learn to catch the ball just using her hands, although she may well wince and look away throughout her kindergarten year or beyond. Mastery of proper catching techniques can be achieved in the primary grades if adults or older children offer their help. At this point, the child can begin to catch smaller balls (a tennis ball, a softball) if she is taught to cup her hands and use her muscles correctly. Games that require plenty of contact with the ball and directed movement experiences in which each child interacts continually with a ball contribute to the elimination of fear and mastery of the catching skill.

Movement experiences for the center and classroom can be divided into four skill areas, although in many games and activities they overlap:

1. *Stability* or balance is "the ability of the body to maintain a stationary position or to perform purposeful movements while resisting the force of gravity" (Kirchner & Fishburne, 1998, p. 52). Stability is a basic necessity for any kind of movement and thus fundamental to the other three skill areas.

Some movement experiences that provide children with opportunities for exploration along with skill attainment include bending, twisting, swinging, landing, and stopping and freezing. Work on balance beams or walking on curbs, climbing in and around inner tubes, or even moving in a variety of ways on a cafeteria or park bench can help children gain stability. As children gain stability, they are able to apply this skill to such activities as gymnastics, jumping rope, and dance.

2. *Locomotor skills* are "the basic motor skills necessary for moving through space and from place to place" (Kirchner & Fishburne, 1998, p. 105). Walking, crawling, running, leaping, jumping, and hopping are basic locomotor skills. These can then be combined in such activities as skipping, galloping, and dodging. Children's abilities in the locomotor skills can be enhanced with the many activities calling for imitation of animals: elephant walk, kangaroo jump, horse gallop, frog and rabbit hops are all examples. Commercial or homemade obstacle courses offer youngsters opportunities to jump, climb, and crawl. Jumpropes can be used in the traditional way but also for simpler challenges such as jumping just once over the rope and back again, hopping over on one foot then hopping back, and so on.

3. *Nonlocomotor skills* "involve movements that do not require transportation of the body through space or from place to place" (Kirchner & Fishburne, 1998, p. 116). Swinging, bending, stretching, twisting and turning, pushing and pulling are the most common examples. Animal movements can be used for nonlocomotor skills as well: The elephant swings its trunk (swinging arms from side to side); the squirrel picks up nuts from the ground (bending); the giraffe reaches for the highest leaves (stretching). Other pantomimes work as well: we are trees blowing in the soft breeze or the hurricane (twisting and turning); we row our boats across the river (pulling); we kayak into the sea (pushing).

4. *Manipulative skills* "involve control of objects, usually with the hands or feet" (Kirchner & Fishburne, 1998, p. 120). They generally require a combination of stability, locomotor, and nonlocomotor abilities. Manipulative skills include throwing, kicking, volleying, striking, rolling, bouncing, trapping, catching, and batting. For younger children, bean bags are less overwhelming than are balls; throwing and catching them in a variety of ways at different targets provides good exploration. Other materials to provide include playground balls, sponge balls, Wiffle balls, yarn balls, lightweight bats, scoops with handles, and frisbee discs. By the primary grades, children should have plenty of opportunities to practice the fundamental manipulative skills if they are to be successful in school and lifelong sports activities.

Girls may shy away from ball-related games, and boys may shun jump roping, but it is important to encourage the development of all skills for both genders. It might be good to note here that, old wives' tales notwithstanding, there is no physiological reason for "throwing like a girl." This is an ideal example of the effects of training or lack of it.

Dance

If all four movement skills—stability, locomotor, nonlocomotor, manipulative— are called into play at once, then combined with rhythm, music, and perhaps more emotion, the possibility of dance and dancelike movement emerges. Despite the complexities of such a combination, youngsters are capable of an initial level of skill from their toddler years onward.

Dance specialist Susan Stinson (1989) maintains:

While preschoolers can learn some simple steps and routines, they have far more important things to learn and do during these years than train for future careers. They need to explore their world and discover what they can do in it. Through such exploration, they build a rich store of sensory experiences, laying a foundation on which abstract concepts and more complex skills can later be built. Such experiences are the most appropriate steps toward future dance training for those children who might desire it. Even more important, these exploratory experiences contribute to the life of every child, not just those little girls who dream of wearing a tutu. (p. 210)

Dance for young children involves body movement and an awareness of that movement from within, which is sometimes (but not always) an expression of emotion: "To dance is to stay aware of what is ordinarily taken for granted, to discover a new world of sensory awareness provided by the kinesthetic sense" (Stinson, 1990, p. 36). As an art form, dance for young children is based on "natural movement rather than on movement of a particular style of the sort that one might see in tap dance or ballet" (p. 36).

Over a 2-year period, researcher Liora Bresler (1992) observed dance education in elementary schools and found little of the natural experience Stinson promotes. Typically, dance experiences were found lacking in any intellectual or aesthetic substance or "tools to explore inner life." Instead, "the infrequent dance sessions were decorative, trivial, and typically associated with the less-important aspects of school life" (p. 20).

Whether in preschool or primary grades, dance experiences for children need to be associated with what is important to children and be developmentally appropriate. Dance is more than fun movement in circle-time sessions (Andress, 1991). It is too important to children's lives for such offhand treatment. Because young children learn about their world, in great part, through exploratory movement and sensory awareness, seriously taken dance can provide concrete experiences "in which children become more aware of the movement they see in their world, try it on for themselves, and notice how it feels" (Stinson, 1990, p. 36).

The second graders in Suzanne's class once found great release from the unexpected sadness they felt during a science experiment in which marigolds, deprived of water or sunshine or soil, predictably died. When the youngsters finally realized that there was no hope of reviving the plants, Suzanne suggested that some children dance out the entire experimental process while others played various homemade instruments. The intensity on the children's faces, along with their enthusiasm for the idea, told her that this was one dance experience that was extraordinarily meaningful (Krogh, 1995).

In their experiences with dance, movement, rhythm, and music, children need to be given a balance of freedom (which provides opportunity for exploration of physical possibilities as well as the development of creativity) and structure (which provides direction and skill development for children at the elementary and mastery levels). Music educator Barbara Andress (1991) suggested three ways in which teachers can interact effectively during more structured experiences: modeling, describing, and suggesting.

Modeling does not mean engaging in movements that are to be imitated by the children. Rather, it involves demonstrating free movement to music, expressing your own ideas. This can and should happen at any time of the day, essentially giving the children inspiration and permission to do likewise. For very young children, use tactile modeling to encourage movement to music. Extend your index fingers for a child to grasp, then sway and move gently to the music, guiding the child to explore movement while providing stability and safety.

Describing is a way of reinforcing children's behavior, helping them to understand and define what it is they are doing. Describing should take place as the movement is happening, not later when it is forgotten. Some typical statements might be:

"Julie and Heather are moving quickly when the music sounds quick."

"Antonio stopped when the music stopped, and he started to move when the music started again."

"Sandy is stamping her feet hard while the music is loud."

Teachers should be careful to describe children's actions in a nonjudgmental way and to include everyone.

Suggesting is useful when you want the children to feel and demonstrate the music in the way it was intended. For example, "Let's Go Fly a Kite" from *Mary Poppins* matches musical mood to words. You might dance and make such comments as, "My kite is flying very high now . . . the wind is moving very slowly . . . now my kite is coming back to earth." Overuse of this technique, however, may lead to teacher-imposed learning and imagination killing. One antidote is to let children, once they are comfortable with the idea, take turns being the "teacher."

During experiences like these, dance and movement are fun and joyful. At other times, they can be quite serious, as was the case with Suzanne's second grade. In any case, they should be important and interesting to the children. Dancing about the change in seasons is natural for children, as demonstrated by Benjamin as he sluffed through the leaves. Experiences from real life, particularly the adult world that children are only permitted to observe, can be meaningful: driving a car, doing the laundry, mowing the lawn. In some ways, such role play has as much in common with drama as it does with dance. As such, it deserves a closer look.

Drama

Just as dance for young children goes a step beyond general movement experiences, drama goes a step beyond dramatic play. Drama for young children is "teacher-initiated dramatic play and can therefore provide a balance between free play and academics." Because it provides experiential learning, children "are more likely to retain information taught through drama because it is multisensory—it gives a visual, physical, and verbal representation of the idea" (Brown, 1990, p. 26).

Drama as a classroom activity can contribute much to children's development. Because it requires interaction, negotiation, and cooperation, and because social themes are often explored, drama promotes social development. Children are encouraged to express their feelings through drama and most children find it a positive experience that promotes self-esteem; consequently, drama enhances emotional development. Creative movement is often a part of drama, providing physical experience. Cognitive development is fostered when drama is integrated with what is happening in the curriculum. Finally, young children's drama experiences provide opportunities for creativity in problem solving, movement, and use of the imagination.

Drama has proven to be particularly effective in enhancing the language arts curriculum. According to Brown (1990), drama activities:

- Promote language acquisition better than many specialized language treatments.
- Enhance speaking skills.
- Foster better reading.
- Encourage verbal flexibility and originality.
- Increase abilities in extemporaneous speaking.

For preschool and kindergarten children, process-oriented drama is a must. Emphasis on product or performance for outsiders defeats the developmental benefits of drama. In the primary grades, process-oriented experiences should continue, but performance-related drama can be added. A few drama experiences that children will enjoy and learn from include acting out:

- The falling rain or snow that is keeping them indoors.
- The math story problem that is difficult to understand.
- A story that is currently being read.
- The television news that their parents are talking about but that is difficult to understand.
- The experiences they recall from a field trip.

You should not be afraid of repetition when using drama. Young children learn much from revisiting dramatic experiences. Repetition can reinforce earlier learning and provide a springboard for new understanding.

EXPRESSIVE ARTS ACTIVITIES ACROSS THE CURRICULUM

The expressive arts lend beauty, sensitivity, and feeling to the curriculum. Without them, life in the center or school can be drab and lack excitement.

The arts are important in their own right, and children should learn to appreciate them individually. At the same time, the arts enhance and integrate well with other areas of learning. The purpose of this section is to give you some guidance in achieving infusion of the arts across the curriculum. Activities are adaptable to many themes and integrated units. See Table 6.1 for a summary of activities for an integrated curriculum.

Art

1. **Shape Drawing or Collage.**   Provide children with paper that has been cut into geometric shapes. Don't confine these to the usual circle, square, and triangle. Children are equally interested in learning about the rhombus, penta-

TABLE 6.1

The Expressive Arts: Activities

Activity	Level*	Curriculum	Adapted From
Becoming Letters and Numbers	P, Py	Reading, Math	Gilbert
Books about Music	P, Py	Literature	Lamme
Box Town	P, Py	Social Studies	
Dancing the Day	P, Py	Math	
Dandelion Time	P, Py	Science	
Drawing and Doing	P, Py	Art	Morningstar
How Animals Protect Themselves	P, Py	Science	Gilbert
Mobiles: Artificial and Natural	P, Py	Science	
Personalized Clipboards	Py	Math	
Predictable Songs	Py	Reading	
Seed Collage	P, Py	Science	Lewis
Shape Drawing and Collage	P, Py	Math	Lewis
Sound Matching	P, Py	Classification	
Water Music	P, Py	Classification	
Where Animals Live	Py	Science	Gilbert

*P = Preschool; Py = Primary

gon, trapezoid, and so on. As they use crayons or markers, or create collages, talk with the children about the shapes of the paper. Tracing the edges with a finger reinforces the learning.

2. **Seed Collage.** On a sheet of drawing paper, children take a long cord and swirl it into an interesting pattern that should contain several loops (to create enclosed spaces that will be filled in). Glue the cord in place and allow it to dry. Meanwhile, have each child classify a collection of various types and colors of seeds according to the child's own observation and choice. Each grouping should be glued in an enclosed space. Informal discussion during this activity might center on identification of each kind of seed and observations of the differences between them.

3. **Mobiles: Artificial and Natural.** Use wire coat hangers and string to make mobiles to be hung from ceiling or doorways. Do this as a two-part project: once with all-natural materials and once with artificial materials. A good source for materials is a nature walk through an area that has litter that can be separated from the natural items. (Be sure any litter that is used in the mobiles is clean and safe.) Discussion of the difference between the two types of materials might lead to an exploration of how some of the materials are made, complete with visits to factories and stores.

4. **Box Town.** Collect large cardboard boxes from stores that sell appliances. Begin with just one or two and expand with children's interest. Have the class paint the outside of the boxes with tempera and either paint or wallpaper the insides. You can lead the children in designing doors and windows and discussing the purpose of each building. Typically, children will begin the project most interested in the painting process and play possibilities. With time, they will become more interested in creating buildings that are functional.

5. **Personalized Clipboards.**   To make clipboards, collect large rectangles of sturdy cardboard. Direct the class in dividing them into smaller rectangles about 10 inches by 13 inches. Primary children can participate in measuring by using nonstandard measuring tools (e.g., a piece of legal-size paper) or with standard rulers if they are learning to read them. A sturdy bread knife is the most effective saw for the board. When the pieces are cut, have children decorate one side with markers or crayons and write their names on the other. Attach two clothespins to the top to secure paper.

Music

6. **Predictable Songs.**   A predictable song is one with repetitive or predictable language. Choose a song with repetition, such as "Old McDonald" or "Mary Had a Little Lamb," or one with a predictable language pattern, such as the traditional ABC song. Sing it to the children several times, and let them join in as they can. Then, write the words on a chart and point to them as they are sung. When the words are familiar, children can take turns doing the pointing. Try chanting the words without the music to focus more on the language. To further develop the reading process, give children strips of words that match a line of the song, or smaller strips with single words on them, and challenge them to find their mates on the chart.

7. **Water Music.**   Fill crystal or other fine glass containers with water to different heights. For preschool children, use no more than two or three glasses. For older children, use eight for a full scale. If you have a classroom instrument, tune the glasses to it. Initially, children wet a finger and rub it around the rim of a glass to explore the sound. Later, they can arrange the glasses from lowest to highest tone or try to create a song. They can also try to find the tones on the classroom instrument that match the tones of the glasses. Primary children (and a few kindergartners) will enjoy the challenge of tuning the glasses to the classroom instrument.

8. **Sound Matching.**   Collect empty film canisters from a photography shop. Fill two canisters with each of several items that make different noises when shaken: rice, sand, dried beans in different sizes. On the bottoms of the canisters, paint dots of different colors, indicating the matching sets. At first, children enjoy shaking to explore the sounds. Next, provide them with just two or three sets to match, increasing the challenge to six or seven sets for older children. A further challenge is to arrange the canisters in rows from softest to loudest tones.

Movement

9. **Dancing the Day.**   At the close of the day, ask children to review the day's activities in the order in which they occurred. Use ordinal numbers to count them. Once the memories have been agreed on, chant or rap them back to the children as they dance or dramatize the events. Be sure to use the ordinal numbers in the chant or rap.

10. **Becoming Letters and Numbers.**   Children use any part of their bodies they choose to illustrate a letter or number. Once they are accustomed to the activity, you can change it to be a cooperative one, with two or three children working together (to form the letter.) Whole words and two- or three-digit numbers can also be created cooperatively.

11. **Where Animals Live.**   As children learn about animals and their homes, ask them to imitate each according to its home. *For example*: Can you show me an animal that lives in a nest? In a den? In the ocean? In the river? In the jungle?

12. **How Animals Protect Themselves.**   Invite children to share ways that animals protect themselves, and add some they don't mention to extend their learning. As each protection is described, children act it out. *For example*: Show me what a bull, elk, or rhinoceros uses for protection. Show me how birds protect themselves. How about tigers or crocodiles? Bees or jellyfish?

13. **Dandelion Time.**   When dandelions start to seed, bring in enough for each child to have one (with a few extras for emergencies). Children blow the seeds, then follow one of them to "become" the seed. Narrate to the children the experiences the seed must have to grow into a new plant: being blown by the wind, being rained on, working down into the ground, and so on.

14. **Drawing and Doing.**   Provide each child with paper and crayon or marker. Before you suggest a movement, children create it on paper. *Examples*: Chant "Dot, dot, dot" as children make dots on their paper. Then, they dance to the chant. Or have children draw a long straight line accompanied by a prolonged note on an instrument. This is followed by making bodies into long straight lines. Lively music can be played as children try scribbles. Replay the music while the children do a scribble dance.

CREATIVITY: A FINAL WORD

The topics of this chapter—music, art, and movement—are often thought of as primary vehicles for creativity. Indeed, we discussed each one within that context. Yet the other areas of the curriculum—language, mathematics, science, social studies—also should be considered in terms of creativity. Thus, the final discussion for this chapter on the expressive arts also pertains to the rest of the curriculum. It also serves to summarize the entire book. We hope that as your career in early education is launched, you will regard your teaching tasks with the utmost creativity and will provide the children in your care with abundant opportunities to learn creatively.

Creativity and Development

It has been argued that the innate creativity of younger children is often effectively, rudely, and unnecessarily destroyed by the education system. There is truth in this criticism, particularly when schools focus only on the "basics" and teach them in a basic way. Yet children themselves also are responsible for this change from enormously creative activity to cautious conformity. Within the framework of their developmental stages, such change is to be expected.

In their earliest years, children must find ways to make sense of their world. Each day they encounter new learning that they must assimilate and accommodate to their knowledge structure. Unless they are inhibited by physical or mental impairments or by overbearing adults, infants and young children spend much of their time exploring and experimenting with each new bit of knowledge. The result, to the adult eye, is vast creativity. Indeed, young children, being inexperienced and lacking in knowledge, have almost no choice but to create. In doing so, they often draw conclusions or make combinations unlike any that the older people around them have seen.

After about 5 years old, however, the world begins to make more sense. Children start to see patterns and connections as they have repeated contacts and experience with various fragments of knowledge. As they start to move into the stage of concrete operations, the excitement they feel toward learning begins to change character. No longer is it interesting just to mess about fancifully with materials, words, and ideas. Now there is an understanding that there are right ways to do and say things, and children want to know what those are and to be able to succeed at them. For many children, it is important to feel comfortable and competent about getting things right before they are ready to think creatively. We might compare this stage to that of the musician who needs to learn theory and the classics before being able to improvise cleverly or the artist who becomes skilled at draftsmanship before experimenting with new art forms.

One example of the way children change over time is their approach to an art medium such as fingerpaint. Three-year-olds who are introduced to it for the first time are fascinated, attracted to, or repulsed by its texture, coolness, and sloppiness. They are not yet ready to create a product but need plenty of time to experiment with the material itself, to see what it will do. Even washing their hands is a learning experience, as the substance disappears and the hands regain their original color. By the time they are 5 years old, most children have overcome any timidity they feel toward fingerpaint and become interested in making designs and pictures. Yet the product may change several times during the creative process, and a short time later, children may not even be able to identify their own pictures. Toward the end of kindergarten and certainly by first grade, most children's interests develop into something quite different. They want to be able to make pictures that really look like something and, unless further instructions are given in the handling of this rather unwieldy substance, children often choose not to use it. Teachers who show them techniques for using the sides of their hands, knuckles, forearms, and fingertips to create specific effects will find that interest in fingerpainting often stays high well into elementary school.

This approach toward fingerpaint demonstrates two stages in creativity development that parallel changes from knowledge gathering to creative expression. In the first stage, the youngest children, faced with a new medium, require time to explore it on its own terms. Process and substance are all-important to them, and little is created. Once they are comfortable with the material and what it does, they begin to create from a limited knowledge base, but with enthusiasm. The second stage is similar in that it begins with a need to gain control before creating. Primary children need to learn how to do things "right" or effectively, and then they feel ready to be creative. Developmentally, primary children do not really lose their creativity. Rather, they pause for a reality check. They are then ready to take their creativity to the next level, in which they make use of their extended knowledge.

Teachers who want to support creativity need to be aware of their children's general level of development. When a new material is introduced, much time should be devoted to experimenting with it. Until children become interested in the product, they should not be forced to focus on it rather than on process. Once the product becomes important to them, however, teachers should not become fearful that creativity will be lost if they provide children with the skills to make the products. There are at least two important ways in which primary teachers can kill creativity in their children. One is to focus almost entirely on "serious" academic work while showing little respect for creativity. The other is to try to prolong the early childhood period in which children are left to their own devices during creative experiences. To avoid either pitfall, primary teachers need to build on the children's desire to do things right by showing them techniques that give them the confidence to develop a more mature approach to creating.

The development that has just been described is related to Piaget's (1972) stage theory previously discussed in which preoperations give way to concrete operations. Thus, art joins other subject areas in which this kind of development takes place. Looking across the curriculum, we see such development:

• *In language.* Children first experiment with sounds, invent their own spellings, create their own versions of stories to accompany their favorite pictures. In the primary grades, they want to read the printed word correctly, spell in a standard way, and speak in a way that makes sense to everyone around them. Their creativity develops as they learn to write their own stories with a beginning, middle, and end; create poetry that they can identify as being different from prose; and, perhaps, give oral reports that entertain their classmates and teacher.

• *In mathematics.* Children first intuit the mathematical attributes of the world around them, count in fanciful ways that may seem creative to adults, and create unusual structures using their limited understanding of spatial relationships. In the primary grades, children need to learn to make change correctly so they can go shopping, measure accurately so they can construct structures that seem accurate to them, and count in a standard way so they can keep score when they play games. When primary children are provided with basic mathematical skills but are then allowed the freedom to invent their own ways to find the answers, they are given an opportunity to be creative. Now, however, their creativity is based on a structure of knowledge that gives them the courage to take risks.

• *In movement.* Children first move instinctively and with whatever physical skill their current developmental level permits them. As they mature, they enjoy learning specific steps that match various songs and musical compositions, yet they also can invent new steps and movements or make new combinations of the ones they have already learned. Similarly, when children first become aware of sports, they make sense of them by wearing the right clothing and mimicking the movements they have seen. Such early creativity toward the playing of sports is later replaced by an interest in following the rules. Still, some creativity is possible as children develop their own effective ways to be skillful.

• *In music.* As in movement, children first participate instinctively and later become interested in learning real songs and other compositions. Once they have learned them, however, children enjoy creating their own lyrics or melodies.

• *In social studies and science.* Many of the interests and skills from other sections apply to social studies and science. For example, children first have a fanciful vision of science that mirrors their view of mathematics. A preschool child might dance about the yard exclaiming that the moon is following his every movement because it wants to keep him company. In the later primary grades, he might become interested in manipulating models of the earth and moon to compare what appears to be reality with actuality.

Fostering and Supporting Creativity in the Center or School

The importance of creative development cannot be overstated. Children who are encouraged to be creative add a dimension to their lives that has influence far into their adult years. They learn to take risks with less fear of failure. They learn to make decisions based on the ability to consider a variety of outcomes. They learn to participate knowledgeably in a democratic society. They eventually are able to bring creative problem solving to their jobs and careers. And they are more likely to enjoy participating (informally or professionally) in any or all of the expressive arts.

Creativity is so important to some children that they will risk everything for it: the annoyance of their teachers who want them to do things in the proper school way, the anger of their parents who wish they would get tasks done and not make such messes, the ridicule of friends who observe that they are "different." Most children, however, gain courage to be creative only when there is someone—even one person—who encourages them. Historically, it has not been teachers who have felt comfortable about being that one special person. In a 1962 study of the childhoods of 400 eminent people, Goertzel and Goertzel found that the families of these creative individuals did not place much faith in traditional education. Some of the children never even were sent to school. Those who did attend school found that "it was a place where creativity was stifled, rather than encouraged" (Wasserman, 1992, p. 134) and that the teachers these children liked the best were those who "let them go ahead at their own pace and who gave them permission to work unimpeded in the area of their own special interests" (Goertzel & Goertzel, 1962, p. 267).

All children deserve to have teachers who give them this freedom. Teachers who hope to promote creativity need to keep in mind, no matter what the pressures, that covering required material, turning out high grades on a standardized test, and preparing children for entrance into school or the next grade are not the ultimate goals for the day. Educating the whole child is the goal, and creativity is an important part of that whole.

To promote creativity, children should be given plenty of time to play—with materials and ideas. Selma Wasserman (1992) wrote:

> The creation of new ideas does not come from minds trained to follow doggedly what is already known. Creation comes from tinkering and playing around, from which new forms emerge. . . . From all of this play, this messing around, serious and new creative forms are brought to life. (p. 137)

Arguing that play should be taken more seriously by educators, who should recognize its benefits, she said:

> Play allows children to make discoveries that go far beyond the realm of what we adults think is important to know. . . . I believe that with play, we teachers can have it all: the development of knowledge, of a spirit of inquiry, of creativity, of conceptual understanding—all contributing to the true empowerment of children. (p. 137)

A final influence on children's creativity that we should discuss is teacher modeling. As with most behaviors and attitudes, children will respond when they see you expressing creative ideas and behaving in creative ways. In turn, your creative behaviors and attitudes will affect your own growth as a person and a teacher. All the benefits that have been listed for children can be yours as well: greater competence in risk taking, decision making, political participation, artistic creativity, and creative thought in all aspects of your life—including, of course, your career as a teacher.

EXTENDING YOUR LEARNING

1. If you play a portable musical instrument, try using it with young children in a variety of ways. Do a guest presentation in which you explain the physics of how it works. (Be sure to let the children touch the instrument while teaching them to handle it with respect.) Play the instrument for children to create their own movement. Play it quietly as children settle down to a nap. Play a tune, and then let the children compose words to go with it.

   If you do not play an instrument, try team teaching these ideas with someone who does. Consider taking up an instrument now. You may find the experience a restful and enjoyable diversion, and the skills you gain will be a definite plus when you begin teaching.

2. If you feel that your artistic growth stopped many years ago, take some time to rediscover and develop your natural capabilities. Buy some art materials and experiment. Visit an art museum and examine just a few works of art very closely. At home, try to replicate some of the feeling and technique that you observed. Perhaps buy a book that encourages the nonartist to develop. An excellent choice is *Drawing on the Right Side of the Brain* by Betty Edwards

(1989). It is written by a college art teacher who has helped nonartists see the world in the ways that artists do, then transfer this capability to drawing skills.

3. Make a collection of songs gleaned from children's music books, from experienced teachers, from children themselves. If you are familiar with musical notation, record the songs on paper. If not, sing them into a tape recorder. Add to your collection, keeping a few favorites in your active memory. When you find yourself with a group of children and a few empty minutes, try introducing one of the tunes to them.

4. You will teach movement activities more easily if you keep yourself agile, strong, and aerobically healthy. Register for a dance or aerobics course. If you currently are working with children, share some of your learning with them.

5. Read the book *Childhood Revealed* (1999), edited by Harold Koplewicz and Robin Goodman, to explore the art of children who show special insights into pain and hope.

6. Go back to the integrated arts activities at the end of the chapter. Choose one and write a lesson plan using the outline in chapter 1. Be specific about your learning objectives.

VOCABULARY

Fundamental Movement Phase.   The period between ages 2 and 7 (approximately) in which children learn the basic movements necessary for later, more complex sport related movements.

Locomotor Skills.   The abilities that humans need to move through space and from place to place.

Manipulative Skills.   The abilities that humans need to control objects, usually with the hands or feet.

Nonlocomotor Skills.   The abilities that humans need to move without transporting the body through space.

Reflexive Movement Phase.   The period that begins before birth and continues until about the fourth month during which many of the infant's movements are involuntary, typically made in reaction to a stimulus such as light or touch.

Rudimentary Movement Phase.   The period between birth and the preschool years in which the infant and toddler learn the most necessary movements for basic survival.

Sport-Related Movement Phase.   The period that begins toward the end of the primary grades in which fundamental movements can be put to use for the complex requirements of sports and games.

INTERNET RESOURCES

Web sites provide much useful information for educators and we list some here that pertain to the topics covered in this chapter. The addresses of Web sites can also change, however, and new ones are continually added. Thus, this list should be considered as a first step in your acquisition of a larger and ever-changing collection.

A+ Schools Reports
www.aplus-schools.org

Arts and Literature: PBS
http://pbs.org/teachersource/whats_new/arts/thismonth_arts.shtm

Music Educators' National Conference
www.menc.org

National Art Education Association
www.NAEA-Reston.org

National Association for Sport and Physical Education
www.aahperd.org/naspe

References

A+ Schools: Schools that work for everyone. (1999). www.aplus-schools.org. Author.

Ackerman, K. (1988). *Song and dance man.* New York: Knopf.

Andress, B. (1991). From research to practice: Preschool children and their movement responses to music. *Young Children, 47*(1), 22–27.

Baker, D. (1990). The visual arts in early childhood education. *Arts in Education, 91*(6), 21–25.

Bayless, K., & Ramsey, M. (1991). *Music: A way of life for the young child.* New York: Macmillan.

Bleiker, C. (1999). The development of self through art: A case for early art education. *Art Education, 52*(3), 48–53.

Bredecamp, S., & Copple, C. (Eds.). (1997). *Developmentally appropriate practice in early childhood programs: Revised edition.* Washington, DC: National Association for the Education of Young Children.

Bresler, L. (1992). Dance education in elementary schools. *Arts in Education, 93*(5), 13–20.

Brown, V. (1990). Drama as an integral part of the early childhood curriculum. *Arts in Education, 91*(6), 26–33.

Clemens, S. (1991). Art in the classroom: Making every day special. *Young Children, 46*(2), 4–11.

Colbert, C. (1997). Visual arts in the developmentally appropriate integrated curriculum. In C. Hart, D. Burts, & R. Charlesworth (Eds.), *Integrated curriculum and developmentally appropriate practice.* Albany, NY: State University of New York Press.

Colbert, C., & Taunton, M. (1992). *Developmentally appropriate practices for the visual arts education of young children.* Reston, VA: National Art Education Association.

Edwards, B. (1989). *Drawing on the right side of the brain.* New York: St. Martin's.

Feierabend, J. (1990). Music in early childhood. *Arts in Education, 91*(6), 15–20.

Gabbard, C. (1992). *Lifelong motor development.* Dubuque, IA: Brown.

Gallahue, D., & Ozmun, J. (1998). *Understanding motor development: Infants, children, adolescents, adults.* New York: McGraw-Hill.

Gardner, H. (1983). *Frames of mind.* New York: Basic Books.

Gilbert, A. (1977). *Teaching the three r's through movement experience.* Minneapolis, MN: Burgess.

Goertzel, V., & Goertzel, M. (1962). *Cradles of eminence.* Boston: Little Brown.

Jalongo, M., & Collins, M. (1985). Singing with young children! *Young Children, 40*(2), 17–22.

Kellogg, R. (1970). *Analyzing children's art.* Palo Alto, CA: National Press Books.

Kenney, S. (1997). Music in the developmentally appropriate integrated curriculum. In C. Hart, D. Burts, & R. Charlesworth (Eds.), *Integrated curriculum and developmentally appropriate practice.* Albany: State University of New York Press.

Kirchner, G., & Fishburne, G. (1998). *Physical education for elementary school children.* New York: McGraw-Hill.

Koplewicz, H., & Goodman, R. (Eds.). (1999). *Childhood revealed: Art expressing pain, discovery & hope.* New York: Harry N. Abrams.

Krogh, S. (1995). *The integrated early childhood curriculum.* New York: McGraw-Hill.

Lamme, L. (1990). Exploring the world of music through picture books. *The Reading Teacher, 44*(4), 294–300.

Lewis, H. (Ed.). (1981). *Art for the preprimary child.* Reston, VA: National Art Education Association.

Lowenfeld, V., & Brittain, W. (1982). *Creative and mental growth.* New York: Macmillan.

Morningstar, M. (1986). *Growing with dance.* Heriot Bay, BC, Canada: Windborne.

Piaget, J. (1972). *The principles of genetic epistemology.* New York: Basic Books.

Schirrmacher, R. (1998). *Art and creative development for young children.* Albany, NY: Delmar.

Stinson, S. (1989). Creative dance for preschool children. *Early Childhood Development and Care, 47*(1), 205–209.

Stinson, S. (1990). Dance education in early childhood. *Arts in Education, 91*(6), 34–41.

Szyba, C. (1999). Why do some teachers resist offering appropriate, open-ended art activities for young children? *Young Children, 54*(1), 16–20.

Wasserman, S. (1992). Serious play in the classroom: How messing around can win you the Nobel Prize. *Childhood Education, 68*(3), 133–139.

Wolf, D., & Perry, M. (1988). *Art, mind and education.* Urbana, IL: University of Illinois Press.

Author Index

Subject Index

A

Activities, *see also* specific academic subjects
    classroom, 10
Activity time, *see* Schedule(s)
Addition, 96–98
Alphabetic principle, *see* Literacy development
Anthropology, 162
Art and development, 188–193
Art appreciation, 195–196
Arts activities, 205–208
Assessment, 18

B

Behaviorism, 49–50
    and Skinner, B. F., 81
Biology, 128–129

C

Chemistry, 127
Child development, *see* Development
Classification, 86, 92–94, 117
Comenius, John, 42–43, 81, 147–148
Communication, 118
Conflict resolution, 165–168
Conservation, 85, 119
Construction, 194–195
Constructivism
    and language acquisition, 50–51
    and mathematics learning, 82–83, 85–87

and Piaget, Jean, 45
and science learning, 116–120
and social studies learning, 153–154
Counting, 95–96, 98
Creativity, 208–212
Culture, *see* Curriculum planning
Curiosity, 132–134
Curriculum guidelines, 8–9
Curriculum planning
    and culture, 55–57, 91, 124, 156–157
    elements of, 14–22
    formats, 13, 23–25
    and preschoolers, 29–31
    and primary grades, 31–34
    and toddlers, 29–31
Curriculum types, *see also* specific academic subjects
    accidental, 8
    canned, 7
    emergent, 4
    enbalmed, 8
    integrated, 3–4
    prescribed, 5–6
    pushed (watered) down, 6
    subject based, 5
    thematic, 4

D

Daily schedule, *see* Schedule(s)
Development, *see also* specific academic subjects
    cognitive, 85–86, 119–120, 150–152, 180
    and gifted children, *see* Giftedness